The Philosopher King and the Pictish Nation

The Philosopher King and the Pictish Nation

Julianna Grigg

FOUR COURTS PRESS

Set in 10.5 on 12.5 point Ehrhardt for
FOUR COURTS PRESS LTD
7 Malpas Street, Dublin 8, Ireland
e-mail: info@fourcourtspress.ie
www.fourcourtspress.ie
and in North America for
FOUR COURTS PRESS
c/o ISBS, 920 N.E. 58th Street, Suite 300, Portland, OR 97213.

A catalogue record for this title
is available from the British Library.

ISBN 978-1-84682-563-7

SPECIAL ACKNOWLEDGEMENT
This book was published with the generous assistance of a
Book Subvention Award from the Medieval Academy of America.

The author is grateful to the Australian Academy of Humanities
for financial support towards the publication of this book.

Printed in England
by Antony Rowe, Chippenham, Wilts.

To Robyn Minnerva, 1944–2013

Contents

PART II

A note on orthography

The orthography used in this book has generally followed current usage among historians of the early medieval period. The names of the Pictish kings, however, are taken from the Pictish king list in the Poppleton Manuscript, Paris, Bibliothèque Nationale de France, MS Latin 4126. Compiled in the fourteenth century, this manuscript does appear to retain the least Gaelic, and possibly oldest, nomenclature of the various extant king lists. The major difference is in the spelling of King Necthon, who appears in Old Gaelic documents as Nechtan mac Der-Ile. Recent convention also uses Bede's spelling of Naiton for this king. In adopting the spelling of the Poppleton MS, my aim is not to confuse but to distinguish the Pictish kings from association with Old Gaelic and Old English/Latin nomenclature. There is, of course, no evidence that the personal names in the Poppleton MS preserve a closer affinity to a Pictish orthography than those used in Old Gaelic texts or in Bede. Instead, my orthographic choice is an attempt to distinguish the Picts from their neighbours by using a nomenclature that is not symptomatic of the notion that the Picts were passive adopters of external cultures.

References to counties and parishes follow the pre-1975 administrative units.

Acknowledgments

I am grateful to the Australian Academy of the Humanities and to the Medieval Academy of America for financial assistance towards this publication. I have been fortunate to pursue this project at a time of increased historical research into the Picts and archaeological excavations that have added significantly to our stock of knowledge. I am especially grateful for the dedication of these scholars in publishing their findings to the wider community. This book has emerged out of my doctoral thesis and I owe a great deal of thanks to all those who offered support and encouragement along the journey to publication. In particular, I received considerable assistance from Simon Taylor, who offered invaluable advice both during my research and on the final manuscript. His insights and generosity steered me clear of a number of pitfalls. Any infelicitous omissions or mistakes are my own. My thanks are also due to my doctoral supervisor Megan Cassidy Welch for her continued support and guidance throughout all the stages of this project. Likewise, I am grateful to Sarah Semple for a number of fruitful discussions as well as her encouragement and support of this publication. I am also obliged to Thomas Clancy, who, as my thesis examiner, provided detailed feedback. For advice, articles in advance of publication and insightful discussions during different stages of this project, I would like to thank Thomas Clancy, James Fraser, Alex Woolf, Nicholas Evans, Richard Oram, Isabel Henderson, Dauvit Broun, Cecily Spall, Martin Carver, Anders Ahlqvist, Meggen Gondek, Dianne Hall, Neil McLeod and members of the Australian Early Medieval Association. I also owe a longstanding debt of thanks to Willie Gillies, who first placed my feet on this path and to Pamela O'Neill, who convinced me to undertake this project and supervised its early stages. I have been grateful for the camaraderie of numerous friends and colleagues whose company and conversation have inspired, at times challenged, and always encouraged me. Thanks also to my family and most of all to Mark Leakey for his unwavering support and everything else. Finally, my thanks to Four Courts Press for taking on this project, and to Michael Potterton, who has guided me through the publication process with patience, support and kind understanding of those unexpected vicissitudes.

Abbreviations

AClon.	*The Annals of Clonmacnoise*, ed. and trans. D. Murphy (Dublin, 1896)
ASC	*The Anglo-Saxon Chronicles*, ed. and trans. Michael Swanton (London, 2000)
AT	'The Annals of Tigernach', ed. and trans. Whitley Stokes, *Revue Celtique*, 16 (1895), 374–419; 17 (1896), 6–33, 116–263, 337–420; 18 (1897), 9–59, 150–303, 374–91
AU	*Annals of Ulster (to AD1131)*, ed. and trans. Seán Mac Airt and Gearóid Mac Niocaill (Dublin, 1983)
CA	*Cáin Adomnáin and Canones Adomnani*, ed. and trans. Pádraig P. Ó Néill and David N. Dumville (Cambridge, 2003)
CCH	*Collectio Canonum Hibernensis*, in Hermann Wasserschleben (ed.), *Die Irische Kanonemsammlung* (Leipzig, 1885; repr. 1966)
CIH	*Corpus Iurus Hibernici: ad fidem codicum manuscriptorum*, ed. Daniel A. Binchy, 6 vols (Dublin, 1978)
CMCS	*Cambridge Medieval Celtic Studies*
CPNS	*The Celtic place-names of Scotland*, William J. Watson (Edinburgh, 1926; repr. 1993)
EME	*Early Medieval Europe*
HE	*Bede's Ecclesiastical history of the English people*, ed. and trans. Bertram Colgrave and R.A.B. Mynors (Oxford, 1969)
IR	*Innes Review*
MA	*Medieval Archaeology*
NMRS	National Monuments Record of Scotland
NSA	*The new statistical account of Scotland: by the ministers of the respective parishes, under the superintendence of a committee of the society for the benefit of the sons and daughters of the clergy* (Edinburgh, 1845)
OPS	*Origines parochiales Scotiae*, ed. Cosmo Innes and J.B. Brichan, 3 vols (Edinburgh, 1851–5)
OSA	*The [old] statistical account of Scotland: drawn up from the communications of the ministers of the different parishes*, ed. John Sinclair (Edinburgh, 1791–9)
PRIA	*Proceedings of the Royal Irish Academy*
PSAS	*Proceedings of the Society of Antiquaries in Scotland*

RCAHMS	Royal Commission for the Ancient and Historical Monuments of Scotland
SHR	*Scottish Historical Review*
VC	*Adomnán's Life of Columba*, ed. and trans. Alan Orr Anderson and Marjorie O. Anderson (Oxford, 1961; rev. 1991)
VW	*The Life of Bishop Wilfrid by Eddius Stephanus*, ed. and trans. Bertram Colgrave (Cambridge, 1927)

Introduction

> To the most excellent and glorious lord, King Naiton, ... we know that whenever rulers themselves take trouble to learn and teach and watch over the truth, it is a heaven-sent gift to God's holy Church. Indeed a certain secular writer has said very truly that the world would be in a happy state if kings were philosophers and philosophers were kings.[1]

When Abbot Ceolfrid penned his missive to the king of the Picts, in the early eighth century, he encouraged the king to rule over his kingdom with wise Christian governance. King Necthon was encouraged. The abbot of Wearmouth and Jarrow's clarification of key liturgical issues offered the king an opportunity to reform and unite churches across Pictland. Indeed, King Necthon's reign arguably reflects the culmination of a strategic process of political consolidation that created a united Pictland under the control of a single dynasty of kings. The process by which this came about is the main concern of this book. Central to this study is an examination of the causal factors that drove Pictish and, to some extent, Insular political consolidation. The roots of this political consolidation can be traced to sixth-century agricultural and settlement transitions that, hand-in-hand with the expansion of Christian foundations, propelled new social and exchange networks. By the late seventh century, the northern Pictish dynasty of Fortriu was able to exploit these networks to expand its territorial control. This book focuses on three kings from the dynasty of Fortriu. In particular, the recipient of Abbot Ceolfrid's letter, King Necthon filius Derelei, navigates the shoals of early medieval politics to fortify and extend his dynasty's control over the burgeoning Pictish kingdom.

Most of our knowledge about the Picts derives from sources external to Pictland. According to the Venerable Bede, what defined the Picts was the language they spoke. As a result, Bede conceived of Britain as four distinct nations linguistically divided; those that spoke English, British, Gaelic or Pictish.[2] Pictish was a version of Brythonic, spoken throughout Britain, although the indications from contemporaneous sources suggest a distinct linguistic identity.[3] This distinction is also found on the Pictish symbol stones, whose distribution and artistic uniformity express a marked cultural identity.

1 *HE* V.21, pp 534–5. 2 *HE* I.1, pp 16–17. 3 K. Forsyth, *Language in Pictland* (1997).

'Pict' began as a pejorative term applied to peoples in the north of Britain during the late Roman period (Latin *Picti* and later *Pictavia*), possibly to indicate their lack of Romanization. The Picts' own name for themselves may have been *Prydyn*, synonymous with the more generic 'Britons' and linked to the Gaelic word for Pict (*Cruithni*) by a common ancestor **Priteni*.[4] By the seventh century they appear to have adopted the Latin *Picti* as an ethnic identifier and inclusive term.[5] The territorial extent of their kingdom, while difficult to determine with exactness, encompassed a similar geographic territory to that of modern Scotland, excluding south of the Firth of Forth and west of the Grampians, or *Dorsum Britanniae*. The Orkney and Shetland islands appear to have participated in a Pictish cultural continuum and overlordship of this region was integral to the geo-political consolidation of Pictland. Documentary sources indicate that Pictland comprised numerous provinces each operating with varying degrees of autonomy; there is no evidence to confirm whether these provinces were analogous to the seven discrete kingdoms recorded in the twelfth-century *de situ Albanie*.[6] Bede's information is more pertinent as he describes a distinct political divide between Picts in the south and those beyond the Grampians (the Mounth) in the north.[7] The Picts first emerge in the documentary sources as a loose confederacy of aggressive tribes in the north of Britain exploiting the Roman withdrawal. According to later historiography, these disparate groups gradually coalesced into a kingdom before being subsumed under a putative Gaelic expansion around the mid-ninth century when the kingdom of Alba was formed.[8] Between the Roman withdrawal and the creation of Alba, a brief flourishing of writings from Insular polities reveals a vital engagement in social and political identity, matched by a move towards centralized government.

There were probably attempts to consolidate Pictland into a unified kingdom under charismatic leadership before the late seventh century but these ventures were unsustained. When documentary sources become available towards the end of the seventh century, however, they reveal a transition to Christian mediated dynastic kingship with its longer-term prospect of consolidation. This transition appears to have been instigated by the Pictish king Bredei filius Bili (*c.*672–*c.*693), who won a pivotal battle against the Northumbrians at Nechtansmere in 685 by uniting numerous Pictish provinces under his leadership.[9] His eventual successor, and probable descendant, Bredei filius Derelei (*c.*697–*c.*706) emerges from the sources as an ally of the clergy of Iona and Gaelic

4 K. Jackson, 'Two early Scottish names' (1954), pp 16–18. Also demonstrated by D. Broun, 'Alba: Pictish homeland or Irish offshoot?' (2005), p. 246. 5 A. Woolf, *From Pictland to Alba* (2007), pp 9–10. 6 D. Broun, 'The seven kingdoms in *De situ Albanie*' (2000). 7 *HE* III.4. 8 See Broun, 'The seven kingdoms in *De situ Albanie*'. See the eleventh-century *Prophecy of Berchán*, which continues to impact on our understanding of the nature of succession in this period: B.T. Hudson, *The prophecy of Berchán* (1996), pp 121–4. 9 The term 'Northumbria' refers to the kingdoms of Bernicia and Deira that, while heterogeneous, were politically consolidated during the reign of King Oswald (634–42) and largely remained so into the eighth century.

groups in Ireland and Dál Riata (whose territory lay in modern Argyll and the Inner Hebrides). Clerical connections figured more prominently during the reign of his brother and successor, Necthon filius Derelei (*c.*706–*c.*724–32), whose diplomatic ties to the Gaelic speakers became less conciliatory. Necthon's impact on his political environment, according to the sources, was actively authoritative. In particular, he instigated church reform within his kingdom.

Political developments within Pictland were neither isolated nor precocious. Pictish institutional transitions occurred during a period when many other kingdoms in the west were moving towards centralized authority. The Picts were participating in the same dynamic political consolidation that saw the Uí Néill in Ireland, the Anglo-Saxon Bretwaldas and the Merovingians of Gaul move towards dynastic theocratic kingship. These kings, however, were not the sole agents driving political transition. External pressures and internal developments encouraged expansionary policies. This is most clear in the textual evidence relating to the reign of Necthon filius Derelei, who used religious reform to mediate territorial and administrative expansion. Existing institutions and social customs similarly intersected with ideological concepts of civil administration that were transmitted through ecclesiastical networks. In addition, the social and institutional developments that were fundamental to the functional exercise of kingship enabled the transition towards a cohesive national identity. The motivations for cultural and political change were multifarious; nevertheless, the impact on existing social institutions by the absorption of Christian ideas on political authority and hierarchy was extensive. The power of these ideas to propel cultural change is amply demonstrated in the proliferation of decorated cross-slabs and churches. Perhaps less obvious was the impact of Christianity on the exercise of secular authority and the consolidation of power.

The paucity of documentary evidence of identifiable Pictish provenance does present a challenge. This absence has led to the assumption that artistic and societal developments in Pictland were purely the result of exogenous influences. Lacking a voice of their own, the Picts have been viewed as a *tabula rasa* upon which neighbouring polities have imposed their script. As a result, any discussion of Pictish political agency requires careful unpicking from the contemporaneous evidence and modern pre-conceptions. It is also the case that due to the slim evidence any study of the Picts must remain subjective. This study is no exception: in attempting to build a 'bigger picture' of Pictish political progress against the constraints of the piecemeal evidence, some inferential leaps are inevitable. There is, however, no reason to be unduly pessimistic. Recent archaeological excavations, techniques and interpretative methodologies substantially augment the stock of evidence on the Picts. This is matched by new historical analysis of the minutiae of political interactions among the early medieval Insular political groups. Indeed, this book owes a debt to Thomas Clancy's seminal study 'Philosopher-King: Nechtan Mac Der-Ilei', which repositioned the way in which Pictish kings and their political agency were examined; particularly the career of the 'philosopher-king' Necthon.[10] Of fundamental importance is the record of contemporaneous witnesses who describe and allude to events in Pictland. These witnesses provide tangible evidence for a dynamic and hierarchical society that was actively participating in the cultural and religious changes affecting other Insular polities. Like Nennius for his compilation of the *Historia Brittonum*, by necessity this study draws on the 'writings of the Irish and the English' to illuminate the history of the Pictish kingdom.[11] These records are sufficiently detailed to indicate the keen interest shown by the Anglo-Saxons and Irish in Pictish affairs, an interest that suggests events in Pictland had the potential to have a wider impact on their neighbours.

Underlying this study is the question as to how a nation is established. It is a question that certainly exercised the minds of Scottish antiquarians but has subsequently excited limited attention from historians. This is not surprising as, leaving no testimony of their own, the historiography on Pictish governmental cohesion has often been driven by contemporary political concerns. Indeed, one of Scotland's earliest surviving histories by John of Fordun, compiled *c.*1360, deliberately downplayed Pictish sovereignty in order to indicate primary Gaelic settlement and suzerainty in the pre-Christian period.[12] Fordun's sources may have derived from documents prepared from 1291 for the 'Great Cause'. This was a defence of the longevity of the Scottish throne in the face of Edward I's claims to sovereignty, which was assembled by Scottish intellectuals after the failure of the direct Scottish royal line in 1290.[13] They were fighting an uphill battle, as Edward's legal advisors and his barons were able to draw upon and manipulate dubious origin myths to support their king's claims to 'British-wide' sovereignty. For Scottish purposes, the distinction between Pict and Briton would have been difficult to argue, it was far more compelling to claim a continuum of Scottish (*Scotti*) rulers. The *Book of Pluscarden*, assembled *c.*1460 at Elgin priory, Morayshire, presents these claims and counterclaims of warring foundation myths.[14] For Fordun, writing in the mid-fourteenth century, Scottish sovereignty remained a live issue and it is not remarkable that he continued to propagate the myth of an Irish origin for the Scottish throne. It is notable that the search for 'origins' remained a dominant paradigm in studies on the Picts until the late twentieth century.[15] In the more conciliatory political environment of 1586, William Camden's *Britannia* did attempt to remove the Picts from the

10 T.O. Clancy, 'Philosopher-king' (2004). 11 Nennius: *British history and the Welsh annals*, ed. and trans. J. Morris (1980), *Praefatio*, p. 50. 12 John of Fordun: *Chronica gentis Scotorum*, 2 vols (1872; repr. Lampeter, 1993). 13 D. Broun, 'The Picts' place in the kingship's past before John of Fordun' (2002). For a discussion of the 'Great Cause', see G.W.S. Barrow, *Scotland and its neighbours* (1992), pp 3–13; A.A.M. Duncan, *The kingship of the Scots* (2002), pp 255–315. 14 F.J.H. Skene, *The Book of Pluscarden*, 2 vols (1880), 2, compares English claims to mythic overlordship (p. 131) to Scots claims of Irish mythic ancestry (p. 164). 15 J.E. Fraser, 'From ancient Scythia to the problem of the Picts' (2011).

yoke of a Gaelic mythological past, asserting that they were indigenous, British and had ruled in Scotland prior to the Scots.[16] It was not, however, until 1729 that Thomas Innes successfully refuted assertions of Gaelic (that is Irish) settlement in Scotland before the Picts in his *Critical essay*, where he claimed that the Picts were related to the Britons, spoke the same language, and arrived together from Gaul to an empty land.[17] Innes' interest in the organization of early medieval Pictish government tapped into ideas on constitutional reform that were stimulating western philosophical debates. From his analysis of early sources, Innes maintained that early Britain was 'governed by little kings' and that after the Roman period the Picts' 'government was hereditary and monarchical' and altogether indigenous.[18] John Pinkerton, writing sixty years later, applauded Innes' approach but could not stomach the idea of the Picts as 'Welsh Britons', instead giving them a Gothic ancestry.[19] Pinkerton viewed the Picts as having a powerful elective monarchy that ruled a territory of greater extent than that held by any other king in Britain, having taken over the north of Britain from a base in Orkney (sometime in the third century). Prior to this, he asserted, they were 'in all probability under democratic government'.[20] George Chalmers had some pithy criticism for Pinkerton's Gothic origins for the Picts. This thesis considerably irked Chalmers who proclaimed that it 'egregiously failed, because falsehood cannot be proved'.[21] Citing numerous authorities, Chalmers reinstated the Brittonic roots of the Picts and, while maintaining that they had an inherent 'principle of disunion', did agree with Pinkerton that after the Romans departed they were under the rule of a single king. The authority of the king, however, he deemed unstable due to the Picts' irregular succession practices.[22]

By the mid-nineteenth century the publication of key primary sources reinvigorated scholarly interest in the beginnings of government and political franchise in early Scotland. In his *Sketches of early Scottish history*, Cosmo Innes attempted to explain the administration of crown lands and administrative officials as well as early social stratification, without quite specifying the antiquity of these institutions.[23] E. William Robertson was similarly engaged in understanding governmental organization in early Scotland and Pictland.[24] Indeed, Robertson's wide-ranging study includes perceptive discussions on land tenure and state formation that, according to James Campbell, are worthy of revisiting.[25] In an earlier publication Robertson suggested that there was an effectively amalgamated Pictish kingdom 'of one state'; instigated under King Onuist filius Urguist (*c*.729–*c*.761) whose military campaigns into neighbouring

16 W. Camden, *Camden's Brittania* (1695). 17 T. Innes, *A critical essay*, 2 vols (1729), 1, pp 70–3. 18 Innes, *A critical essay*, 1, pp 99, 165. 19 J. Pinkerton, *An enquiry into the history of Scotland* (1789), pp 240, 271. 20 Ibid., pp 253–61, 277. 21 G. Chalmers, *Caledonia* (1807; repr. 1887), pp 231–2. Chalmers details the historiographical debate as to the origins of the Picts as Brittonic or otherwise, pp 225–33. 22 Ibid., pp 199, 204–5. 23 C. Innes, *Sketches of early Scottish history* (1861). 24 E.W. Robertson, *Historical essays* (1872). 25 J. Campbell, 'A nearly, but wrongly, forgotten historian of the Dark Ages' (2008).

territories were well chronicled.[26] A close colleague of Cosmo Innes, William F. Skene published an edited collection of manuscript material relating to early medieval Scotland.[27] He followed this with a discursive history of *Celtic Scotland* over three volumes, making an expansive attempt to discuss the social hierarchies and their development.[28] Nevertheless, as historians such as Geoffrey Barrow have found, projecting medieval administrative structures back onto earlier medieval societies is anachronistic and potentially limiting.[29] Skene also proposed that kingship evolved from an occasional elective war leader, selected from a member of the hereditary nobility, to gradations of kings determined by territory and clients.[30] According to Thomas O'Rahilly, Skene's prejudice against Irish origin myths and 'obsession in favour of the Picts' resulted in 'patriotic Pictomania'.[31] This criticism seems misplaced, for Skene did not hesitate to attribute the Christianization of the Picts to Columban Gaelic missionary activity; unlike others who, like Archibald Scott, took a more sectarian approach by attributing the conversion of the Picts to a native Briton, and therefore non-Gaelic, saint Ninian.[32] Hume Brown summarizes the sentiments of his day that 'in rejecting Iona for Rome, they entered a world at once ethically and intellectually superior to that which they left'.[33] By addressing the evangelical influence on the Picts as consistently exogenous, and of late development, the cultural passivity of the Picts was emphasized.[34] Indeed, this assumption continues to have some currency in relation to the influence of Columban missionary activity on the political progress of Pictland.[35]

Recent topical studies do, however, assert a greater degree of political coherence and cultural dynamism for the Picts than previously proposed and suggest the existence of a Pictish hegemony led by the dynasty of Fortriu.[36] This, nevertheless, raises a number of questions as to how the hegemony came about; the nature of its constitution; whether it maintained its initial political consolidation, and how it functioned territorially. Likewise, the term hegemonic provides limited descriptive light on this period of dynamic socio-political transformation. Finding an appropriate term to describe political phenomena of the early medieval period is undoubtedly problematic. Concepts such as 'centralized government', 'nation' and 'state' are ideologically loaded towards modern definitions of the heavily bureaucratic administrative structures which most of us live

26 E.W. Robertson, *Scotland under her early kings*, 2 vols (1862), 1, p. 38. 27 W.F. Skene, *Chronicles of the Picts, chronicles of the Scots* (1867). 28 W.F. Skene, *Celtic Scotland*, 3 vols (1876–80). He also provided an extensive discussion on the administrative workings of early Scottish society as an appendix to: John of Fordun: *Chronica Gentis Scotorum*, 2, pp 441–60. 29 G.W.S. Barrow, *The kingdom of the Scots* (1973). 30 Skene, *Celtic Scotland*, 3, pp 140–50. 31 T.F. O'Rahilly, *Early Irish history and mythology* (1946), p. 379, n. 374. 32 A.B. Scott, *The Pictish nation* (1918). 33 P. Hume Brown, *History of Scotland* (1909), p. 25. 34 See C. Kidd, 'The ideological uses of the Picts' (2002). 35 For instance: K. Veitch, 'The Columban church in northern Britain' (1997), particularly the assumptions of a Columban confederacy over Pictish churches, pp 635–9. 36 Most notably by J.E. Fraser, *From Caledonia to Pictland* (2009).

within. Neither has there been complete agreement among scholars as to the definition and applicability of these concepts for medieval polities.[37] In effect, these terms summarize the 'end result' of an opaque political process. While these terminological issues are discussed in chapter two, this book concentrates on the process of political consolidation. This process is examined through the institutional and political changes that occurred among the Insular polities. By incorporating the documentary and material evidence for a Pictish *regnum*, it is possible to map a complex political trajectory for the Picts as they, like their neighbours, developed the apparatus of nationhood.

Understanding the process by which Pictish polities were consolidated can illuminate their constitutional foundations and the underlying mechanisms that extended executive authority. The manifestation of governmental organization in Pictland similarly offers a paradigm for the concurrent operation of authority among other Insular polities. This study reappraises the comparative evidence for political transition among the Picts in conjunction with the material evidence for amalgamation. The book is divided into two parts. Part one comprises a survey and re-examination of the prevailing conditions and institutions that expedited centralizing government. These issues are approached over the first three chapters, from the ground up with an assessment of the economic and settlement conditions extending to the integration of Christian institutions and their influence on kingship. In part two these theoretical insights are applied to the political career of King Necthon filius Derelei. Necthon's reign offers an illustration of centralizing authority against which to test theories of geo-political expansion and theocratic kingship. Chapter four addresses his succession and the challenges to his political authority and Pictish autonomy. The final chapter investigates Necthon's attempts at religious reform and the potential impact reform had on political cohesion.

In considering the political transition of Pictish polities towards a territorially defined collective kingdom, it becomes clear that there was a concomitant transition in the nature and executive function of kingship. Moreover, effective kingship required a means to enact territorial control for which the political assembly offered a focus from which to expedite and endorse the operation of governance. Likewise, the formative potential of Christian political ideologies intersected with existing institutions to encourage pro-state developments. The king's increasing executive powers, his employment of the political assembly and Christian political exemplars, contribute to the dynamism of this period. By incorporating the evidence for social transition, this study offers a new reading of geo-political expansion in order to evaluate the governmental evolution in Pictland alongside similar developments in the Insular world. Ultimately, this construct of Pictish political autonomy aims to add to the debates on early medieval governance and the emergence of the nation.

37 L. Scales and O. Zimmer, 'Introduction' (2005), pp 3–13.

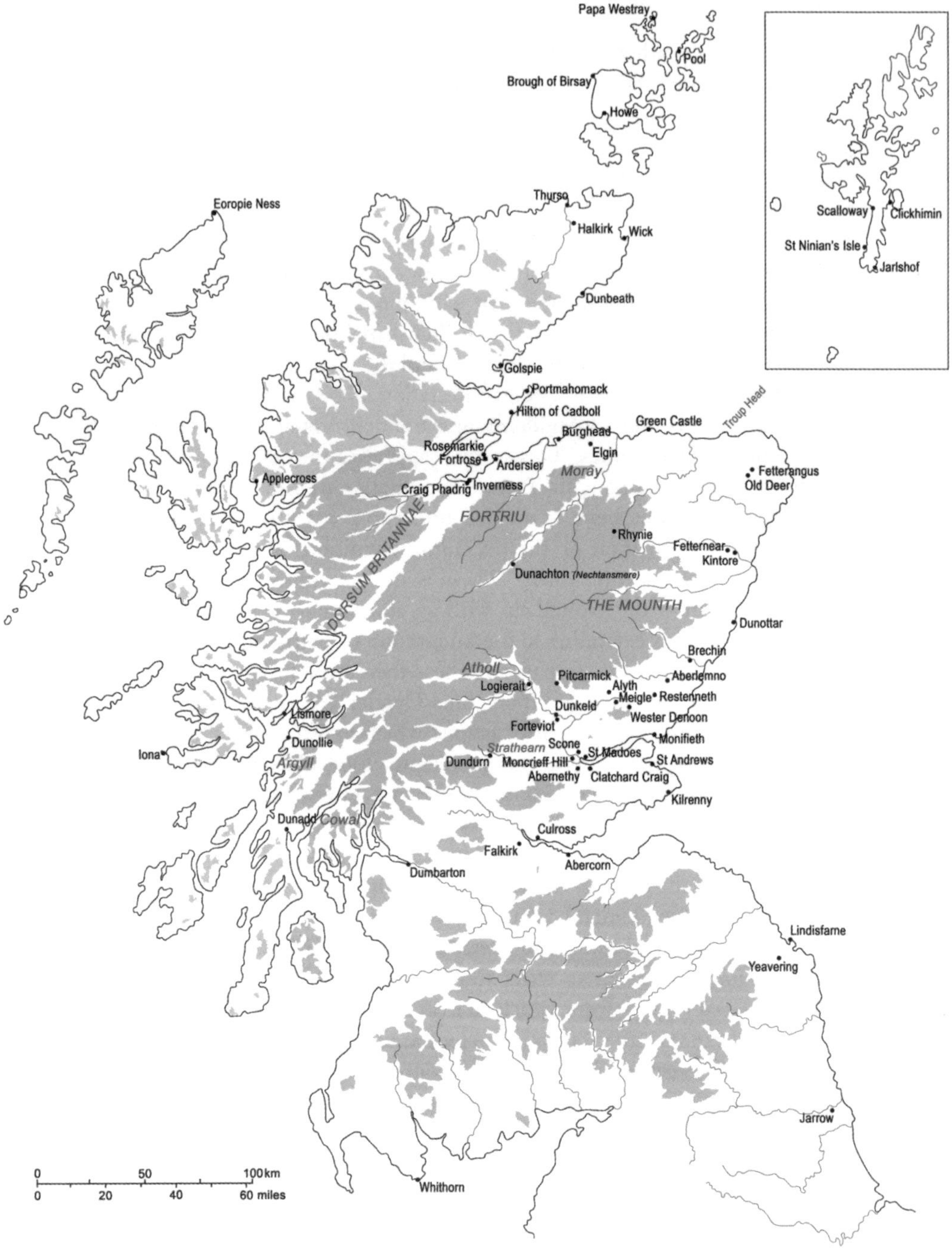

1 Sites referred to in the text.

PART I

I

Economics of power

Documentary evidence points to a Pictish political community of people who, from the late seventh century, were the subjects of a king.[1] While this attests to the existence of kingship and normative hierarchies by this period, it raises questions about the manner and extent of their authority, and how that authority was consolidated. In order to answer these questions it is necessary to understand the conditions that led to the construction and maintenance of a layered hierarchical society and the means and extent by which authority was transferred upwards. For this reason, the economic and settlement history of the region is an important place to begin, as political authority was primarily manifested through the control of resources, settlement being contingent upon the exploitation of these resources. Economic developments and, indeed, downturns are therefore socially and politically transformative. Evidence for these economic changes is primarily archaeological. Recent developments in archaeological method have significantly expanded our understanding of day-to-day conditions for the early medieval period, with analyses of faunal and cereal remains adding to settlement and funerary evidence. Nevertheless, excavation in Scotland has been patchy with a concentration on high-status sites, particularly along the north Atlantic, and only the most recent excavations have collected diagnostic evidence for agrarian practices. Attempting a synthesis of the evidence for settlement and agrarian transitions is therefore challenging. There is, however, sufficient evidence to detect a broad pattern of economic change and cultural shifts that appear to coincide with the establishment of an ecclesiastical presence in Pictland.

The level of economic stability, surplus or subsistence can predicate the extent of hierarchical and geo-political expansion – surplus encouraging increased hierarchical expansion. In this scenario, the control of resources also presumes control of land and its productive potential. As Wendy Davies and Paul Fouracre assert, for Insular groups in the early medieval period 'land equalled power' and the area controlled 'correlated with the power one wielded'.[2] Similarly, Tom Saunders emphasized that coercive control, through exploitative rents and taxes, increased hierarchical power that maintained its control through payments to retainers and armies.[3] This functional paradigm envisions a 'top down' exploitative and militaristic relationship that led to the

1 *HE* I.1, V.21; *VC* II.33–5, 37, 42. 2 W. Davies and P. Fouracre, 'Introduction' (1995), p. 2. 3 T. Saunders, 'Class, space and "feudal" identities' (2000).

coalescence of fixed, vertical hierarchal relationships between king and regional ruler, regional ruler and landlord, and landlord and tenant.[4] This theory assumes an existing control of land and military force rather than explains how it was achieved. Moreover, it takes a limited account of the reciprocal nature of economic relationships that formed the basis of social negotiation rather than purely exploitative patterns. While the territorialization of power by elite groups was a manifestation of their economic control, this control also initiated a sense of communal identity that was reinforced by the impact of neighbouring power structures.[5] The economic exploitation in Pictland, as it emerged in the late seventh century, can be seen to underlie its transformation into a consolidated kingdom.

Unlike most regions of western Europe, including southern Britain, Pictland was substantially free of Roman incursion and incoming political groups. Continuity of population in early medieval Europe was, as Chris Wickham has argued, likely to result in continuity of 'daily practice' and 'social exchange'.[6] This is not to suggest a conservatism that prevented administrative structural change or new exchange systems being developed. The influence of Christianity did have a deep impact on political and social structures, as did neighbouring polities and trade networks. Nevertheless, in many regions of Pictland patterns of land use, customary law governing land rights and the control of land by consanguine noble families had been present from the Iron Age. Indeed, Tacitus describes an aristocracy mustering its army in Pictland (the Caledonians 'beyond the Forth') during the Agricolan campaigns.[7] At the same time, social and environmental fluctuations had an impact on economic viability, which was at the core of a maturing administrative system. Because of these pressures, stratified hierarchical control would not always progress to a centralized government or a stable state.[8] Developmental models for this type of historical analysis have often approached the period through modern theories of commodity versus gift-exchange economies.[9] Instead, it is worth considering that production, consumption and exchange are interrelated aspects of the economy by which territorial control shifted from a fixed geographic area to become an actively mobile expression of power. In the case of Pictland, the long-term existence of relatively stable, territorially defined, communities could promote the upward transfer of authority and resources. Undoubtedly, some degree of territorial consolidation was achieved through militaristic action. This does not negate the way in which existing institutions enabled the upward transfer of power. Likewise, the institutionalization of Christianity over all aspects of the social

4 W. Davies, *Patterns of power in early Wales* (1990), pp 28–31, 83; S.M. Foster, 'Before Alba' (1998), p. 5. 5 See R. Hodges, 'Peer polity interaction' (1986). 6 C. Wickham, *Framing the early Middle Ages* (2005), p. 12. 7 Tacitus: *The Agricola and the Germanica*, ch. 29. 8 I.B. Ralston, *The hill-forts of Pictland* (2004), p. 43. 9 J. Moreland, 'Concepts of the early medieval economy' (2000), p. 32.

environment further encouraged the rise of hierarchical authority and political consolidation.

Hierarchical expansion relied on the effective exercise of power and authority which, by its nature, consolidated hierarchical control. Both power and authority are interrelated, where 'power' can be seen as the imposition of the will of a ruling group who recreate the socio-cultural values that support their own political agendas through which they are able to claim 'authority'.[10] Power can therefore be viewed as an 'informal influence' that enabled the exercise of authority in the form of a 'socially sanctioned "right" to make decisions binding on others'.[11] For instance, the exercise of power in the form of military enforcement, if successful, results in the enforcer having dominant authority over those subjugated. Military might, however, was just one form of power that could be deployed. The source of this power, as Fouracre and Davies assert, came from wealth and that wealth from the ownership of land. Economic wealth, through the control of land, was not an end in itself; instead, it provided the opportunity to gain access to the dominant social groups as well as the maintenance of dominant status. As a consequence, personal alliances with members of the dominant group created the opportunity for the exercise of authority.[12] The possession of land may have endowed the owner with status or inherited nobility, but power and authority were achieved through the creation and maintenance of relationships, usually of dependency. Wealth provided the means to create these advantageous relationships, so control of the productive landscape remained necessary for the maintenance of political authority. In addition, the exercise of power and authority was only possible through the compliance of dependent members of the political communities. Of course, this compliance may be equally enforced through military, legal or economic coercion.

THE AGRICULTURAL ENVIRONMENT IN TRANSITION

Successful exploitation of the environment through a range of agricultural practices was central to the development of sustained hierarchies during the medieval period. Political organization was intimately tied to production and demand, where power was gained, constructed and exerted through the accumulation of resources.[13] Intriguingly, the piecemeal archaeological evidence from Scottish sites, spanning the Iron Age to early medieval period, does indicate an increase in surplus production and agricultural innovation. This is tied to a shift in agricultural practice that may have had a significant cultural impact. The

10 T.L. Thurston, *Landscapes of power, landscapes of conflict* (2001), p. 263. 11 M.C. Erler and M. Kowaleski, 'Introduction: a new economy of power relations' (2003), p. 2. 12 M. Innes, *State and society in the early Middle Ages* (2000), p. 93. 13 U. Näsman, 'Exchange and politics' (2000), p. 64.

agricultural surplus produced certainly appears to have become a commodity and its complex employment in initiating and fortifying social exchange offered an opportunity to alter the dynamics of power.

Environmental conditions improved dramatically around the British Isles from the fifth century AD. Michael Ryan, citing pollen records of forest decline and climatic amelioration, found corresponding evidence for improved and intensive farming practices in Ireland from this period.[14] Pollen analysis from a number of sites in eastern Scotland similarly confirms widespread forest clearance, broadly dating between AD500 and 1000.[15] This evidence should be treated with some caution as the pollen records also indicate a widespread and dramatic loss of oak trees from across Europe dating to *c.*540 that cannot be the result of intensive farming.[16] Nevertheless, archaeological evidence does point to an increased use of timber for building purposes and craft production that had an impact on forest resources.[17] In his Life of St Columba, Adomnán of Iona referred to the felling and transportation of pine and oak trees from the west of Scotland, for use as house beams and in shipbuilding.[18] Similarly, abandoned cultivation ridges at 400m above sea level in Scotland have revealed intensive agricultural exploitation potentially dating to the early medieval period.[19] Cultivation terraces were also identified on the hillsides around Dundurn hillfort, Perthshire, which were probably in use during the occupation of the fort.[20] Leslie Alcock has also cited evidence for a change from squarish fields to long narrow fields during the same period.[21] Long narrow ard marks with plough pebbles found at Portmahomack, Ross and Cromarty, substantiate this innovation and they date to the earliest period of monastic settlement, *c.*AD600.[22] The appearance of plough pebbles is significant, as they represent an important improvement in agriculture. These pebbles were embedded into the wooden mouldboard of a plough to increase its strength and durability. A plough augmented in this way was sturdy enough to be drawn by teams of horses or oxen and resulted in deeper furrows and increased crop yield. Evidence for the extensive use of this mouldboard technology was found at Whithorn, Wigtownshire, dating to the later fifth century, where an apparently green-field site was developed for the early *monasterium*.[23] Suggestive links with Gaul were also found at this site indicating the possible route by which technologies, trade

14 M. Ryan, 'Furrows and browse' (2000), p. 32. 15 P.E. O'Sullivan, 'Pollen analysis and radiocarbon dating' (1976), p. 301; L. Alcock, E.A. Alcock and S.T. Driscoll, 'Reconnaissance excavations of early historic fortifications' (1989), pp 221–2. 16 R. Tipping, A.L. Davies and R. McCulloch, 'Introduced woodlands in northern Scotland' (2006). 17 Ralston, *The hill-forts of Pictland*, p. 19. 18 *VC* II.45. 19 M.L. Parry, 'Secular climactic change and marginal agriculture' (1975). 20 Alcock, Alcock and Driscoll, 'Reconnaissance excavations of early historic fortifications', p. 221; see also A. Graham, 'Cultivation terraces in south-eastern Scotland' (1939), p. 305. 21 L. Alcock, 'The Rhind Lectures, 1988–9' (1988), p. 333. 22 M. Carver, *Portmahomack* (2008), pp 51, 73, 75. 23 P. Hill, *Whithorn and St Ninian* (1997), p. 28.

goods and evangelization were imported.[24] Certainly, the use of mouldboard technology required knowledge, organization and resources that were beyond the reach of an ordinary farmer; making it likely that the technology was imported by ecclesiastics along with other agricultural improvements.[25]

The agricultural shift to long, narrow fields in parts of Gaul towards the end of the Roman period has been attributed to the introduction of new plough technology.[26] The new plough was able to dig a deep furrow, rather than merely scratch the surface. The aeration of the soil resulted in a better crop. Adoption of this plough technology would certainly explain the change to long fields in Scottish contexts, as oxen pulling the plough could not easily turn in the shorter square fields. It seems likely that the adoption of better agricultural tools in Pictland also increased crop yields, altered field layout and, as indicated by pollen records, opened up new sites for cultivation. Moreover, the introduction of this technology appears to coincide with the expansion of Christianity. There was also extensive evidence for ironworking, seasonal repairs and exploitation of local haemetite (bog-iron), on most occupation sites in Scotland from the Pictish period.[27] This reveals the importance of tool manufacture and maintenance at a local level and there is no indication that the quality and technology of ferrous metalworking at these sites differed from contemporary sites across Britain and Ireland.

The fruit of this technological improvement was in the production of surplus. The transformation of raw grain into useful commodities encouraged trade and supplied the regular renders required under clientage conditions. Excavations at Dunadd, Argyll, revealed evidence for organized grain processing with fifty-three rotary querns; some with handles while others appear to show an understanding of horizontal mill technology.[28] Excavation at Raystown, Co. Meath, Ireland, has uncovered a settlement based around eight successive water-mills that were in use from at least the seventh to the twelfth century, indicating the deliberate and centralized processing of grain.[29] In this context it is interesting to note that, according to Sharpe's translation of the Life of St Columba, St Columba's Uncle Ernán expired on Iona in front of a 'corn kiln'.[30] Adoption of the corn-kiln greatly enhanced the potential for preserving grain. Monastic sites, like Iona, operated as extensive self-sufficient farms; with the advantage of monastic and lay labour, access to new technologies and the re-investment of resources. The Rule of St Benedict stipulated that monastic sites were to be

24 Ibid., p. 12. 25 Ibid., 39; R. Faith, *The English peasantry and the growth of lordship* (1997), p. 17. 26 K. Brunner, 'Continuity and discontinuity of Roman agricultural knowledge' (1995), p. 25. 27 J. Grigg, 'The role and status of the metalworker in Scotland and Ireland' (1997), pp 93–5. 28 A. Lane and E. Campbell, *Dunadd* (2000), pp 30, 185. 29 M. Seaver, 'Silent mills' (2006); M. Seaver, 'Against the grain: early medieval settlement and burial on the Blackhill' (2010) 30 R. Sharpe (trans.), *Adomnán of Iona*, pp 142, 308–9, n. 195. *VC* I.45 [*Unde in eodem loco ante januam canabae crux infixa est*].

equipped in a similar self-sufficient manner – with specialized water management, a mill, garden and workshops – as has been found at Portmahomack.[31] In a secular context, the drying and storing of grain occurred at settlements such as the complex multi-period site of Pitcarmick, Perthshire, with its hut circles set on terraces, enclosures and broad cultivation ridges in use during the early medieval period.[32] These sites represent the homestead of a wealthy farmer – having enclosures for livestock, pasturage and intensively cultivated fields with nearby tenant farms – similar in layout to the multi-period raths of Ireland. Descriptions of this latter type of farm are found in the list of possessions of a *bóaire* in the early eighth-century Irish status text *Críth Gablach*, and include a kiln, a barn and a mill, the latter being leased out to neighbours.[33]

Cereal and faunal record

An innovation for which we do have widespread evidence is the supplementation of the barley crop with oats. Evidence for the cultivation of oats at Pool, Orkney, indicates the widespread uptake of the crop from the fourth century.[34] Unlike barley, oats grow in poor un-manured soil, resulting in a useful low-maintenance crop with long storage capacity that was edible by human and animal alike. Oat harvesting occurs late in the year, even during winter.[35] The excavation at Pool has shown an increase in cereal production between the fifth and the eighth century, with over 60 per cent of samples tested being of oats. This was also the case for Scalloway, Shetland.[36] A similar picture has emerged from Dunadd, Argyll, where the excavators noted that the predominance of oats reflects its importance as a crop from the seventh century AD onwards across western Britain.[37] It is notable that the rise in oat production appears to match the increased presence of horses at early medieval sites on Orkney.[38] Having sufficient fodder to keep livestock over winter had long-term economic benefits for a community, with animals to till the soil, provide flesh and milk, leather and trade goods. Oat production could therefore provide radical economic benefits to the expansion of trade; let alone the increased chance of survival for the human population who had sufficient resources to apply economic innovations.

Aside from oats, staple cereal crops continued to be required for food and, in particular, for beer production, which is attested in early Irish law tracts.[39] Barley was certainly cultivated at Pool throughout this period but with some indications of early harvesting, perhaps to ensure against poor weather or as surplus.[40] During the same period there is evidence for the cultivation of flax at Pool and

31 *The Rule of Benedict* (1994), ch. 66.6, pp 303–5; M. Carver, 'Sculpture in action' (2005), p. 26. 32 NMRS: NO05NE 6, NO05NE 21. 33 *Críth Gablach*, §16, p. 8. 34 J.M. Bond, 'A growing success?' (2003), p. 107. 35 Parry, 'Secular climactic change and marginal agriculture', p. 4. 36 Bond, 'A growing success?', p. 107; Lane and Campbell, *Dunadd*, p. 230. 37 Lane and Campbell, *Dunadd*, p. 230. 38 Bond, 'A growing success?', p. 107. 39 F. Kelly, *Early Irish farming* (2000), pp 332–5. 40 Bond, 'A growing success?', p. 109.

Howe, Orkney, with the appearance of new species of weeds indicative of expanding cultivation.[41] Flax growing intensified at Pool prior to Viking settlement and the excavator of the site noted that both flax and oat production in this settlement reflected innovation away from subsistence cultivation.[42] Likewise, Martin Carver pointed out that the production of flax during the late Saxon period was potentially a cashable surplus crop that was easy to transport and trade.[43]

Analysis of faunal remains, like that of cereals, relies on how much of a sample can be retrieved during excavation, which makes conclusions problematic. For instance, while the proportion of cattle bones to other animals may be expressed as a percentage the result is dependent on the size of the sample and from where it was taken. Indeed, the concentration of excavation on high-status sites and the fact that the examination of cereal and faunal remains is a recent research strategy makes any but the broadest conclusions untenable. The findings do, however, indicate that there was diversification on a number of sites with cattle, sheep and pigs present and managed to varying degrees depending upon the terrain. Overall, there is evidence for a heavy reliance on cattle that corresponds with its apparent social importance in Irish saga texts. The percentage of cattle remains against all faunal evidence found at Dundurn, Perthshire, was 61 per cent; Dunadd, Argyll, 59 per cent and Pool, Orkney, 40 per cent.[44] The age at which the cattle were slaughtered at Pool suggested to James Bond that dairying was practised with ancillary leather production.[45] This may also have been the case at Dunadd, although the excavators were unwilling to assert this on the basis of the evidence.[46] Two chapters in the Life of St Columba are devoted to St Columba's judgment and blessing of milk; it would be extraordinary for herders not to exploit this seasonal surplus.[47] Evidence for the practice of transhumance can also be found in residual Pictish place-names.[48] In addition, the monastic settlement site at Portmahomack revealed evidence for the organized production of vellum as well as other crafts; with the *floruit* of production around the mid-seventh to early eighth century.[49] Indeed, the growth of ecclesiastical settlements would have made the supply of animal skins for the production of vellum a lucrative activity. For instance, the three Pandects completed at Wearmouth and Jarrow in 716 required an estimated 1,500 animals.[50] This clerical book production had economic benefits that could also facilitate relationships with secular rulers and other ecclesiastical houses. With

41 J.R. Hunter, *A persona for the northern Picts* (1997), p. 19. 42 Ibid. 43 M. Carver, 'Environment and commodity in Anglo-Saxon England' (1994), p. 5. 44 Alcock, Alcock and Driscoll, 'Reconnaissance excavations of early historic fortifications', p. 222; Lane and Campbell, *Dunadd*, p. 226; Bond, 'A growing success?', p. 107. 45 Bond, 'A growing success?', p. 108. 46 Lane and Campbell, *Dunadd*, p. 231. 47 *VC* II.16, 17. 48 G.W.S. Barrow, 'The uses of place-names and Scottish history' (1998), pp 62–7. 49 M. Carver and C. Spall, 'Excavating a parchmenerie' (2004); Carver, *Portmahomack*, p. 208. 50 R. Marsden, *The text of the Old Testament in Anglo-Saxon England* (1995), pp 100–1.

less intensive production requirements than vellum, leather was a preeminent trade commodity. Artisans could create a range of leather products, including harness straps, coracles, storage vessels, clothes and footwear; a finely worked example of a high-status shoe was uncovered at Dundurn.[51] Maddicott referred to leather as 'the plastic of the Middle Ages' and its commercial use was ubiquitous.[52] According to Alcock, Gallic sailors traded with the Picts for furs and hides, as raw and finished products.[53] Trade in products from western Gaul between the fifth and early eighth century is demonstrated by the presence of E Ware (wheel-turned) pottery at sites such as Dunadd, Argyll, and Craig Phadrig, Inverness-shire.[54] Significantly, a fragment of sixth-century Mediterranean amphora has recently been excavated at Rhynie, Aberdeenshire, which expands the possibilities for far more complex and extensive trade links between the Picts and Europe than previously speculated.[55]

The faunal record also points to the amassing of food renders for the local elite at high-status sites. Livestock was easily transportable and formed a typical tribute or a render similar to that required for the Irish cow-land unit (*tír mbó*) of the *bóaire*.[56] In this way, livestock and agricultural produce was commodified. The use of cattle as currency was, of course, not an Irish innovation. As Karl Brunner has noted, the Latin monetary unit *pecunia* is from *pecus* (cattle) and the Old High German term *fehu* (cattle) became 'fief'.[57] The predominance of cattle remains at these sites is suggestive of the regular render required from farms under clientage and tenancy obligations to the local elite. Another monetary unit that appears to have extensive currency in Ireland was the female slave.

Slavery, surplus and silver

The ubiquity of slavery in this period had an economic and social impact.[58] Irish law texts described the female slave (*cumal*) as a unit of currency, alongside other currency units such as the cow and silver.[59] Although by the period in which these laws were transcribed the *cumal* appears to represent a monetary unit rather than an actual person to be exchanged. The extent of enslaved labour and manumission in this period is difficult to discern. Insular documentary sources provide limited insight until the ninth century, when an increase in land charters shows evidence for a tied labour force.[60] Earlier evidence of slavery is patchy and cannot support a comprehensive assessment of the percentage of slave labour. Nevertheless, while slavery was never as extensive as in the Classical period, it

51 Alcock, Alcock and Driscoll, 'Reconnaissance excavations of early historic fortifications', p. 219. 52 J.R. Maddicott, 'Two frontier states' (2000), pp 33, 37. 53 L. Alcock, *Kings and warriors, craftsmen and priests* (2003), pp 90–1. 54 G. Ritchie and A. Ritchie, *Scotland: archaeology and early history* (1991), p. 145. 55 G. Noble and M. Gondek, 'Symbol stones in context' (2011), p. 319. 56 A.R. Easson, 'Ouncelands and pennylands' (1987), p. 6; Foster, 'Before Alba', p. 7. 57 Brunner, 'Continuity and discontinuity of Roman agricultural knowledge', p. 28. 58 J. Henning, 'Slavery or freedom?' (2003), p. 274. 59 F. Kelly, *Early Irish law* (1988, rep. 1991), p. 112. 60 D.A.E. Pelteret, *Slavery in medieval England* (1995).

was a feature of agrarian production. Slave raids appear to have been a regular occurrence – which was the fate that befell St Patrick – and the appearance of Angles from Northumbria at a slave market in Rome suggests that slavery was a lucrative trade across western Europe.[61] Frisian traders appear to have had a sideline in the purchase or ransom of the vanquished enemies of Anglo-Saxon kings.[62] Closer to home, in his letter to Coroticus, Patrick rails against the enslavement of his converts, some of whom are sold to 'the most unworthy apostates and Picts'.[63] Other than prisoners of war, slaves were also sourced from payments for debt or from the sale of children due to familial impoverishment.[64] This latter transaction may have reduced the practice of infant exposure and initially flourished more vigorously under Christianity, which was traditionally opposed to exposing newborns.[65] Christian ideals on equality appear to have had some currency, with St Wilfrid baptizing and granting freedom to some 250 male and female slaves whom he received as part of a property settlement in Sussex.[66] St Columba reputedly freed an Irish female slave from the court of the Pictish king Bridei filius Mailcon, as he 'had pity on her as a fellow human being'.[67] These instances suggest that there were clerical attempts to alter social customs. That these events were included in the hagiographies of these saints suggests that the actions of these prelates were unusual and slavery was a culturally embedded practice. Initially, Christianity appears to have had a limited effect on the practice of slavery, although the sixth-century *Penetentials of Vinniani* did attempt to prevent the sexual exploitation of female slaves.[68] Similarly, the laws of King Ethelberht penalized sexual dalliance with a maiden belonging to the king, or his grinding slave, but this may relate to a generalized protection of royal property.[69] Irish laws lay out a gender-specific division of labour, with male slaves (*mug*) doing menial farm work and female slaves confined to the quern and kneading trough.[70] While the female slave appears more valuable, both were vital to economic prosperity. Fergus Kelly suggested that social custom and taboos prevented the release of slaves, as they were integral to the cosmological, and economic, sustainability of lordship.[71] In Insular honour culture, slaves were non-persons having no legal presence or corresponding political power. Slaves were, however, useful gifts or trade commodities that could be used to strengthen alliances. Negotiations over enslaved prisoners of war could foster improved relations, advantageous trading rights as well as fiscal advantages. Adomnán's appeal to King Aldfrid of Northumbria for the return of Irish prisoners of war

61 *HE* II.1. 62 *HE* IV.22. 63 'Epistola ad milites Corotici', *Liber epistolarum Sancti Patricii episcopi*, ed. and trans. D.R. Howlett (1994), §15, pp 34–5 [*Praesertim indignissimorum . pessimorum apostatarumque . Pictorum*]. 64 Kelly, *Early Irish law*, pp 95–6. 65 C.J. Clover, 'The politics of scarcity' (1988). 66 *HE* IV.13. 67 *VC* II.33. 68 'Penitential of Finnian', *The Irish Penitentials*, ed. and trans. L. Bieler (1975), §§39, 40, pp 88–9 [*Si qui(s) intrat ad ancellum suam, uenundet eam et annum peniteat*] [*Si genuerit filium ex ea, liberat eam*]. 69 *English historical documents*, ed. D. Whitelock (1955), §29.10–11, pp 391–2. 70 Kelly, *Early Irish law*, pp 95–6. 71 Ibid., pp 96–7.

provided him with an opportunity to develop diplomatic ties with the newly installed king.[72] As a gift to sweeten the negotiations, Adomnán gave the king a copy of his book *De Locis Sanctis*, which appealed to Aldfrid's respect for scholarship. Adomnán received gifts in return, but the success of his mission ensured his status among his own people and a continuing diplomatic role with Northumbria that was politically advantageous to Iona. Aldfrid generously circulated the book on holy places and by doing so he reinforced his stature and authority as a cultivated Christian king with his kingdom's ecclesiastical foundations such as Wearmouth and Jarrow. This type of cultural capital was as useful as pecuniary measures in facilitating beneficial relations through which power could be accumulated and expressed.

The accumulation of resources was not an end in itself but a means to access advantageous socio-economic connections. As a consequence of the increased exploitation of agriculture – including the practice of dairying – a surplus of production became regularized and commodified. Some of this surplus, according to Rhys Jones, formed food renders to local elites in exchange for the maintenance of social order and tenancy rights.[73] In the case of the Brough of Birsay, Orkney, food renders would have been necessary as this prestige site appears to have been a tidal island with no associated arable land.[74] Surplus could also be ritualized to endorse hierarchy, as seen in the feasts provided to the lord by his clients. Nerys Patterson's discussion on the social implications of providing feasts highlights their use as tools of social domination through the elite's capacity to demand surplus from their clients.[75] In this way, being able to demand food render reinforced the political status of the elite and entrenched food render and labour obligations as a regular social custom. Food renders were pivotal in sustaining a military presence to physically buttress the local elite's standing. These renders also fed the visiting artisans and poets who created material and metaphysical expressions of their patron's position. The exploitation of regular food render regulated the pattern of a noble's circuit of his clients and tenants, which was vital to the success of itinerant lordship.

Surplus that was used as a trade commodity considerably expanded both networks of communication and power. The acquisition of trade goods endows the recipient with cultural and political authority that, in turn, would encourage the political leadership to formalize restrictions on trading rights.[76] If Maddicott is correct, the impetus that fuelled cultural growth and consolidated hierarchies was not only the trade of agricultural produce, livestock and slaves but access to precious metals such as silver.[77] The presence of silver is well testified in Pictland, and possibly derived from Roman loot collected during incursions into

72 *HE* V.15. 73 R. Jones, 'Mann and men in a medieval state' (1999), p. 70. 74 Foster, 'Before Alba', p. 20. 75 N. Thomas Patterson, 'Self-worth and property' (2000), p. 66. 76 M.W. Helms, *Craft and the kingly ideal* (1993), pp 163–6. 77 Maddicott, 'Two frontier states', p. 31.

Britain.[78] Trade in precious metal is also evident from the standardized size of silver ingots found at Clatchard Craig, Fife, and the Brough of Birsay, Orkney.[79] At these sites the silver ingots were associated with the production of prestige items and indicate the concentrated activity of artisans in workshops. Ecclesiastical foundations such as the monastery at Portmahomack also have evidence for the manufacture of prestige items, including altar vessels and sacral items.[80] Workshops were often located adjacent to ecclesiastical and secular prestige sites. The concentrated effort in skilled craftwork is shown in the numerous hoards of early medieval fine metalwork that have been found in Scotland. The extant quantities of prestige silver objects from this period (that now rest in various museums) represent, as James Graham-Campbell has pointed out, only a small portion from those hoards recovered over the last few centuries.[81] Indeed, one of the few intact hoards was discovered on St Ninian's Isle, Shetland, from an ecclesiastical context. Among other items, this hoard contained a number of finely detailed silver penannular brooches dating from the seventh to the eighth century.[82] From the seventh century, prestige metal-working, particularly in silver, appears to have flourished in workshops under ecclesiastical and high-status secular control. The possession of precious metal-work was a sign of status but also materially facilitated the creation of socio-political relationships, and could be used as sureties in legal procedures. Elite control of precious metalwork and trade provided physical and ideological prestige that underscored their authority and aided dynastic longevity.

From the sixth century, discernible transitions in the agricultural environment indicate a move to surplus production. Technological improvements appear in the material record in the same period that ecclesiastical foundations become more prominent in the physical and cultural landscape. These improvements offered numerous opportunities for increased agrarian production, specialized goods manufacture and trade. The beneficiaries of economic surplus were those best placed to exploit and control the resources, ensuring the consolidation of their authority. Cultural expressions of this upward transfer of resources and authority can be found in the production of fine metalwork. Surplus production had a social impact that can be read in the settlement record suggesting a shift in the competition for the control of resources.

78 G. Henderson and I. Henderson, *The art of the Picts* (2004), pp 87–121; C. Spall, 'All that glitters' (2006), p. 45. 79 J. Close-Brooks, 'Excavations at Clatchard Craig, Fife' (1986), p. 167; C.L. Curle, *Pictish and Norse finds from the Brough of Birsay* (1982), p. 19. 80 Spall, 'All that glitters', pp 46–7. 81 J. Graham-Campbell, *Pictish silver: status and symbol* (2002), p. 10. 82 A. Small, C. Thomas and D.M. Wilson (eds), *St Ninian's Isle and its treasure* (1973).

SETTLEMENT IN TRANSITION

Where evidence from southern Britain points to the growth of nucleated, or proto-urban, settlements from the sixth century the opposite seems true for most of the Pictish zone.[83] In this region the habitable size of prestige settlements appears to contract from the fifth to the ninth century. Sally Foster has noted that in Orkney and Caithness newly built structures of this period were not fortified and were on a smaller scale than previous dwellings.[84] This reduction in the size of settlements has been interpreted as a result of the consolidation of power into fewer centres with control over dispersed agrarian sites.[85] At the settlement sites of Pool and Howe, Orkney, the reduction in the size of dwellings occurred around the seventh to eighth century, implying a reduction in the population living on the site and the increase of dispersed farms in the surrounding landscape.[86] This contraction at high-status centres represents the onset of dispersed settlements with implications for deliberative land division and organization. According to Ian Armit, settlement contraction is clearly shown at Jarlshof and Clickhimin, Shetland, and he explained this as the result of the centralization of power, resulting in fewer centres of administration controlling dispersed settlements.[87] Contraction was also apparent on some of the hillforts in eastern and northern Scotland. Indeed, Ian Armit suggests that this trend occurred in the pre-Roman period but the Roman presence appears to have hampered a more widespread move to open settlements.[88] It is therefore of interest that the reoccupation of hillforts in the early medieval period enclosed a much smaller area than that used by the Iron-Age occupants.[89] The distribution of these prestige hillforts has led Michael Spearman to suggest that they represented 'regional economies under political control'.[90] This contraction in high-status sites may have gained impetus under the coercive, confederating activities of King Bredei filius Bili. The targeted attacks by this king on high-status sites, discussed in the next chapter, had implications for the centralization of regional power. His successful sieges at these prestige sites may have enabled him to gain widespread political adherence. Bredei's attacks may underline the necessity of defensive structures in this period but the putative confederation of the north would also lead to a more peaceful population. It may be that the continued recourse to hillforts by elites symbolically reinforced their status by imposing their authority topographically, not necessarily militarily.

The northern broch sites have received intensive archaeological interest and

83 Saunders, 'Class, space and "feudal" identities', pp 215–21. 84 S.M. Foster, 'Pins, combs and the chronology of the later Atlantic Iron-Age settlement' (1990), p. 170. 85 Foster, 'Before Alba', pp 18–19. 86 Hunter, *A persona for the northern Picts*, p. 14. 87 I. Armit, 'Epilogue: the Atlantic Scottish Iron Age' (1990), pp 201–2; L.R. Laing, *Settlement types in Post-Roman Scotland* (1975), p. 36. 88 I. Armit, *Celtic Scotland* (1997), p. 65. 89 Ralston, *The hill-forts of Pictland*, pp 44–5. 90 M.J. Spearman, 'Early Scottish towns' (1988), p. 99.

present a case study for the centralization of power, arguably due to the coalescence of political groups.[91] Instead of brochs representing the apogee of late Iron-Age northern culture and their decline narrating systems collapse, recent research indicates that most of the sites continued in use with new forms of domestic building that were under construction by the beginning of the seventh century.[92] The abandonment of the broch, but not the site, has provided archaeologists with evidence for a dramatic cultural shift that occurred in other areas of northern Britain concurrently. This evidence suggests that brochs were a form of monumental architecture deliberately built to bolster new power structures in an unstable political climate.[93] The reduction in monumental architecture and their ancillary defences therefore implies an increasingly stable society. The trend towards this consolidation of authority would have necessitated diplomatic, over militaristic, relations with neighbours.[94]

The geography of Scotland dictates both the settlement site and the building type to a greater degree than is found in southern Britain. Considerations such as available resources, local security and access to trade routes resulted in a range of architectural styles and sites. Hillforts were elite centres of local control and coastal promontory forts, like those further inland, were strategically located in the landscape to exploit local economic resources and control land and water routes.[95] This is evidenced in hillforts such as Dundurn, which guarded a strategic pass between the Dál Riata and the Picts, while the promontory forts of Green Castle, Kincardineshire, and Burghead, Morayshire, are still used as harbours to the present.[96] Indeed, Burghead may have been a pivotal trading centre to which cattle and manufactured goods were brought as trade as well as tribute.[97] Given the incidence of coastal forts, elite protection of maritime trade networks is likely, alongside investment in coastal and riverine vessels. Early ecclesiastical sites were also co-located on trade routes or by harbours and the single *sceatta* found at Portmahomack hints at the broad contacts available to and exploited by monastic centres.[98] For instance, the ecclesiastical sites of Abernethy (and St Madoes which sits directly opposite on the north bank of the Tay), Perthshire, and Rosemarkie, Ross and Cromarty, are located within the Tay and Moray firths respectively. From this vantage point they had oversight of any trading vessels coming into the firths. The strategic placement of these ecclesiastic sites points to a necessarily collaborative relationship with local secular rulers for protection and trading privileges. Many of the excavated

91 Armit, 'Epilogue: the Atlantic Scottish Iron Age', p. 207. 92 Ibid., 194; I. Henderson, *The Picts* (1967), p. 22; Laing, *Settlement types in Post-Roman Scotland*, p. 16. 93 Armit, 'Epilogue: the Atlantic Scottish Iron Age', p. 201. 94 N. Sharples, 'From monuments to artefacts' (2003), p. 160. 95 L. Alcock, 'The activities of potentates in Celtic Britain' (1988); I.B. Ralston, 'The Green Castle and the promotory forts of north-east Scotland' (1980). 96 L. Alcock, 'A survey of Pictish settlement archaeology' (1984), pp 19, 24; Alcock, Alcock and Driscoll, 'Reconnaissance excavations of early historic fortifications', p. 196. 97 NMRS: NJ16NW 1 and NJ16NW 5. 98 Carver, *Portmahomack*, pp 139, 197.

prestige sites have produced evidence for manufacture and trade in luxury goods and raw materials, reflecting local control of markets and trade routes further inland via rivers.[99] Elite patronage stimulated trade in high-end commodities, suggesting an established pattern of lordship with the capability of expanding their economic base from agrarian exploitation. A broad view of the settlement record indicates a transition from the early seventh century: larger territories were controlled by fewer elite centres with an intensive exploitation of agrarian resources. From the seventh to the ninth century, farms such as those excavated at Pitcarmick, Perthshire, appear to become a feature of the landscape, often exploiting upland sites.[1] These dispersed farmsteads, usually comprising one to three rectangular dwellings, are notable for their enclosed fields, suggesting the organized division of the productive landscape.

Land tenure

The division of land into productive units had a long antecedence and by the seventh century a basic unit of land became an assessable unit of 'tax', render and service.[2] This suggests the commodification of the agrarian landscape, not just its produce. Both survival and economic expansion were reliant on agriculture and the control of its productive potential was an imperative well before the early medieval period. By the beginning of the seventh century, however, archaeological testimony indicates that agrarian productivity was accelerated throughout the British Isles. Changes in field systems increased yields, which provided a measureable and assessable benefit. As a consequence, fertile land became potential economic capital. The 'tax' implications of land measurements from late medieval Scottish charters such as 'ouncelands' and 'pennylands' are obvious but they may also overlie pre-existing land divisions of an early medieval date.[3] Intriguingly, the *davach*, a place-name element of problematic interpretation mainly occurring in the Pictish zone, appears to relate to a unit of land imposed on the landscape under conditions of 'extensive lordship'.[4] Extensive lordship, in this context, implies the overarching political control of territories by a ruler to whom the local, territorial leaders owed a degree of compliance. This would suggest that regional lordship controlled land division and the occurrence of this place-name element, while of uncertain date, may imply the exercise of centralized control. Pictish land measurements and tenure arrangements, however, remain ambiguous, although comparisons with Anglo-Saxon and Irish agrarian land units suggest a standard overall pattern that could be

99 A. Lane, 'Trade, gifts and cultural exchange in Dark-Age western Scotland' (1994); Spearman, 'Early Scottish towns', p. 101. For a wider view, see N. Middleton, 'Early medieval port customs, tolls and controls on foreign trade' (2005). 1 C. Dalglish, 'Scotland's medieval countryside: evidence, interpretation, perception' (2012), pp 280–1. 2 T.M. Charles-Edwards, 'Kinship, status and the origins of the Hide' (1972), p. 4. 3 Easson, 'Ouncelands and Pennylands', p. 3. 4 A. Ross, 'The Dabhach in Moray' (2006). See *CPNS*, p. 183; A. McKerral, 'What is a Davach?' (1947–8).

applicable to the Pictish context. Bede specifies that the Anglo-Saxon unit of land measurement was the 'hide' and, in the same period, early Irish legal texts minutely codified land organization and divisions.[5]

In general, the possession of land was a status requirement for an Anglo-Saxon freeman (*ceorl*) and Irish freeman (*bóaire*). Both *ceorl* and *bóaire* could legally increase their status by increasing their land holding.[6] Land was divided equally between the sons, the eldest gaining the main house. Referred to as partible inheritance, the custom was practised by the Anglo-Saxons, Irish and Welsh, making it likely to have been the custom among the Picts. This partible inheritance could eventually result in the control of regions by kin groups. Theoretically, the continual partition of land among heirs would eventually put pressure on available resources. Thomas Charles-Edwards suggested that the pressure of land partition, causing an ever diminishing supply of arable land, was behind the creation of a new status of semi-freeman in the seventh century – the *ócaire* in Ireland and the Anglo-Saxon *hlāfæta*.[7] On the other hand, the legal provision that status could be increased by increasing landholdings could also imply the availability of arable land. Certainly, increasing status from a tenant to a semi-freeman through the purchase of land or clearing an assart would be desirable. The obligations of a freeman and semi-freeman to their lord were less onerous than that of an unfree worker, who was required to provide his labour in exchange for land tenure.[8] Instead, the freeman had obligations of hospitality, food render and participation in his lord's hosting. Agnatic lineage in Ireland also shrank from four to three generations, thus reducing the onus on the lineage to ensure all members retained their status through appropriate land qualifications; or risk lowering the status of the whole kin group.[9] Likewise, the reduction in agnatic lineage could offer some protection against the diffusion of property to remote generations.

Both the expectation that a *bóaire* could accumulate more land and the creation and expansion of new ecclesiastical sites suggest more complex pressures were affecting social customs, like agnatic lineage, than the paucity of land. The earliest Irish laws were concerned with inheritance and property rights.[10] At a local level, the status tract *Críth Gablach* indicates that a *bóaire* had the right to adjudicate on farming law (*mruigrecht*), which provided legal protection against trespass and restitution for property damage.[11] *Mruigrecht* translates as 'land law' and was part of the 'law of neighbourhood' (*comaithches*) protecting property and foraging rights, thereby protecting social order.[12]

5 *HE* I.25, II.9, III.4, IV.3, 13, 16, V.19; Ryan, 'Furrows and browse', p. 32. 6 Charles-Edwards, 'Kinship, status and the origins of the Hide', p. 56. 7 Ibid., pp 13–14, 20. 8 T.M. Charles-Edwards, *Early Christian Ireland* (2000), p. 71. 9 Charles-Edwards, 'Kinship, status and the origins of the Hide', pp 17–18. 10 K. Hughes, *Early Christian Ireland: introduction to the sources* (1972), p. 45; Kelly, *Early Irish farming*, pp 6–7. 11 *Críth Gablach*, §13, p. 7. 12 E. MacNéill, 'Ancient Irish law' (1923), pp 308–11; D.A. Binchy, 'An archaic legal poem' (1971),

These laws detail penalties for every infringement on the productive landscape, pointing to established land division and the commodification of production by this period. While partible inheritance acted as a control mechanism that maintained kin groups, tensions in social stratification are evident in the upward transfer of wealth and the legal prescriptions on social mobility point to transformations in status. In addition, ecclesiastical foundations and their attached lands were not partible, establishing a different precedent for the conception of land ownership rather than inherited 'stewardship'.

Social mobility

In Ireland, an *ócaire* was generally a client of a higher-status lord, who provided him with eight cows in exchange for food-rent and services. By producing a surplus and increasing land and livestock holdings he could rise to the next rank of *bóaire*. An increase in status brought increased legal privileges and honour price, greater access to plough teams, new land and less onerous obligations of service.[13] Nevertheless, Irish customary law regulated upward mobility by ensuring that, despite an increase in wealth and clients, a commoner such as the *bóaire* could not rise to the status of lord until the third generation, his grandson.[14] Likewise, social customs ensured that marriage to a higher-status partner was economically disadvantageous.[15] In what appears to be an innovation, *Críth Gablach* allowed a *bóaire* to use his surplus wealth, when unable to obtain more land, to lend as capital in order to acquire clients at which point he is named a *fer fothlai*, a 'man of withdrawal', as he was neither commoner nor lord.[16] Although he is not ranked a noble, the number of clients under his protection provided him with increased prestige and political input. Likewise, the Anglo-Saxon *ceorl* retained their inherited status without the property qualification, reflecting a remarkable alteration in the importance of land possession bestowing status.[17]

The Irish *nemed* grades also allowed for social mobility through skill rather than the possession of land and their various social grades were codified by the early eighth century in the *Bretha Nemed* tracts.[18] In Old Irish texts, a person who is designated a *nemed* is 'a privileged person', due to their rank or profession, or a 'dignitary'.[19] The *Bretha Nemed* tracts calculate a persons' honour price according to their status in the same way tracts such as *Críth Gablach* delineate status. The concern of the *Bretha Nemed* tracts, however, is in categorizing status according to profession and skill rather than agricultural possessions. As

152–68. 13 Kelly, *Early Irish law*, p. 10. 14 Ibid., p. 12. 15 Ibid., p. 73. 16 *Críth Gablach*, §19, p. 10. 17 Charles-Edwards, 'Kinship, status and the origins of the Hide', p. 14. 18 Kelly, *Early Irish law*, pp 43–67, 267–9. The legal tracts describing the *Nemed* grades include: *Uraicecht Becc*, *CIH* 1590–1618, 634–55; 2318–35; *Bretha Nemed Toísech*, *CIH* 2211–32; *Bretha Nemed Déidenach*, *CIH* 1111–38. See L. Breatnach, 'Canon law and secular law in early Ireland' (1984). 19 *Bechbretha*, ed. Charles-Edwards (1983), p. 108.

the *Bretha Nemed* tracts were produced in Munster, Patterson suspected that these tracts and *Críth Gablach* described two separate modes of economic organization that were territorially specific; with Munster exploiting local resources from mines.[20] This theory, of two separate legal systems, has been disputed by Michael Ryan who suggested the *Bretha Nemed* laws merely reflect regional specializations and resources.[21] Certainly regional specialization occurred, however, it is clear that the two sets of laws are primarily concerned with different social contexts. The provisions of *Críth Gablach* present a model of political franchise based on membership within the túath and, primarily, agricultural possessions and land tenure. The *Bretha Nemed* tracts, on the other hand, detail a far more complex society of political function beyond the confines of a single túath and pay limited attention to status based on the possession of land. While their basis for calculating a *nemed* persons' honour price follows the basic hierarchical system of *Críth Gablach* (so that the noble ranks are the same) they also calculate a persons' worth based on their skills and knowledge. This makes sense, when it is considered that not every person of means or skill fits tidily into the agricultural model of *Críth Gablach*. For instance, the highest *nemed* status, the *sóer-nemed* (free, or noble, *nemed*) included ecclesiastics who did not possess land individually yet were accorded similar legal privileges and rights to that of rulers. The *Bretha Nemed* tracts, therefore, reconcile the realities of politically important personages who, despite not possessing individual land holdings, were accorded significant social status. Whether this was an innovation due to the increased political presence of ecclesiastics or an adaptation of existing status qualifications, the *Bretha Nemed* tracts divorce status from land possession. The lower rank of *nemed* persons, the *dóer-nemed* (subject, or non-noble, *nemed*), included such persons as poets, doctors, lawyers, ferrous and non-ferrous smiths, woodworkers, sculptors and persons of every art (*dán*). Their social mobility was controlled by restricting *dóer-nemed* status to the third generation, or more, to practise a *nemed* skill. Nevertheless, as *Uraicecht Becc* makes clear 'everyone [may become] free by his wealth' so that a *dóer-nemed* person may buy 'land or rights by his art or by his husbandry or by his talent that God gives him': ergo 'a man is better than his birth'.[22] This group were integral to the maintenance of the hierarchies and, as will be discussed, were agents of political consolidation. It is notable that a *dóer-nemed* person was not legally assessed or contractually liable through their possession of land, but through their professional skills; these were formalized to ensure the assessment of commensurate legal compensation. Moreover, a *dóer-nemed* required patronage to practise their skills and had special freedoms to move outside of their home territories without losing legal franchise. The presence of skilled artisans in Pictland, some

20 D.A. Binchy, 'The date and provenance of *Uraicecht Becc*' (1958); N. Thomas Patterson, *Cattle-lords and clansmen* (1994), pp 45–6. 21 M. Ryan, 'Early medieval Ireland: some archaeological issues' (1996). 22 *CIH* 1594.5–32.

producing high-status jewellery at elite sites, suggests that Pictish artificers acquired similar social and legal privileges to a *dóer-nemed* person. In Pictland, the increased production of prestige items of personal ornament coincided with the alteration in building practices away from monumental architecture.[23] The Brough of Birsay, Orkney, has produced extensive evidence for the production of pins and penannular brooches, dated typologically from the seventh to the eighth century AD.[24] In the same period, Clatchard Craig, Fife, and Dunadd, Argyll, had a phase of high-status metalworking activity, including the manufacture of penannular brooches.[25]

The manufacture of penannular brooches displays an intriguing conformity across the sites, and their apparent socio-political use is examined in the next chapter. This production indicates a shift from communal expressions of power, through architecture, to individual displays of prerogative both in areas under Pictish control and among neighbouring polities.[26] The evidence points to elite control over the production of prestige items, reflecting status by personal displays of wealth and gift giving. The political implications of gift giving rest in the social obligations created in the exchange that, as a consequence, fostered the development of a complex network of relationships.[27] This increased craft production – for trade and to enhance personal status – required specialized artisans with their own obligations of patronage and status. Artisans of prestige items were integral to their patrons' exercise of status, as were those providing necessary services such as blacksmiths who may have been encouraged to permanent settlement by the provision of mensal land.

Rather than fixed by the possession of land, status was mobilized by the accrual of wealth, clients, patronage and the acquisition of specialized skills. At the same time, customary law was adapted to control physical and social mobility and integrate those members of society who did not gain status through the inheritance of property. Economic diversification encouraged the upward transfer of authority and the consolidation of hierarchical control over resources. The ideological attachment to property as a source of status was changing in the seventh century; no doubt assisted by Christianity and the development of church hierarchies patterned on existing social structures but without the heritable land qualifications. The physical and cultural shifts in settlement and social custom suggest an increasing level of political organization at a local and regional level. The operation of local administration represents a building block for regional control and sheds light on the way in which communities were organized internally and expanded their social networks outwards.

23 Armit, 'Epilogue: the Atlantic Scottish Iron Age', p. 202. 24 Curle, *Pictish and Norse finds from the Brough of Birsay*. 25 Close-Brooks, 'Excavations at Clatchard Craig, Fife'; Lane and Campbell, *Dunadd*, p. 234. 26 Sharples, 'From monuments to artefacts', pp 159–60; M.R. Nieke and H.B. Duncan, 'Dalriada: the establishment and maintenance of an early historic kingdom' (1988), pp 6–8. 27 Sharples, 'From monuments to artefacts', p. 161.

UNITS OF LORDSHIP

Despite the potential for social status to become detached from land possession, agriculture remained the fundamental economic basis of social organization. Documents from the seventh to eighth century – such as the Anglo-Saxon *Tribal hidage* and law codes, Old Irish status texts like *Críth Gablach*, and the Dál Riatan muster record of the *Míniugud Senchasa Fher nAlban* – refer to systematized territorial assessments that were used to calculate tribute, dues and service as well as compensation. They reveal the obligations of each status level to a superior rank according to the proprietorship or tenancy of land and, as the period progresses, moveable wealth. Theoretically, the control of territories by kin-groups could have developed naturally with the land held by a 'tribal corporate body of kin' fixing the geographic boundaries.[28] Allodial, partible inheritance could therefore restrict ownership of a relatively static territory within a kin-group, yet the kin-group itself was hierarchical. Communal service to an elite is archaeologically attested from the Bronze Age to the medieval period: monumental building works were organized for the benefit of a community's leaders. Cooperative activities were therefore controlled by the operation of lordship, which ordered and protected kin-group rights. By the early medieval period social and political relations and rights within territorially defined kin-groups were mediated through a local lord who thereby controlled production and resources. Fixed territorial divisions allowed for a regularized assessment of property, production and manpower aiding the upward transfer of resources. In turn, these territorial units could be amalgamated into a wider network of obligation.

The postulated antiquity of these territorial units led William Hoskins in 1955 to declare that 'I believe that boundaries are one of the most ancient features in the English landscape – parish, county, hundred, estate'.[29] While Hoskins credited aspects of the regularized partitioning of land in England to Roman estate networks, Glanville Jones, some twenty years later, claimed these divisions as a native feature pre-dating Roman settlement.[30] Finding that similar territorial divisions existed in Wales as well as in England, Jones determined that a regular division included a main or manorial estate settlement with a number of satellite settlements, a complex he described as a *multiple estate*. Moreover, the *multiple estate* division may have been trans-cultural and approximated the size of a parish. At roughly 1,024 acres, dependent upon fertility and resources, they represent the smallest unit over which lordship was exercised.[31] Rosamond

28 S.T. Driscoll, 'The early historic landscape of Strathearn' (1987), pp 110, 299. 29 W.G. Hoskins, *The making of the English landscape* (1955; repr. 1985), p. 13. 30 G.R.J. Jones, 'Multiple estates and early settlement' (1976), p. 17; G.R.J. Jones, 'The Dark Ages' (1989). For the possible antiquity of field boundaries, see S. Oosthuizen, 'The roots of the common fields' (2000). 31 R.A. Dodgshon, *Land and society in early Scotland* (1981), pp 58–60.

Faith, however, contests the use of a *multiple estate* for the earlier period suggesting it relates to a 'unit of ownership'. This she claims was a later evolution, preferring the Old English term *scīr* ('shire') that more effectively expressed a 'political unit'.[32] There is some relevance to this argument. Faith uses a contemporary term that in medieval Scotland correlates to the later 'shire' and 'thanage', although there is no evidence that these terms were current or had equivalents in seventh-century Pictland.[33] Nevertheless, Faith was following the theory of Barrow who found evidence that the medieval Scottish 'shire' and 'thanage' corresponded to a potentially early administrative unit of lordship.[34] Control over these territorial units may be ancient; Tacitus referred to the Icenian chiefs as deprived of their hereditary estates by the Romans.[35] Any attempt to locate a regularized pattern of *multiple estate*, 'shire' or 'thanage' on the modern landscape is problematic; and is probably indicative of a gradual and fluctuating coalescence of control over an irregular landscape. Likewise, the extent to which *multiple estate* equates to 'shire' or 'thanage' is difficult to determine with any degree of accuracy. An assessment of the 'thanage' of Kintore, Aberdeenshire, determined that it consisted of six 'parish-sized' estates under ecclesiastical control, although when the 'thanage' or ecclesiastical control was established is unknown.[36] In his recent analysis of the toponyms in and around the parish of Deer, Aberdeenshire, Simon Taylor detected a possible Pictish administrative territorial term in *fetter* (Fetterangus, Aberdeenshire). Pictish **uotir* (*fetter*) is related to Welsh *godir* meaning district, which is found in other place-names in north-east Scotland. Moreover, Taylor suggested that the toponymic appearance of *fetter* was coincident with the *caput* (administrative centre) of late medieval baronies and could indicate the headquarters of early Pictish secular administration.[37] The territorial extent of this term is yet to be determined but was probably larger than a parish. Further examination of its incidence could substantiate an earlier development of administrative officials than the evidence currently supports.

The premise of some studies that discuss the development of the *multiple estate*, 'shire' or 'thanage' in Britain is that there was a general control over the distribution of land by the king with his stewards and thanes maintaining royal estates that were distributed around the kingdom.[38] Faith's contention that this was a later evolution in concepts of land ownership nevertheless presents a simplified progression of what would have to have been a more complex series of social exchanges.[39] King Oswiu granted a profitable estate to his thane, and

32 Faith, *The English peasantry and the growth of lordship*, p. 11. 33 E.W. Robertson, *Historical essays in connexion with the land, the Church &c.* (1872), pp 112–33; Barrow, *The kingdom of the Scots*, pp 7–68. 34 G.W.S. Barrow, *Kingship and unity* (1981), pp 8–10. 35 Tacitus: *The annals of imperial Rome*, trans. M. Grant (1996), ch. 12, p. 328. 36 RCAHMS, *In the shadow of Bennachie* (2007), p. 132. 37 S. Taylor, 'The toponymic landscape in the Gaelic notes in the Book of Deer' (2008), pp 277–8. 38 Jones, 'Multiple estates and early settlement', p. 15. 39 Faith, *The*

later monastic founder, Benedict Biscop after the successful completion of his military duties, which he was to maintain on behalf of the king for his lifetime.[40] Oswiu would have perceived the property as his possession yet its political usefulness as a gift transcended its mere productive capacity and allowed Biscop to re-enter the social hierarchies in a new capacity, able to marry and contribute politically. There may indeed have been a similar arrangement in Pictland. It is, however, unlikely that royal estates (*villae regiae*) dotted the landscape in quite the profusion as was possible within territories won so recently by the sword, such as Bernicia. Indeed, Alex Woolf has suggested that the manorial aspect of *multiple estates* was a later development encouraged by the increase of ecclesiastical estates.[41] In the case of Pictland, Alexander Grant has suggested that provincial rulers instigated the establishment of thanages with principal *villae regiae* to provide hospitality during their annual circuits of their provinces. These *villae regiae*, Grant argued, were then appropriated by the king in order to consolidate his territorial control during the unification of Pictland.[42] Rather than the imposition of a new organizational model, this would see the gradual appropriation of a provincial caput, and perhaps subordination of the local leadership. A more effective use of authority would be for the ruler to extract hospitality from his clients rather than deplete his own putative estates; but appropriating a regional caput would certainly be a quick way for a king to impose his authority over the area. Thomas Charles-Edwards assembled evidence for this type of appropriation of *villae regiae* from client kingdoms by Irish high-kings. This ensured the high-king's oversight of the region and announced his purview over the local administration, as the evidence points to the *villae regiae* being synonymous with the caput of client kings.[43] The regional ruler retained the use of their caput but would owe the king hospitality and a greater render of surplus production and military participation. According to Insular social custom, the king ensured his regional lord's compliance through hostages rather than direct possession of the caput. By whatever means compliance was achieved, the presence of regional centres exercising some level of control over a distinct territory would expedite political consolidation and centralization.

In his analysis of territorial organization in Sutherland and Caithness, Malcolm Bangor-Jones established congruence between existing territorial units and the 'shire' pattern, which he postulated was present prior to Norse settlement.[44] Studies investigating the antiquity of territorial divisions in Perthshire

English peasantry and the growth of lordship, p. 11. **40** Bede: *Lives of the abbots of Wearmouth and Jarrow*, ed. and trans. D.H. Farmer and J.F. Webb (1965, repr. 1998), ch. 1, p. 187. **41** A. Woolf, 'Apartheid and economics in Anglo-Saxon England' (2007), p. 121. **42** A. Grant, 'The province of Ross and the kingdom of Alba' (2000), pp 64–5. **43** T.M. Charles-Edwards, 'Celtic kings: "priestly vegetables"?' (2009), pp 72–6. **44** M. Bangor-Jones, 'Pennylands and Ouncelands in Sutherland and Caithness' (1987), p. 20.

parishes likewise found similarities to the 'shire' pattern of England that could represent an early, territorially defined, unit coincident with the Pictish period.[45] John Rogers refers to these 'shires' as 'units of lordship', a term that takes into consideration their communal and political identity as discrete territorial divisions.[46] Nevertheless, these territorial divisions should not be mistaken for a pattern of comprehensive regularity. They are, however, useful as a theoretical framework to understand communal social organization within a landscape over which hierarchical control could be manifest. Lordship, therefore, did not exert its authority through direct land ownership, but through a dominant relationship over people.

As a self-contained entity, a unit of lordship required sufficient resources to support its community, as well as surplus for food renders and labour duties to the lord's estate. These latter transactions of dependency to the lord maintained the social relationships that were nevertheless reciprocal as the dependents received protection, the administration of justice and sometimes land. The local lord was connected to his community by both kin ties and 'paternal' responsibility that may have ameliorated coercive rule. Communal identity and social status was reinforced by regular assemblies at which consensus, or at least the appearance of consensus, could be maintained. While no Pictish assembly site has been definitively identified, Stephen Driscoll's regional study of meeting sites in Scotland has led him to conclude that they were an early 'common feature of the political landscape' throughout Britain and Ireland.[47] Early medieval political assembly, particularly on monumental mounds, was practised throughout north and north-west Europe.[48] As sites of political maintenance it would follow that every territorially defined polity would require one. Indeed, Barrow's desktop study on the toponym 'cuthill' (Old Irish *comdál*, Gaelic *comhdhail* – assembly, meeting) found that these administrative sites were usually on a mound or flat-topped hill and there was never more than one to a parish, indicating local open-air justice and assembly.[49] Oliver O'Grady has augmented this research to include the toponyms *eireachd* (Gaelice *airecht* – court, gathering) and *mòd* (Gaelic *mhòid* from OE *mōt*, later *moot* – a court, trial, meeting); the latter often including the Irish and Welsh toponymic *tom*, meaning 'hillock'.[50] These place-names are Gaelic and therefore later than the Pictish period. No equivalent Pictish place-name for assembly has been established, although given comparative evidence for early medieval assembly among Insular

45 Driscoll, 'The early historic landscape of Strathearn'; J.M. Rogers, 'The formation of the parish unit and community in Perthshire' (1992), pp 114–16; and 'The formation of parishes in twelfth-century Perthshire' (1997); Foster, 'Before Alba', pp 21–2. 46 Rogers, 'The formation of parishes in twelfth-century Perthshire', p. 91. 47 Driscoll, 'The early historic landscape of Strathearn', p. 324. 48 O.J.T. O'Grady, 'The setting and practice of open-air judicial assemblies' (2008), pp 67–8. See A. Pantos and S. Semple (eds), *Assembly places and practices in medieval Europe* (2004). 49 G.W.S. Barrow, 'Popular courts in early medieval Scotland' (1981). 50 O'Grady, 'The setting and practice of open-air judicial assemblies', pp 134–42.

groups, it may be conjectured that some of these place-names were traditional meeting places from the Pictish period. Assembly sites were the foci of political action and had a long antecedence commensurate with the defined territory. Regular assembly fostered community identity and ensured all contracts and judgments were accepted and held within the communal memory. The mechanism of assembly was fundamental to government at this period and assembly at this local level suggests that the unit of lordship represents a microcosm for social organization and administration. A study of these territorial units may assist in understanding their basic economic and communal organization and how these units were incorporated under regional control.

Present parish organization in Scotland, despite numerous boundary changes over the centuries, may sometimes retain a hint of an earlier territorial organization.[51] Driscoll and Rogers concentrated their analyses of territorial units in the south of Scotland where they found a syncretism between early medieval territorially defined self-administering units and later parishes.[52] This correlation is fundamental to uncovering the manifestation of early communal organization at a parish level and the functions of local governance. As Barrow's study on court hill sites suggests, each parish appears to have possessed a place of communal and judicial assembly from which active governance could occur.[53] It is notable that many of these sites indicate a continuity of use throughout the medieval period. There is, furthermore, the possibility that a topographic analysis of a northern parish can reveal details of early civic organization similar to the parish studies of southern Scotland. A wider view of the act of assembly may also be appropriate in order to discern the nature of communally negotiated boundaries and sites of communal bonding. The following is a brief look at a northern parish – Ardersier in Inverness-shire – to show the potential that these sites may retain for understanding earlier communal organization (fig. 2). This parish is strategically positioned along the Moray Firth with two boundaries fixed by its coastal location. Its eastern boundary appears to be marked by a sculptured cross-slab. A boundary marker that may reflect the parish's long-standing affiliation with the bishopric of Ross, as Ardersier was the most easterly parish within the diocese of Ross. While any conclusions as to the antiquity of communal organization from the evidence of one parish must remain conjectural, even a cursory examination offers potential avenues for inquiry.

Situated in the north-east, the parish of Ardersier is close to an important early medieval political centre and a prominent ecclesiastical site. The parish was also in an ideal location to observe and support the activities of the Fortriu dynasts and their allies. Sources indicate that the counties of Inverness-shire, Moray and Ross and Cromarty were the focus of concentrated political authority

51 H. Shennan, *Boundaries of counties and parishes in Scotland* (1892). 52 Driscoll, 'The early historic landscape of Strathearn'; Rogers, 'The formation of parishes in twelfth-century Perthshire'. 53 Barrow, 'Popular courts in early medieval Scotland'.

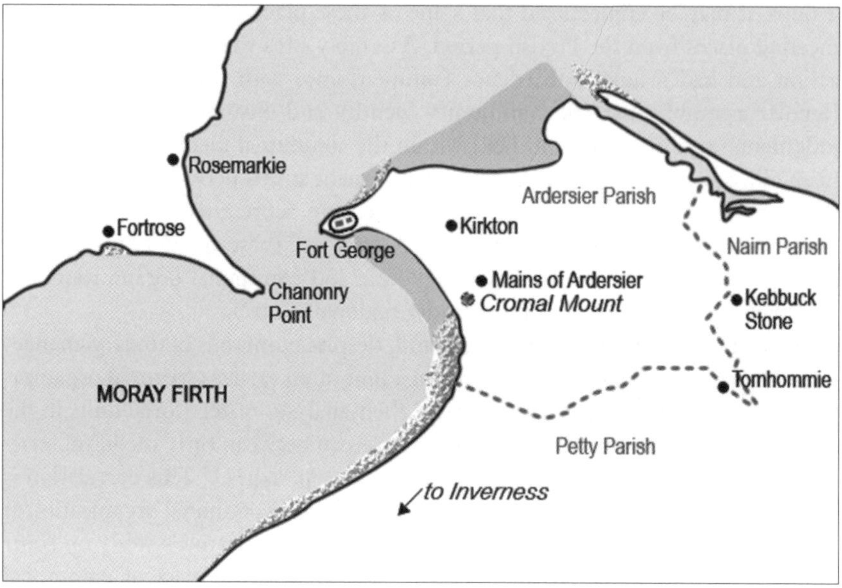

2 Ardersier parish.

during the seventh to early eighth centuries. The Life of St Columba places the Pictish king Bridei filius Mailcon in a hillfort in the immediate vicinity of Inverness.[54] This would have been one of a number of forts used by the king, but may have held prominence on his annual circuit. Bridei's fort has not been located – the previously favoured vitrified fort at Craig Phadrig has been ruled out – but Adomnán's description points to a location close to, if not in, modern Inverness.[55] In re-siting the Battle of Nechtansmere (685) north of the Mounth, Woolf has provided convincing evidence that the Fortriu dynasty were based in this region.[56] Although this dynasty would have held a number of forts within their territories, the strategic location of Inverness made it ideal for a northern king's caput. Inverness offers an excellent harbour that is protected by the Moray Firth, and sits at one end of the Great Glen, a major route connecting Dál Riatan Argyll with the head of the Moray Firth. The Great Glen functioned as an important trade route in earlier periods and it was in the interests of any local ruler to control traffic through the glen, whether diplomatic, military or evangelical. A hillfort at Inverness could control access to this route and the dissemination of goods and people into Pictish territories. Similarly, Inverness is ideally placed to take advantage of maritime traffic utilizing the Moray Firth.

54 *VC* II.33. 55 Ritchie and Ritchie, *Scotland: archaeology and early history*, p. 171. 56 A. Woolf, 'Dún Nechtain, Fortriu and the geography of the Picts' (2006).

This advantage would be compounded by control over the entrance to the firth. At approximately sixteen kilometres north-east of Inverness, the ecclesiastical site of Rosemarkie does overlook the entrance to the Moray Firth with the parish of Ardersier on the opposing bank. Chanonry Point and Ardersier Point project into the firth to funnel, and potentially halt, marine traffic. A regular ferry operated between Ardersier Point and Chanonry Ness and has been attested as early as 1508, but was likely to have been in operation when Ardersier formed a prebend of the bishopric of Ross, if not earlier.[57] The shingle beach along the west shore of the parish makes an ideal landing site for shallow boats. The presence of Fort George on Ardersier Point – constructed in 1748 in the aftermath of the 1745 uprising – underlines the parish's tactical position in relation to the highlands and maritime access to the firth. The size of the parish has been estimated at 1,985 acres, comparable to estimations for a more agriculturally fertile *multiple estate* at around 1,024 acres.[58] Sixteenth-century documents refer to the parish as a Mairdom.[59] The office of Mair appears equivalent to that of the medieval Thane, but stems from Brythonic/Goidelic *maer*, itself a loan from Latin *maior*, attesting to an early development.[60]

The parish of Ardersier is first mentioned as belonging to the bishopric of Ross in 1227, 'as their predecessors formerly held it', with its diocesan seat moving from Rosemarkie to nearby Fortrose soon after this period.[61] A weathered sculptured cross-slab – known as the Kebbuck Stone and similar to eighth-century cross-slabs found at Rosemarkie – is located just outside the parish's eastern boundary in Nairn parish, which also forms the Nairn/Inverness county boundary.[62] The Kebbuck Stone sits on a small prominence alongside a track-way that links Ardersier Point with the town of Nairn. According to early Irish legal practice, stone crosses were used to confirm legal oaths or compacts.[63] This would involve a public declaration at the cross to the assembled community, or communities. Current theories on the placement of Pictish symbol stones and cross-slabs argue that they can mark the boundaries of older territorial units, sometimes co-extensive with current parish and county boundaries.[64] The Kebbuck Stone may have acted as a meeting point between the two parish communities. There is a further hint as to the importance of this stone as a boundary marker with Allen and Anderson's reference to a cist grave of an adult that was found 'within a few yards of the stone'.[65] A cist burial close to a territorial boundary evokes comparison with similar burials found at

57 *Treasurer's accounts*, cited in *OPS*, 2, pt II, p. 596. 58 *OSA*, iv, pp 89–90; Dodgshon, *Land and society in early Scotland*, pp 58–60. 59 *OPS*, 2, pt II, p. 595. 60 Barrow, *The kingdom of the Scots*, p. 67; D. Broun, 'The property records in the Book of Deer' (2008). 61 *Registrum episcopatus Moraviensis*, no. 75, p. 81; cited in *OPS*, 2, pt II, p. 571. 62 J. Romilly Allen and J. Anderson, *The early Christian monuments of Scotland*, 2 vols (1993), 2, pp 117–18. 63 Kelly, *Early Irish law*, pp 198–9. 64 RCAHMS, *In the shadow of Bennachie*, pp 134–5. 65 Allen and Anderson, *The early Christian monuments*, 2, p. 118.

boundaries in Ireland that have been interpreted as marking the ownership of a territory by the kin-group of the person interred.[66]

The parish's most important topographical feature is a substantial flat-topped mound, known as Cromal Mount (also in Gaelic: *Tom Mhoit*), beside which is the demesne farm the Mains of Ardersier and the nearby old parish church of Kirkton (fig. 2). This demesne farm, having the same name as the parish, was the primary estate within the parish; its location next to Cromal Mount further underlines its importance. Cromal Mount not only acted as a focus of local political power for the parish, but its vantage point at the head of the firth had wider importance for those seeking to control access to the firth and beyond. At 47m above sea level, the view from the top of the mound encompasses up to seven modern counties.[67] Evidence for an enclosure on Cromal Mount suggests late Iron-Age occupation and local lordship; this flat-top hill conforms to other *mòd* sites in Scotland.[68] Cromal Mount was the focus of internal assembly for the parish. Nearby, the church at Kirkton also provided an opportunity for communal engagement. To the south, the intriguing Tomhommie farm, which extends into the old parish of Brackley (now combined with Petty parish) may also represent a site of assembly at the boundary between parishes. The place-name has no direct associations with assembly but its situation on the parish boundary and the rounded hill, standing above marshy terrain, is evocative of a venue from which to expedite and formalize diplomatic relations between territories. In addition, Ardersier Point and Chanonry Ness, on opposing banks of the Moray Firth, are geographically strategic to the counties of Morayshire, Ross and Cromarty and Inverness-shire. This suggests that there were early connections between the communities of Ardersier and Rosemarkie and a governing interest by the elite residing in the vicinity of Inverness.

Territorial boundaries defined this unit of lordship, restricting and controlling social exchange internally and externally. The collective identity of the community and its political horizon was made manifest by the physical boundary. Additionally, the local lord could mediate travel and social alliances between the units of lordship ensuring the dependency of the community. As a site of assembly, Cromal Mount points to a self-contained local polity over which a further level of administration could be effected as political control was enlarged and consolidated over the parish by the church and potentially by the crown. The church at Kirkton may also be considered for its role as a forum for communal assembly where relationships within the parish were formalized by custom and liturgy. Due to their strategic location, ties between Rosemarkie and Ardersier would have been early: the bishop of Rosemarkie being of superior status to a local ruler of Ardersier. While the tenants of Ardersier owed render

66 T.M. Charles-Edwards, 'Boundaries in Irish law' (1976). **67** *Ordnance Survey original name books for Scotland* (1868–73), Inverness-Shire no. 8: parish of Ardersier. **68** NMRS: NH75NE 2; O'Grady, 'The setting and practice of open-air judicial assemblies', p. 141.

and services to their lord, possibly at the Mains of Ardersier, their lord owed similar service and hospitality to the bishop of Rosemarkie who in turn owed respect, if not obedience, to the king. The unit of lordship facilitated normative social customs that were communally negotiated and enforced, consolidating lordship and the upward transfer of authority. Moreover, the administrative organization of these units aided their incorporation under regional authority with limited changes at local level: the local lord represented his people on the larger political stage.

Territorialization of power

Territorial power, according to Matthew Innes, is defined as the 'rights of command over land that one did not own'.[69] Political authority over the inhabitants of a territory would, as a consequence, allow the lord to exert his right to the services and render of the inhabitants due to their dependent relationship. Local lords connected their territorial communities through dependent relationships to a superior lord. It is also likely that any diplomatic alliances between lordships would rarely have been, or remained, equal. Ancient tribal ties may have established these connections but political expediency also shaped allegiances between territories. Likewise, land granted as benefices to distant ecclesiastical establishments resulted in obedience to a distant lordship. Alliances with neighbouring lordships ensured that borders and their assembly sites remained physically active, fixing them within the communal psyche. The urge for lordships to form dependent or superior connections with others, for protection or economic advantage, is evident from the conceptual understanding of Alba's regional consolidation documented from the ninth century.[70] The social mechanism of clientage, addressed in the next chapter, allowed for greater flexibility in creating advantageous political connections between territories. An analogous development among the early medieval Anglo-Saxons points to the construction of regional identities and collective identity emerging in the sixth century, coinciding with increased economic control by institutional structures such as the Church.[71] Tom Saunders identified the emergence of lordship with an increase in economic control and he saw this as a Europe-wide development by the seventh century.[72] During this period Anglo-Saxon settlements became physically bound and regulated betokening organized settlement distribution under local landlords who thereby controlled increased resources by their 'territorialization of power'.[73] Within this definition of Anglo-Saxon nucleated settlement, hierarchy of social order emerged from a hierarchy of land rights. In

69 Innes, *State and society in the early Middle Ages*, p. 93. 70 Broun, 'The seven kingdoms in *De situ Albanie*'. 71 J. Moreland, 'Ethnicity, power and the English' (2000), p. 43; Saunders, 'Class, space and "feudal" identities', p. 213. 72 Saunders, 'Class, space and "feudal" identities', p. 213. 73 Ibid., pp 215–21.

early medieval England, as elsewhere among Insular polities, the pattern of local, regional and kingdom-wide rulership emerged from economic control.

The evidence from Pictland indicates that a unit of lordship represented a territorial building block, tied into other such units by mechanisms of dependency, but retaining a level of administrative autonomy through their local assembly. Political ascendency over a regional agglomeration of these dependent political entities constituted a province; with the potential for overlaying further tiers of authority over territories, coercively or diplomatically. Certainly, by the late seventh century Adomnán writes of the *regulus* of Orkney being able to vouch for the safety of an Irish cleric travelling through this ruler's extensive territory. Significantly, this *regulus* was himself a dependent of the Pictish king.[74] Ties of dependency were usually personal and fluctuations in political ascendency occurred regularly, particularly where the social transaction was not necessarily dependent on gifts of land. Perhaps mitigating this instability was the change in the pattern of dependent lordships created by grants of estates and territories to churches. This would cause an alteration in the chain of dependency and a redrawing of traditional social status and customary law, as bishops and clerical officers were shoe-horned into the social ranks. Life as a tenant on an estate newly bestowed on a cleric, however, may have altered little if local allodial rights were respected. If, however, it was a 'green-field' settlement then relationships with neighbouring territories would need to be created resulting in a change to the local political balance. Faith contends that the enclosure of land by monasteries would result in local resentment, which may underestimate the facility of installing a member of the local, leading kin-group to high-clerical office.[75] Indeed, the manner in which Christianity impressed itself upon the existing social structures provides an insight into its political utility in assisting the consolidation of hierarchical control over territories.

FUNERARY PRACTICES AND RELIGIOUS TRANSFORMATION

Bede asserts a geographically defined dual conversion of Pictland when he describes the south being converted by St Ninian and the north by St Columba.[76] The Grampians, or the Mounth, divide north and south Pictland, although this geographic determinant is undermined by the well-established routes through this putative barrier. Rather than as a barrier, the Mounth could be viewed as a geo-political boundary between territories. This would suggest that the different agents of religious conversion followed a political division of Pictland that in Bede's period was becoming less important. There is no evidence that this political division was of sustained antiquity. Instead, Bede's

74 *VC* II.42. 75 Faith, *The English peasantry and the growth of lordship*, p. 16. 76 *HE* III.4.

description of the sixth-century Pictish king Bridei filius Mailcon as *rex potentissimus* hints at wide-ranging territorial authority. A late gloss on a Pictish regnal list describes his successor as Nectonius *magnus filius Wirp rex omnium prouinciarum Pictorum*; which may suggest that these kings' authority were not confined by the boundary of the Mounth.[77] Nevertheless, early conversion tradition, as reported by Bede, conceptualized a political division between north and south Pictland that had relevance in the early eighth century.

St Ninian and the southern conversion

Bede understood St Ninian's diocese to stretch south of the Mounth and from the west coast to the east coast. In a rare encomium, Bede describes St Ninian, a Briton, as a most reverend bishop and holy man educated in Rome.[78] The appropriation of St Ninian's foundation at Whithorn by the Northumbrians may explain some of Bede's singular praise for a British cleric. Possession of Whithorn may have provided legitimacy to Northumbrian claims of religious suzerainty over the southern Picts, particularly after they lost their bishopric at Abercorn after 685.[79] Whithorn's new Northumbrian tenants erected shrines and buildings from *c.*730, perhaps leading to its elevation as an episcopal see.[80] Clancy's convincing argument for identifying St Ninian with Bishop Uinniau, Columba's teacher who died in 579, places the saint's activities in the sixth century.[81] Moreover, Uinniau's cult in Renfrewshire and Ayrshire was in close proximity to the Strathclyde rulers of Al Clud, Dumbarton. Clancy may dismiss Bede's St Ninian as 'hagiographical propaganda' but he supports the possibility of an earlier native life of the historical saint from which details of the mid-sixth-century king of Al Clud, Tudwal, were drawn.[82] It is therefore likely that Uinniau had a relationship with the ruling house of Al Clud, with religious contacts and influence in western British territory and in Ireland. As Anglo-Saxon and Irish analogies indicate, conversion was usually top-down and initiated through dynastic marriages between neighbouring and distant kingdoms. Moreover, the Strathclyde Britons' relationship to the southern Picts, who undoubtedly spoke a similar language, would have resulted in marriage ties through which it was possible for Christianity to be spread. Indeed, the tenth-century *Betha Adamnáin* ascribes the paternity of the Pictish king Bredei filius Bili (672–93) to the king of Al Clud.[83] This post-dates Christian conversion in Pictland but it does indicate that alliances between the kingdoms occurred and were accepted in terms of kingship qualifications. On his paternal side, Bredei filius Bili's grandfather was Neithon map Guipno, who, it has been suggested,

77 M.O. Anderson, *Kings and kingship* (1973), p. 144 and 'Regnal list A', p. 247. 78 *HE* III.4. 79 T.O. Clancy, 'The real St Ninian' (2001), pp 7, 27. 80 Hill, *Whithorn and St Ninian*, pp 40–8; NMRS: NX44SW 5. 81 Clancy, 'The real St Ninian'. 82 Ibid., 23; *Ailred of Rievaux's Life of St Ninian*, trans. W.M. Metcalfe (1895), ch. 4, pp 11–13. 83 *Betha Adamnáin*, ed. M. Herbert and P. Ó Riain (1988), §14, pp 58–9.

was the same Nectonius *magnus filius Wirp* king of Pictland.[84] It is certainly open to question whether the inhabitants of the southern regions of Pictland, in the sixth century, defined themselves as Picts or had a unified political consciousness. Nevertheless, linguistic affiliation connected the people of southern Pictland to the Strathclyde Britons as easily as to the northern Picts, facilitating conversion. Geographically, however, the Great Glen offered a direct and well-established route between the Irish Sea provinces and northern Pictland that may have expedited conversion from this direction.

It is difficult to determine whether there was a *cultus* of Uinniau that stretched into south-east Pictland by the end of the sixth century, or, indeed whether there was any earlier history of proselytizing among the southern Picts. There had been a short-lived Roman settlement and interaction in Fife and Perthshire that caused the Iron-Age forts at Abernethy and Clatchard Craig to be abandoned. This activity, however, appears to have exploited riverine and maritime routes rather than penetrating inland. Similarly, the Roman activity in the region appears primarily military and concentrated in the third century AD, making it an unlikely conduit for evangelization. The presence of a rare *chi-rho* motif on the Skeith stone at Kilrenny, near Anstruther in Fife, has parallels to a similar motif on a late fifth-century pillar gravestone at Whithorn and points to a common religious influence.[85] It is, however, unlikely that members of Uinniau's *familia* established his *cultus* this far and the Skeith stone evidence for this particular contact is problematic. Nor was such extensive conversion the work of a single cleric or his *familia* expanding the *cultus* of their founder. On the other hand, it is likely that the Strathclyde Britons and southern Picts had quondam geo-political connections that were riven in the early seventh century both by Northumbrian dominance of the region under King Oswiu and by Dál Riatan expansion. This break between the Strathclyde Britons and the Picts may have been lasting. James Fraser has suggested that, after the mid-seventh century, relations between the two were mediated through the Cenél Comgaill of the Dál Riata.[86] As in the rest of Britain, conversion would have been both sporadic and multifarious, with the memory of individual saints usually surviving due to the efforts of later hagiographers promoting their founders.

The evidence for church-related place-names in the southern Pictish zone does indicate direct Pictish or British influence. The survival of the place-name element 'both' in parish names in Fife and Strathclyde points to a native development: possibly contiguous with the small clusters of Gaelic 'cill' names along route-ways used by Iona clerics.[87] A poem to St Columba, the *Amra Choluimb*

84 P.C. Bartrum, *Early Welsh genealogical tracts* (1966), p. 10; A.P. Smyth, *Warlords and holy men* (1984), pp 63–5; A.O. Anderson, *Early sources of Scottish history*, 2 vols (1922), 1, pp 116, 122, 145; A. Macquarrie, 'The kings of Strathclyde' (1993), pp 8–9. 85 R. Trench-Jellicoe, 'The Skeith Stone' (1998). 86 J.E. Fraser, 'Strangers on the Clyde' (2005), p. 105. 87 S. Taylor, 'Place-names and the early church' (1996), pp 100–3; S. Taylor, 'Seventh-century Iona abbots in

Chille, composed soon after the saint's death in 597, alludes to the saint teaching the tribes of the Tay (*túatha Toí*).[88] Here *túatha* has been interpreted as 'tribes' but its meaning more commonly refers to territorial kin-groups, regionally confederated. As the small kingdoms in Ireland were also named *túath* it could suggest that a similar hierarchically arranged agrarian society is implied for the 'tribes' of the Tay. The poem provides no indication of the local political hierarchy but it is notable that the Pictish regnal lists ascribe the foundation of the monastery of Abernethy on the River Tay to either Gartnart filius Domelch (d. 601/2) or Nectu nepos Uerb (?d. 621).[89] It is tempting to see a core of truth in these legends, and that these putative historic kings were directly promoting Christianity and endowing foundations in the area. Moreover, Abernethy is situated by the confluence of the rivers Earn and Tay, along a possibly ancient county border making it the type of 'prime real-estate' that was under elite control and its liminality suggestive of sacred topography. St Columba's posterity in this region is not, however, evident in commemorations despite the claims of the *Amra*. Rather, propinquity and linguistic similarities would suggest the early conversion of southern Pictish regions by Brythonic speakers, possibly introduced through marital and trade alliances.

St Columba and the northern conversion

Place-name evidence is particularly slender regarding St Columba's legacy in Pictland.[90] The earliest documentary evidence, the *Amra*, alludes to Columba teaching people living along the Tay and its tributaries, whereas Bede places him firmly in the north. Adomnán made far-reaching claims for Columba's influence over the Pictish king Bridei filius Mailcon both in the king's northern fortress and over Iona's putative monastic foundations in Pictland.[91] Adomnán claims that the presence of Columban monasteries in Pictland protected the inhabitants from plague but omits to name the foundations. The evidence suggests, however, that any connections with Iona or Columban foundations were the work of successive Iona abbots. For example, commemorations to Abbot Cumméne (657–69), who wrote an earlier Life of St Columba from which Adomnán took much of his material, appear in church dedications in Morayshire and Inverness-shire.[92] It is worth reiterating Bede's statement that Iona was chief among northern Irish and Pictish monasteries, 'exercising supervision over their communities'.[93] Iona's supervisory capacity should not be interpreted as a monopoly over the establishment of ecclesiastical foundations in northern Pictland. Columban dedications are, after all, rare in northern Pictland for this

Scottish place-names' (1999), p. 48. 88 T.O. Clancy and G. Márkus, *Iona: the earliest poetry of a Celtic monastery* (1994), pp 104, 118–19. 89 Anderson, *Kings and kingship*, pp 92–101, 247, 249, 262, 266, 272, 287. 90 Taylor, 'Seventh-century Iona abbots in Scottish place-names', p. 40. 91 *VC* II.46. 92 Taylor, 'Seventh-century Iona abbots in Scottish place-names', p. 56. 93 *HE* III.3.

period. Instead, it appears that Adomnán forged the Columban connection with the Fortriu dynasty for mutual political advantage; it is this hagiographical account of a near-contemporary political relationship that informs Bede's understanding of northern Pictish conversion. Bede also stressed the indebtedness of Northumbrian Christianity to the activities of Iona clerics, which the Picts shared. Nevertheless, as Bede emphasizes, this debt was undermined, if not quenched, by the insistence of Iona clerics on un-Roman liturgical practices until wise counsel prevailed at Whitby and through Ceolfrid's advice to the Picts. With Iona as the clear protagonist, Bede's narrative construct was an attempt to assert Northumbrian theological superiority. Adomnán's claim that the Picts were spared from plague on account of Columba's monasteries, perhaps tellingly, is followed by his complaint that the Picts fail to recognize Columba's protection.[94] Clerics from Iona were certainly present in northern Pictland but, equally, clerics from Bangor or the *familia* of Brendan may have made the journey from the west through the Great Glen into northern Pictish territory. Funerary evidence may suggest that the uptake of the new religion in Pictland was gradual and concentrated in regional centres of political power, rather than an organized and expansionary individual mission of conversion from an external ecclesiastical base suggested by Bede's dichotomous conversion story.

Funerary practice

The corpus of hagiographical and legendary materials can paint only a limited and subjective picture of the Christianization of Pictland. The archaeological evidence relating to funerary practices is therefore useful in order to gauge the possible extent and impact of Christianity on social customs. This evidence is, however, problematic. As Adriáno Maldonado has pointed out, there are significant discrepancies in type, size, gender and age distribution, and communal ritual intent in burials found across Scotland. Nevertheless, he suggests a broad chronology where new forms of burial types (cairns, barrows and long-cists often associated with prehistoric monuments) come into use from the fifth to the seventh century, after which there is a shift to inhumations within cemeteries.[95] The socio-cultural issues surrounding the deposition of human remains are complex and alterations in mortuary practice do not necessarily represent religious change. A case in point is the distinct change detected in funerary practice that appears in Britain from around the second century with extended inhumations.[96] No obvious socio-political transitions can be linked with this change. Extended inhumations, however, are not apparent in Scotland until the sixth century when long-cist burials become evident, making the change in burial custom more credibly linked to religious influences. The limited excava-

94 *VC* II.46. 95 A. Maldonado, 'Burial in early medieval Scotland' (2013), p. 27. 96 E. O'Brien and C. Roberts, 'Archaeological study of church cemeteries' (1996), p. 160.

tion evidence from long cists (identified with Christian burial practice) displays a distinct cluster around the firths of Forth and Tay and a smaller grouping around the Moray Firth, following the coastline up into Orkney; a cluster has also been located around Whithorn and in Strathclyde.[97] According to this distribution, there does not appear to be a distinct chronological difference in funerary rites between the Strathclyde Briton region, southern Pictland or northern Pictland. If the presence of long cists does suggest the adoption of Christian funerary practices, as orientation and lack of grave goods suggest, then their eastern distribution indicates that the transmission of Christianity most likely occurred through maritime activity.[98] This could as easily have been from native missions as from external ones, exploiting existing trade and communication networks. It may also be possible to identify contemporaneous centres of political authority by the distribution of long cist clusters: particularly in the northern regions such as at Dunbeath,[99] Wick and Thurso, in Caithness and around Golspie, Sutherland.[1]

The Fife cluster of long cists suggests that the region may have embraced new burial practices under concerted communal agreement, pointing to a single leader initiating change. Long cist cemeteries in Fife have been identified at Lundin Links, Leuchars, Kilminning, Old Haiks, Kirkhill and Hallow Hill.[2] The excavation at Hallow Hill, St Andrews, Fife, found a change from crouched or flexed inhumations (often with north–south orientation) to extended inhumations orientated east–west dating from the sixth to the ninth century AD.[3] This was obviously a local cemetery that continued to be used by the community after conversion; there are indications that this was a site of pre-Christian religious significance.[4] In addition, Hallow Hill was previously named Eglesnamin attesting to an early Pictish attribution for a church at this site with the Latin-derived element *eglés*.[5] This change in burial ritual points to communal acceptance and observance that was probably authorized by the local ruler. Changes to the orientation of inhumations in this cemetery were followed by the appearance of dug graves at nearby Kirkhill, St Andrews, in the seventh to eighth century.[6] Kirkhill is only two miles from Hallow Hill and appears to have

97 See distribution map: E. Proudfoot, 'Excavations at the long cist cemetery on the Hallow Hill' (1996), p. 445. 98 E. Proudfoot, 'The Hallow Hill and the origins of Christianity in eastern Scotland' (1998), pp 66–71. 99 A penannular brooch was found at Dunbeath: NMRS: ND13SE 30, with a possible early medieval monastery nearby: NMRS: ND13SE 18. 1 J. Close-Brooks, 'Excavations in the Dairy Park' (1981). Two more long cists with Class I fragments were found in the vicinity: NMRS: NC80SW 9 and NC80SW 24. 2 NMRS: NO40SW 13, NO42SE 2, NO60NW 8, NO61SW 2, NO51NW 38, NO41NE 8. 3 Proudfoot, 'Excavations at the long cist cemetery on the Hallow Hill'. 4 S.M. Foster, 'Discovery, recovery, context and display' (1998), p. 44. 5 S.Taylor, 'Place-names of Fife' (2000), p. 212. 6 Close-Brooks, 'Pictish and other burials', pp 89–94; Foster, 'Discovery, recovery, context and display', p. 43; I. Smith, 'The archaeology of the early Christian Church in Scotland' (1996), p. 28. Although the excavation records were poor, this seems to be the case for St Ninian's Isle cemetery: Small, 'The

been established *de novo* as a Christian cemetery. There is also a large cluster of burials dating to the late seventh century associated with an early church near the modern cathedral.[7] Kirkhill's proximity to Hallow Hill suggests that the local communities gradually transferred their allegiance from an older ritual site to the new cemetery. The evidence points to Christianity becoming normative in the region by this period: authority over the dead reflecting the dominant religion of the living.

At Pictland's northern extremity, excavations on Orkney have revealed a similar development with a long transitional period during which ancestral burial mounds continued to occur alongside a move towards communal burial at church sites.[8] No burials are associated with broch sites and the earliest inhumations began in the mid-fifth century.[9] From then until the seventh century, east-west orientated long cist inhumation and inhumation under cairns were favoured, followed by a move to cemeteries.[10] Within a monastic context, an enclosed cemetery was established at Whithorn, focused on an early cist grave. A distinct change from lintel (cist) graves to log coffins occurred in the early seventh century.[11] In this period the graveyard was extended and the excavator suggested that this material alteration reflected a change in cultural influence due to closer connections within the Irish Sea province.[12] The cemetery was in use over a number of centuries and the 118 identified graves were laid out in organized serried rows mostly aligned east-west with indications of a reorganization at the beginning of the eighth century that extended the burial ground.[13] This religious site can be usefully compared with the monastic site of Portmahomack. Here, the cist graves of, mostly, middle-aged males have been radiocarbon dated to *c.*AD565–700, with the continued use of cist graves, some with stone pillows, to *c.*700–800.[14]

Comparative evidence from Ireland dates the onset of long cist inhumations to around the fifth century AD, with a move towards east-west orientated burials in cemeteries from the seventh to eighth centuries AD. It is notable that the practice of high-ranking personages being buried in their ancestral burial mounds continued well after Christianization.[15] This burial practice has been detected in northern Pictland with long cist inhumations found under cairns or mounds associated with Class I Pictish symbol stone fragments.[16] Class I Pictish symbol stones are a category of sculpture with simple incised designs, from a small corpus of symbols, on undressed stones that are sometimes megaliths of

site: its history and excavation' (1973), pp 5–7. **7** Close-Brooks, 'Pictish and other burials', p. 96; Foster, 'Discovery, recovery, context and display', p. 45. **8** J. Mulville, M. Parker-Pearson, N. Sharples, H. Smith and A. Chamberlain, 'Quarters, arcs and squares' (2003), p. 32; P.J. Ashmore, 'Orkney burials' (2003), p. 40. **9** Ashmore, 'Orkney burials', pp 35–6. **10** Ibid., p. 41. **11** Hill, *Whithorn and St Ninian*, p. 70. **12** Ibid., p. 37. **13** Ibid., 103–11; NMRS: NX44SW 5. **14** M. Carver, 'An Iona of the east' (2004), p. 11. **15** E. O'Brien, 'Burial practices in Ireland' (2003), p. 66. **16** P.J. Ashmore, 'Low cairns, long cists and symbol stones' (1978–80).

Neolithic or Bronze Age origin. The symbols represent a distinct cultural character with the limited corpus suggesting an agreed symbolic language. The inhumation of local families around an ancestor grave would legitimize and bolster the families' responsibility over the land and territory. The association of Class I Pictish symbol stones with these burials reflects familial territorial possession. Unfortunately, as Class I symbol stones have not been securely dated they are not a chronological determinant.

Long cists appear in the mid-fifth century and reflect a new funerary pattern that may represent the influence of Christianity. The long cist grave had a wide distribution and was not necessarily associated with a nearby church, but their Christian associations have largely been determined by orientation and lack of funerary artefacts.[17] There was a trend between the sixth to eighth centuries AD in which isolated clusters of long cist cemeteries were abandoned in favour of cemeteries at churches.[18] The slow move away from ancestral cemeteries, seen particularly in the establishment of Kirkhill and in the continued use of Hallow Hill, may reflect a change in the ideological attachment to land and territory. Ancestral cemeteries may have continued to be used by the elite as part of a requirement to assert and legitimize their dominance over a physical territory.[19] Yet the move away from ancestral burial grounds similarly suggests that rights over land were being institutionally recognized with less need to reinforce claims by burial. From the seventh century, churches with cemeteries (such as Kirkhill) were founded to serve communities with the land removed from customary claims and transformed for sacred obligation. Some sites, such as Hallow Hill, were altered from pre-existing sacred precincts to Christian ones. Churches were claiming ownership of the body after death with the promise of bodily resurrection on the day of judgment thereby over-riding the traditional use of ancestral burial mounds and graves. This widespread late seventh-century trend in church burials suggests a deliberate religious policy by a corporatized institution. This was the period in which Insular monastic establishments and ecclesiastical scholars drew novices and students from distant communities and polities while clerics travelled freely across borders encompassing numerous territories in their pastoral remits. An inscribed stone from Portmahomack has a distinct script, similar to that used in the early eighth-century Lindisfarne Gospels, which points to the monastery also producing manuscripts with attendant *scriptoria* and *schola*.[20] The funerary evidence indicates that, by the end of the seventh century, Christianity had become integrated in Pictish society, its clerics and monks perpetuating the religious life within their enclosures and throughout their communities. They possessed the bodies of the dead awaiting final judgment, thereby controlling the hope of the living.

17 Close-Brooks, 'Pictish and other burials', p. 96; Smith, 'The archaeology of the early Christian Church in Scotland', p. 20; Proudfoot, 'Excavations at the long cist cemetery on the Hallow Hill', p. 402. 18 Close-Brooks, 'Pictish and other burials', p. 95. 19 R. Bradley, 'Time regained' (1987), pp 10, 14–15. 20 J. Higgitt, 'The Pictish latin inscription at Tarbat' (1982).

CONCLUSION

The archaeological evidence indicates a transition in agriculture and settlement from the sixth century to the successful exploitation of local resources in a period of climatic amelioration. The introduction of oats had a pivotal impact on community survival by expediting a shift from subsistence to surplus production. Nor can the benefits of new agricultural technologies be underestimated for this shift to surplus production. Contraction in the size of settlements and elite dwellings indicates a cultural shift to an organized, dispersed agrarian economy that used this new technology to increase yields and extend cultivation to marginal areas. This exploitation appears to have been managed by a small elite who ensured the upward transfer of resources through social customs and laws that assisted their consolidation of authority over communities. The territorialization of authority by local lords encouraged communal identity and the commodification of land. This was assisted by social and familial relationships that enforced hereditary rights to land and status. The unit of lordship facilitated the incorporation of these 'building-blocks' into larger territories of obligation to superior lords. In addition, economic surplus offered opportunities to diversify and increase beneficial alliances and networks of authority. Accrual of wealth and, by extension, military power and dominant relationships promoted the incorporation of larger territories under the control of an elite. A gradual shift in the equation of land possession with status points to the mobilization of freemen for active service to the elite. This was expressed in the increased cultural investment by wealthy patrons in skilled craftwork. Judges, doctors and legal experts assisted the physical consolidation of political administration. Coincident with these socio-political transformations was the Christianization of Pictland, most likely through the top-down conversion seen in other insular societies. Christianity offered new models of political organization and the religion appears to have been swiftly integrated into the social fabric. It is impossible to extricate the social transformations that occurred in Pictland during the sixth to early seventh centuries from the introduction and dissemination of Christianity. Existing organizational structures such as the units of lordship assisted a political shift towards the centralization of authority, bolstered by Christian models of hierarchical control. The Pictish kings who emerge in the contemporary documents of the late seventh to eighth century display prerogatives over the social and economic environment. These kings continued to use existing organizational supports, such as assembly and itinerant circuits, but their closer affiliation with senior clerics created dynamic opportunities to consolidate their kingdom.

2

The emergent state

Where transitions in the economic environment had consequences for settlement and the upward transmission of authority, so too did the impact of Christianity. Coterminous with economic advances Christianity began to affect social organization and consolidated its physical presence over both landscape and society. The institutional hierarchy of Christianity offered new insights into the benefits of political consolidation that improvements in economic conditions made desirable. The particular strength of Christianity was in its ability to accommodate itself with existing institutions. One of these institutions was clientage. Clientage allowed the establishment of social networks outside of kin relations and facilitated the extension of authority and political consolidation. It was this system that created close ties of dependency which endorsed the exercise of territorial authority without direct proprietorship. Clientage encouraged elite mobility and patronage, which, in turn, was maintained by political assemblies and articulated through displays of status.

Late seventh-century records mark the beginning of a Pictish historical period, when kings emerge in the documentary sources and their political aims of consolidation become apparent. Recent, concerted interest in the activities of these kings has produced a clearer narrative of political interaction.[1] Their political progress, however, should be examined in relation to the institutional structures that supported the kings' accumulation of power and the way in which their authority was enacted. It is these social and institutional structures that enabled the operation of kingship and endorsed the transfer of authoritative power so that, by the eighth century, King Necthon could enact religious reform. Necthon and his predecessors could also call on the support of established nobility whose leading members were likely to have recent or ancient consanguine ties with this dominant dynasty. Where existing social systems supported political consolidation and the expansion of a communal identity, beyond the local territory, ecclesiastical institutions introduced new concepts of centralization and patriarchal rule into communal consciousness. Indeed, the increasing social role of senior churchmen reflects the increase in ecclesiastical foundations and communal religious participation. The ability of bishops and other senior clerics to transcend local and regional boundaries facilitated the king's expanding authority. Their mutual role in political organization, evident at the assembly,

1 Fraser, *From Caledonia to Pictland*; Woolf, *From Pictland to Alba*; Clancy, 'Philosopher-king'.

underpinned the king's territorialization of power. While the evidence for Pictish assemblies remains inferential, comparison with neighbouring polities and later evidence indicates that the assembly was the primary arena for the exercise of a ruler's executive functions and governmental agency. Assembly offered an ideal means to publicly negotiate and exert authority, reinforcing hierarchical control. One potential Pictish assembly site at Rhynie in Aberdeenshire appears to bear similarities to the Northumbrian royal assembly site at Yeavering. This would suggest that the political assembly in Pictland similarly offered a platform for the exercise of regional and supra-regional governance where royal authority could be manifest. In effect, the assembly was a site of government action that facilitated centralization. The form that this centralization may have taken should, however, be identified against a geo-political framework. This allows a closer evaluation of the terminological usefulness of 'hegemony' against current debates on the defining principles of state and nation formation. The activities of the Pictish kings, described in the documentary sources, indicate that they followed deliberate strategies that promoted dynastic legitimacy and political consolidation. The conscious adoption of origin myths and objects reflecting status encode a concerted intent to construct a nation.

THE HISTORIC HORIZON

Contemporary sources indicate that major political changes occurred in Pictland during the later seventh century that cemented a communal Pictish identity. Prior to 685 the Northumbrians held southern Pictland under tribute conditions for at least a generation; it is likely that most of Lothian, and parts of Fife were witness to Anglo-Saxon settlement.[2] An attempt to reverse their subordination in 672, under the Pictish king Drest filius Donuel (*c.*664–72), was thwarted and a defeated Drest removed from office.[3] This battle was described by Stephanus in his Life of St Wilfrid, which includes the evocative detail that innumerable peoples of the north gathered from every nook and corner of Pictland to throw off the yoke of Nothumbrian domination.[4] A parallel could be drawn with Tacitus' description of the mustering of the Caledonii to remove the Roman threat.[5] Similarly, the revolt of 672 appears to have been more an inchoate alliance of regional rulers uniting against a common enemy than a single nation fighting off an oppressor. Nevertheless, Drest's failure appears to have provided a point of unity and engendered a communal desire for autonomy.

According to Irish chronicles Bredei filius Bili gained the kingship in the wake of this Pictish defeat. It is possible that Bredei initially received

2 *HE* IV.26. 3 *AU* 672.6; 678.6. 4 *VW* XIX. Cf. Gildas: *De excidio Britonum*, ed. M. Winterbottom (1978), §19. 5 Tacitus: *The Agricola*, ch. 29, p. 79.

Northumbrian support due to his familial connection to the new Northumbrian king Ecgfrid.[6] In a decidedly political volte-face, however, Bredei and his supporters appear to have set out on major military campaigns across Pictland from *c.*679. Bredei is definitively named as the protagonist who effectively subjugated Orkney around 681.[7] This is one of a number of aggressive contests for authority witnessed by the Irish chroniclers. These military engagements targeted high-status sites: first Dunbeath in Caithness then Orkney and, in the next year, Dunottar by Stonehaven in Kincardineshire.[8] With northern dissent subjugated, two key southern sites were besieged in the same year, Dunadd in Argyll and the important border fort of Dundurn, Perthshire.[9] Winning Dundurn provided a key tactical advantage in southern territories and may have allowed Bredei and his confederates to antagonize Northumbrian rule without coming into direct conflict and to negotiate assistance from interested groups in Dál Riata. In 684, King Ecgfrid had sent an army into Ireland, laying waste to churches and monasteries in Meath, which earned the disapproval of his clerics and Bede's enduring censure.[10] It is likely that this action inspired ideas of retaliation among the allies of the Uí Néill king of Brega; ideas on which Bredei may have capitalized. Bredei may also have received support from his grandfather's relatives among the Strathclyde Britons.[11] The entries in the Irish chronicles suggest that Bredei filius Bili was gathering a confederacy of provinces by sword and, no doubt, by alliance. If so, the sites targeted by his campaign suggest that they were the centres of independent provinces that may have refused to acknowledge his rights to a more extensive kingship. The corollary of the sites targeted by Bredei may suggest that the counties of Inverness-shire, Ross and Cromarty, Morayshire and Aberdeenshire were either allied to the king's interests or were already part of his dynastic territories. It is of interest that the Irish annal reference to Bredei's attack on Orkney uses the word *deletae* indicating forceful subjugation. This implies a comprehensive attack including the complete subordination of the local elite to Bredei. Adomnán of Iona, writing his Life of St Columba at the end of the seventh century, indicates a contemporary political condition when he places a *regulus* of Orkney under the authority of the Pictish king Bridei filius Mailcon. Bredei's attack on Orkney highlights the extent of Pictish maritime mobility making it likely that the king had control of a fleet of vessels, which may have been moored at the numerous harbours along the Moray Firth and at Burghead. Orkney was obviously of key strategic value.

On the strength of these chronicled references to Pictish battles, Fraser has proposed that Bredei filius Bili's reign established a Pictish hegemony. This

6 M. Miller, 'Eanfrith's Pictish son' (1978), p. 55; A. Woolf, 'The Verturian hegemony' (2001), p. 108. 7 *AU* 681.4. 8 *AU* 679.5; *AU* 680.5. See A. Morrison, 'Field survey and excavation at Dunbeath, Caithness' (1993). 9 *AU* 682.3. 10 *HE* IV.26. 11 *Betha Adamnáin*, §14, pp 58–9.

hegemony, Fraser argues, was built of client provinces owing allegiance and tribute to Bredei filius Bili as king.[12] This form of hegemonic control had advantages, encouraging cooperating groups to eventually identify themselves with a single polity. It would also ease the way for a single ruler with popular support to establish dynastic control. Unless successive rulers retained a relationship of dominance with their provincial leaders, however, unity could easily dissipate under this political model. The successful domination and mustering of Pictish forces by Bredei filius Bili is borne out by his win over King Ecgfrid's army at the Battle of Nechtansmere (also recorded as Linn Garan and Duin Nechtain), now identified by Woolf with the place-name Dunachton, Inverness-shire.[13] Here, in 685, Bredei finally broke the Northumbrian overlordship over Pictish provinces.

Nechtansmere was a remarkable battle according to both Anglo-Saxon and Irish chronicles and Bede's own account is scornful of Ecgfrid's foolhardiness.[14] Ecgfrid's decision to approach Pictish forces in their own territory suggests that the Northumbrian king was fired by the need to repress Pictish pretensions and expected success in his venture. Bede laments that after this defeat 'the hopes and strength of the English realm began to waver and slip backward ever lower'. Northumbrian control over Pictish territory was ended and the English occupying Pictish territory, according to Bede, were killed, enslaved or, like Bishop Trumwine, forced to flee.[15] The probable tribute conditions that the Northumbrians had exerted over Dál Riatan septs and the northern Britons came to an abrupt end, potentially resulting in significant political upheavals among all the northern polities. Nevertheless, Northumbria retained control of Whithorn and parts of Cumbria. The battle has all the necessary elements of a heroic epic and the victory would have stimulated a proliferation of stories among the Picts. No heroic sagas of the battle are extant in written form but this event may well be the narrative carved into the eighth- or ninth-century Aberlemno cross-slab in Angus.[16] If this is the case then the sculptural depiction of a battle scene preserves a deliberate reminder of the conquest and is indicative of the affiliations of the commissioning patron. It may be notable that Aberlemno is located approximately half-way between the potentially early episcopacy of Brechin and the foundation of Restenneth, Angus, which is attributed in a later Life of St Boniface to a donation by King Necthon.[17] Warfare can act as a powerful tool to shape national identity and inform a community's self-image, particularly when the enemy is an incursive socio-political group.

12 J.E. Fraser, 'Ministry, mission and myth' (2003), pp 164–6. 13 Woolf, 'Dún Nechtain, Fortriu and the geography of the Picts', p. 185. 14 *ASC*, at 685; Winchester MS 638 and Peterborough MS 639; *AU* 686.1; *HE* IV. 26. For further reports, see Anderson, *Early sources of Scottish history*, 1, pp 192–3. 15 *HE* IV.26. 16 NMRS: NO55NW 28.00; G.D.R. Cruickshank, 'The Battle of Dunnichen and the Aberlemno battle-scene' (2000). 17 A. MacDonald, *Curadán, Boniface and the early church of Rosemarkie* (1992), p. 16.

Anthony Smith has analysed numerous historic conflicts and the way in which they shaped and promoted a sense of cohesive community. He found that wars generate a stratum of propaganda such as myths of cohesion that serve to legitimize the centralization of power.[18] In addition, contemporary Insular advice texts, such as the Old Irish *Audacht Morainn* and the ninth abuse in the seventh-century treatise *De duodecim abusiuis saeculi* equate the success in defending territories from outside enemies with a 'just' notion of kingship ordained and favoured by God.[19] By mustering the Pictish provinces to prosecute a successful war Bredei filius Bili would have capitalized on this sense of a collective win against a mutual opponent. To a Christian populace, Bredei's success in the face of the Northumbrian's superior forces provided a divine sanction for his rule.

Bredei's success as a military leader validated his rights to the kingship. This was also true for the Anglo-Saxon, Irish and the Merovingian rulers in this period.[20] All these groups attempted to consolidate extensive territorial control under single charismatic leadership. War being the obvious outcome of territorial expansion, a tactical and powerful war leader gained legitimacy through successful military engagements. Even without the impetus of territorial expansion, a leader needed to protect his territory. According to contemporary political manifestos, such as the ninth abuse in *De duodecim abusiuis saeculi*, the king had a contractual obligation to protect the physical welfare of his people from invasion or suffer cosmological failure.[21] *Críth Gablach* also outlines an Irish king's right and obligation to call a hosting in times of physical threat – such as the Northumbrian invasion of Mag Breg in 684 – and the mutual acceptance of the king's authority by his people condoned this muster of forces.[22] Similarly, the late seventh-century census, *Míniugud Senchasa Fher nAlban*, calculates the men available for muster in Dál Riata, indicating the necessity for an organized and responsive militia.[23] Binchy noted that in early medieval Ireland '[v]alour in battle was the supreme test of rightful kingship'.[24] Cowardice in battle, on the other hand, could result in a king losing his status.[25] Furthermore, a king's failure to protect his people could signify God's disfavour and provide a legitimate reason for his deposition. Failure in war may have caused the exile of the Pictish king Drest filius Donuel, who led the disastrous campaign against the Northumbrians in 672.[26] Deposition was not an unusual occurrence for a Pictish king. Irish chronicles list a number of Pictish kings expelled from office and/or

18 A. Smith, 'War and ethnicity' (1981), p. 391. 19 *Audacht Morainn*, ed. and trans. F. Kelly (1976), §15, pp 6–7; Pseudo-Cyprian: *De duodecim abusiuis saeculi*, ed. S. Hellmann (1909), ix rex iniquus, lines 9–10, 15, p. 52. 20 Y. Hen, 'The uses of the Bible' (1998), pp 286–8. 21 Pseudo-Cyprian: *De duodecim*, ix rex iniquus, lines 9–15, p. 52. See also L.H. Keeley, *War before civilization* (1996). 22 *Críth Gablach*, §37, p. 20. 23 J. Bannerman, *Studies in the history of the Dalriada* (1974), pp 41–9. 24 D.A. Binchy, *Celtic and Anglo-Saxon kingship* (1970), p. 17. 25 K. McCone, *Pagan past and Christian present* (1991), p. 122; *Críth Gablach*, §40, p. 21; Kelly, *Early Irish law*, p. 353. 26 *AU* 672.6.

exiled. The records of these kings' expulsion imply a legal procedure, possibly including physical confinement, to ensure they could not regain their leadership rights. This appears to be the case for the short-lived reign of Taran filius Entifidich who was expelled from the kingship in 697 and fled to Ireland two years later.[27] It may not be coincidental that the Life of St Columba describes a visit to the saint of an exiled Pictish noble named Taran.[28]

Kings who were successful in battle were able to consolidate their hold on the kingship and promote the interests of their own dynasty. The record of Bredei filius Bili's death in 693 refers to him as *rex Fortrend* (Fortriu), an apparently new designation potentially reflecting a similar ideological concept of kingship to that of the king of Tara.[29] Muirchú's Life of St Patrick refers to Tara as 'the capital of the realm of the Irish'.[30] An earlier reference to Fortriu in 664 (*Bellum Lutho Feirnn, .i. i Fortrinn*) relates to a territorial designation, albeit a distinct one.[31] The title *rex Fortrend* suggests that Bredei retained control of confederated provinces and promoted a potentially new conceptual framework for kingship with dynastic ambitions. It is likely that his successor kings, Bredei filius Derelei and Necthon filius Derelei, emphasized their relationship to Bredei filius Bili in order to legitimize their retention of authority over the provinces. Bredei filius Derelei, soon after the forcible expulsion of his predecessor Taran filius Entifidich (*c.*693–7), was styled *rí Cruithintuathi* (king of the Picts) in the guarantor list of Adomnán of Iona's *Cáin Adomnáin* (*lex innocentium*).[32] The guarantor list was updated with the titles of the guarantors at some point after the ratification of this law, but they appear to reflect roughly contemporary titles.[33] The Old Irish construct *Cruithintuathi* is genitive singular and implies that the king (*rí*) represented a single polity rather than a single province of the Picts. As Fraser observes, after Ecgfrid's defeat documentary references to the Picts were to the singular *gens*, where previously they were in the plural *gentes*.[34] The documentary evidence points to an initial forcible confederation of provinces under Bredei filius Bili that, by the reign of Bredei filius Derelei, was conceptualized as a single polity under a single ruler.

Retaining and legitimizing political control in the hands of a single ruler required not just coercive threats but the careful use of ideas and propaganda to express unity and consolidated authority. Control was also augmented by the possession of hostages from rulers of subordinated provinces, which ensured the territorial expansion of a king's authority. This was a traditional means of gaining support that, in the seventh century, was augmented by ideological constructs of identity and cultural unity. This is apparent in the invention and

27 *AU* 697.1; 699.3. 28 *VC* II.23. 29 *AU* 693.1. 30 *The Patrician texts in the Book of Armagh*, ed. and trans. L. Bieler (1979), 'A. Muirchú', §I.10 (9), pp 74–5 [*imperator barbarorum regnans in Temoria, quae ‹tunc› erat caput ‹regni› Scotorum*]. 31 *AU* 664.3. 32 *CA* §28. 33 M. Ní Dhonnchadha, 'The guarantor list of the *Cáin Adomnáin*' (1982). 34 J.E. Fraser, *The Battle of Dunichen* (2002), p. 28.

promotion of 'nation-building' ideologies in the form of origin myths and dynastic pedigrees which invested claims to kingship with a further layer of legitimacy. The creation and maintenance of confederated provinces beyond the single reign of Bredei filius Bili, however, required existing institutional supports through which political control could be consolidated and unification gain popular support. Clientage was one of these institutions. As a means of forging dependent yet reciprocal relationships across all levels of society, clientage offered a means to effect dynamic social control and geo-political authority.

THE INSTITUTION OF CLIENTAGE

Client/patron relations affected most levels of early medieval Insular society. A system of clientage prevailed among the Iron-Age Gauls and a codification of this system underpinned early Irish legal custom.[35] The kin-group as a closed system of relations was unsustainable given the exigencies of marriage and the changes imposed on social networks through births, marital alliances and deaths.[36] The clientage system, however, was integrative. It allowed for alliances outside of the kin-groups and could ultimately establish a system of interlocking alliances and hierarchies that transcended the local to create and support political centralization. This system did not invalidate the role of kinship ties: the Irish law text, *Cáin Aicillne*, regards a contract of base clientage with a kinsman as the ideal.[37] Contracts between kinsmen had the advantage of retaining property and wealth within a kin-group and preserving the inherent protection offered to its members, particularly for those of lower status. Clientage, however, bolstered the hierarchies' authority over land and personnel by fixing the client into a relationship of, usually, economic obligation to a noble of higher status. At the most basic level, a noble would grant their lower-status client cattle or land in exchange for regular food render, military support and labour. The noble, in return, would protect the client's interests, legally and physically.[38] The more clients a noble accrued, the greater their control of resources from render, labour and legal prosecutions which, in turn, allowed the noble to maximize their wealth and prestige through military retinues, trade and patronage. The client was not legally coerced into this relationship, as either party could end the relationship, but without the support of a noble a base client had restricted legal access and limited social participation.

According to Roymans, there were at least three levels of client relations among the pre-Roman Gauls: those between nobles and plebs, which forged

35 N. Roymans, *Tribal societies in northern Gaul* (1990), pp 39–45; Kelly, *Early Irish law*, p. 29. 36 A. Woolf, 'Community, identity and kingship in early England' (2000), p. 92. 37 Kelly, *Early Irish law*, p. 29; *CIH* 485.16–17, 19–20. 38 See M. Gerriets, 'Economy and society' (1983).

vertical relations; between differing levels of the nobility, also predominantly vertical relations; and those between tribes, indicated by hostages and tribute.[39] The possession of clients allowed the nobility to exert political control and increase their social status. One of the flaws in the client system was that, in general, for the continuation of relations the patron must offer gifts to bind the client into a dependent relationship. The pursuit of political status, and concomitant power, therefore required increasing wealth and control of prestige goods. The prestige goods model of socio-political competition, whereby top-rank gifts circulated exclusively among the elite as insignias of high status, resulted in a highly competitive hierarchy. The giving of prestige goods facilitated dependent vertical relations but also endorsed the hierarchies, as possession of these gifts was the preserve of the elite. Prestige gifts, in the form of personal ornament, also acted as insignias of status and affiliation over a wide geographic area: the wearer making visible their political obligation to the person from whom they received the gift. The penannular brooches, mentioned in the previous chapter, would easily fulfil the role of insignias of high status and their organized manufacture appears conducive to socio-political competition.[40] Manufactured during a period of historically attested political consolidation, penannular brooches were ideal gifts to relevant levels of the nobility to forge a social contract between the donor and the recipient.

Penannular brooches and political agency

Evidence for penannular brooch production at the Brough of Birsay, Orkney, Clatchard Craig, Fife, and Dunadd, Argyll, provides an intriguing uniformity in chronology and type.[41] At both Dunadd and Clatchard Craig the production of penannular brooches occurred in a single short phase, and this may also have been the case at the Brough of Birsay. R.B.K. Stevenson dated this intensive period of production of these 'material manifestations of wealth' to the end of the seventh century, and suggested that their production was stimulated by increased contacts between Pictland, Ireland, Northumbria and the Continent.[42] This intensive phase of production indicates the deliberate manufacture and commissioning of penannular brooches to fulfil an immediate social function.[43] The concurrent manufacture of these prestige items at Pictish and Dál Riatan sites suggests a growing need to publicly display personal status and social affiliation in response to changing socio-political conditions.[44] As Margaret Nieke

39 Roymans, *Tribal societies in northern Gaul*, p. 39. 40 Hodges, 'Peer polity interaction', p. 71. 41 J. Grigg, 'Conquest and conformity in penannular brooch manufacture' (2007). 42 R.B.K. Stevenson, 'The Celtic brooch from Westness, Orkney' (1989), p. 265. 43 Moreland, 'Ethnicity, power and the English', p. 39. 44 Sharples, 'From monuments to artefacts', p. 162; Nieke and Duncan, 'Dalriada: the establishment and maintenance of an early historic kingdom', p. 11; L. Alcock, 'Pictish studies: present and future' (1987), p. 85; Armit, 'Epilogue: the Atlantic Scottish Iron Age', p. 203.

has observed, possession of prestige items that reflect social status was a feature of societies across Europe in this period and control of this signifier of status usually rested with the king.[45] A thesis advanced by Mary Helms equates this type of craft production to the creation of tangible objects that make manifest new social orders; these objects would enhance dominant political ideologies and 'assist in the recognition of influential persons as foci for political order'.[46] The period of manufacture, which appears to occur after Bredei filius Bili's success at Nechtansmere and the apparent continuing consolidated control under the brothers Bredei and Necthon filii Derelei, argues for the penannular brooch being a purpose-made, politically charged object that enhanced a new political ideology. As a top-rank gift, the penannular brooch manoeuvred the recipient into political obligation towards his or her patron.[47] The obligations engendered on the part of the recipient worked particularly well in cementing non-kin client relationships. Indeed, as Tina Thurston notes, the bestowal of prestige gifts 'may be directly related to the subverting of kinship as a primary form of alliance by replacing kin obligations with socio-political obligations'.[48] Penannular brooches are undoubtedly high-status items. Moreover, their wide distribution indicates their facility to connect members of the elite into dependent relationships that encouraged identification with authority and its centralization.

Typologically similar penannular brooches were also produced in Ireland during this period.[49] The Irish law text *Bretha Nemed Toísech* attests to their integration into social custom when it defines status according to the varying sizes and metal compositions of the brooches.[50] This text has led to the inference that the brooches represented 'badges of honour'.[51] Similarly, they were used as pledges in early Irish legal proceedings and contracts.[52] Pledges were not just security deposits against potential default but were symbols of legal stability and hierarchical authority which had currency among other Insular polities.[53] The use of pledges, or sureties, among the Britons may be supported by their mention in the *Elegy for Gwallawg ap Lleenawg*, a sixth-century ruler.[54] The paucity of sources makes it difficult to establish the level of correlation in the practice of customary laws across the Insular polities. It is significant, therefore, that Gildas' criticism of kings and judges in sixth-century Britain reflects the same authoritative dichotomy of king and separate judiciary as that found in early Ireland.[55] This arrangement offered a means to check royal power and, as

45 M.R. Nieke, 'Penannular and related brooches' (1993), pp 128–9. 46 Helms, *Craft and the kingly ideal*, pp 25–6. 47 J. Carrier, 'Gifts, commodities and social relations' (1991), p. 124; J.F. Sherry, 'Gift giving in anthropological perspective' (1983), p. 157. 48 Thurston, *Landscapes of power, landscapes of conflict*, p. 49. 49 For example, see J. Bradley, 'Moynagh Lough: an insular workshop' (1993), pp 77–9. 50 C. Etchingham and C. Swift, 'English and Pictish terms for brooch' (2004), pp 32, 44–8. 51 Nieke, 'Penannular and related brooches', p. 128. 52 Kelly, *Early Irish law*, p. 164. 53 J. Bemmer, 'The types of pledges in early Irish law' (2013), p. 5. 54 T.O. Clancy, *The Triumph Tree* (1998), pp 92–3. 55 Gildas: *De excidio Britonum*, §27, pp 29, 99.

texts such as *Uraicecht Becc* indicate, establish constitutional directives for the exercise and delegation of authority.[56] This text indicates that kings and judges shared in rights of adjudication and legislative reform. Gildas' pairing of tyrannical kings with wicked judges may also indicate a collaborative relationship, and Barrow has argued that the office of *judex* in Scottish twelfth-century records represents a position of some antiquity. Welsh sources similarly attest to the ubiquity of professional judges.[57] The evidence from this later period indicates that *judices* were present in the king's retinue and in every province where they were responsible for creating and witnessing charters, formulating law and enacting judgment.[58] It may be argued that the office of *judex* was a later innovation, introduced into Scotland with Gaelic settlement. However, the promulgation of the *Cáin Adomnáin* under the aegis of Bredei filius Derelei would suggest that, as in Ireland, similar customary laws with judicial oversight were in effect in Pictland in order to ensure the *cáin's* integration. Indeed, Frederic Seebohm found evidence for a relatively uniform system of honour-price and wergild reckoning of status among British, Irish, Anglo-Saxon and Scandinavian polities in the early medieval period.[59] Their purpose often related to calculating suitable compensation in cases of injury. Lisi Oliver also found a broad syncretism across the 'barbarian' law codes in her analysis of personal injury legislation.[60] This would suggest that, across western Europe, these polities formed a similar set of legal procedures to circumstances requiring status to be considered in terms of compensatory worth and trust. Status would therefore be upheld by a legal system based on compensation and culturally encoded by a – potentially – semi-independent judiciary. A pledge, under this circumstance, not only reflects the honour-price of the person offering the pledge but the compensatory value for the loss of face incurred by reneging on a contractual agreement. The evidence is inferential and, in the case of the Welsh laws, late, but Irish law provisions would suggest that the codification of pledges to guarantee contracts was a widespread practice. It therefore follows that the ability to make contracts and access advantageous legal decisions was expedited through pledging a top-rank gift. Access to legal support was necessary in order to continue social participation, to make influential contracts and to maintain, as well as increase, prestige. That similar styles of penannular brooches were manufactured in both Scotland and Ireland in the same period is suggestive of close political ties. This type of status and affiliation marker allowed its wearer to advertise their position wherever they travelled. The cross-cultural mobility of clerics in this period would suggest that for this group, at least, wearing a penannular brooch expedited travel through unfamiliar territories. If the posses-

56 See J. Gardner, *Law as a leap of faith* (2012), pp 89–94. **57** J. Beverley Smith, 'Judgement under the law of Wales' (2005). **58** Barrow, *The kingdom of the Scots*, pp 69–72. **59** F. Seebohm, *Tribal custom in Anglo-Saxon law* (1911). **60** L. Oliver, The body legal in Barbarian law (2011).

sion of a penannular brooch represented inclusion, not receiving one indicated exclusion from the main political arena, limiting social participation and mobility.

While the sites of manufacture that have so far been discovered in Scotland appear secular, the religious centres of Nendrum and Armagh in Ireland both have evidence for brooch production.[61] This makes it likely that wealthy ecclesiastics were controlling production in a similar fashion to the king. The filigree designs on the more elaborate brooches have been interpreted as instructive Christian messages.[62] They offered senior clerics an ideal vehicle for articulating their status outside their regions of jurisdiction. There are representations of penannular brooches on the Pictish sculptured crosses of Hilton of Cadboll in Ross and Cromarty, and Monifieth and Wester Denoon in Angus.[63] Significantly, these representations are of women wearing the brooches. Evidence also suggests that the penannular brooch continued to be worn and adapted into the ninth century.[64] This suggests that the social significance and utility of the brooch was sustained over a long period and that some Pictish women (some of whom may have been abbesses) had a level of political agency. The trans-cultural production of penannular brooches implies the deliberate participation in a wider cultural *milieu* where the brooches provided a way to articulate status outside personal familiarity. Persons operating at a community level worked within a system in which knowledge of and familiarity with their neighbours reduced conflict, as local social networks were intimately binding. Therefore, to leave your 'home' territory would result in a loss of personal and communal familiarity that substantially dissipated your social agency. Woolf links this diminished cognisance, engendered by movement across territories, with the appearance of 'ethnic signifiers'.[65] In the instance of penannular brooches, rather than being indicators of difference they signified inclusiveness outside personal territories of power. There was an implied agreement as to the meaning and use of these brooches over large territories indicative of social and physical mobility. This implies that there was a degree of political consolidation among the territorial elite that was most likely assisted by the supra regional mobility of ecclesiastics.

The cultural and economic investment required to manufacture the brooches suggests that, in Pictland, they were the preserve of a king who was able to control production.[66] While we do not have a complete record, the Orkney and

61 Nieke, 'Penannular and related brooches', p. 130. **62** C. Thomas, 'Sculptured stones and crosses from St Ninian's Isle and Papil' (1973), p. 25. See also Nieke, 'Penannular and related brooches', p. 130; Nieke and Duncan, 'Dalriada: the establishment and maintenance of an early historic kingdom', p. 14; R.B.K. Stevenson, 'Further notes on the Hunterston and "Tara" brooches' (1983), pp 469–70. **63** Allen and Anderson, *The early Christian monuments of Scotland*, 2, Hilton of Cadboll pp 61–3 and Monifieth pp 229–30. Wester Denoon NMRS: NO34SE 16. **64** Henderson and Henderson, *The art of the Picts*, pp 96–107. **65** Woolf, 'Community, identity and kingship in early England', p. 105. **66** Nieke, 'Penannular and related

Fife manufacturing sites, with their similarity of design yet geographic distance, indicate a uniform political purpose at the instigation of a king. In controlling a monopoly on top-rank gifts, the king could legitimize and preserve his status while increasing access to external power bases and profitable social networks.[67] Personal ornaments, such as penannular brooches, had ideological significance beyond their economic value. As tangible items, Helms suggests, they reflect 'the intangible prestige, worth and valour of the leadership itself' and clearly identify the political leadership.[68] Like the Roman *fibula*, the penannular brooch articulated the wearer's administrative capacity and participation in the aims of a dominant political leadership.[69] The presence of manufacturing sites at the geographic extremities of Pictland, in Orkney and Fife, during a period of political consolidation points to the imposition of new cultural forms. The short production period attests to the deliberate creation of the brooches to fulfil a political function. Moreover, their concurrent manufacture in Ireland and Dál Rita demonstrates close links between Pictland and the Gaelic-speaking world most likely facilitated by high-status clerical mobility. Clerics were able to create extensive high-status and long-distance networks that transcended local social boundaries. Affiliation with the secular authorities enabled churches to be founded within communities and to then establish territories of spiritual jurisdiction that facilitated political identification and consolidation.

BISHOPS AND ECCLESIASTICAL ORGANIZATION

We have no direct evidence for church organization in Pictland for the early medieval period. By comparison, recent discussion on the ecclesiastical organizational development in Ireland suggests a model of eclectic foundations that were integrated into hierarchies of authority reflecting territorially defined jurisdiction.[70] Abbots and bishops were at the top of the clerical hierarchies, able to affect political change through their temporal holdings and spiritual oversight. Abbots, in particular, had a crucial diplomatic role in fostering relations between kings, kingdoms and churches. Bishops, in general, had wide-ranging jurisdiction over ecclesiastical foundations within their territories. A bishop's territory represented a number of confederated local polities, often tied through kinship, which were not necessarily geographically contiguous. With the emergence of territorially consolidated kingdoms a hierarchy among bishops developed. Evidence from Ireland and Anglo-Saxon England indicates that bishops maintained episcopal centres but were defined by the political groups to whom

brooches', pp 128–9. **67** I. Morris, 'Gift and commodity in archaic Greece' (1986), p. 9. **68** Helms, *Craft and the kingly ideal*, p. 14. **69** D. Janes, 'The golden clasp of the late Roman state' (1996), p. 129. **70** C. Etchingham, *Church organisation in Ireland* (1999), pp 456–61.

they ministered.[71] In his summary, Bede lists seventeen episcopal territories in Anglo-Saxon England, not including the archbishopric at Canterbury, that were territorially determined by kingdom and population.[72] Northumbria, like Ireland, displayed a similar mix of bishoprics, monasteries and personally endowed foundations; personal foundations growing in number from the end of the seventh century.[73] The Irish evidence, from the *Collectio Canonum Hibernensis*, supplies a formula for the extent of a bishop's territory of jurisdiction, the *provincia*. This text, collated in the first half of the eighth century, defines a *provincia* as having ten *civitates*, one king with three minor rulers under him, one bishop and various clerics and ten justices.[74] The king may have had authority over a number of provinces but the description of hierarchical control at province level suggests that an episcopal presence could certainly have assisted territorial and political consolidation. Moreover, it appears that royal initiative could be behind the establishment of episcopal sees and the division of bishops' territories of jurisdiction.[75]

The successful exercise of ecclesiastical jurisdiction was dependent on the relationship formed between bishop or abbot and secular leaders. As a result, episcopal precedence would have fluctuated dependent upon the secular political situation.[76] Similarly, while theoretically the bishop of a *paruchia* had oversight of all ecclesiastical establishments within their territory of jurisdiction, Anglo-Saxon evidence indicates that proprietor interests were wresting control (particularly of monasteries) from presiding episcopal sees. Bede's letter to Bishop Egbert outlines some of the problems stemming from the proliferation of proprietor foundations but he also emphasizes the judicial rights of the bishop over all ecclesiastical foundations in his territory.[77] At the Synod of Hertford in 673, Archbishop Theodore ruled that 'no bishop shall interfere in any way with monasteries dedicated to God'.[78] This follows a statement that bishops were not to intrude on each other's diocese, which suggests that Theodore was attempting to establish and preserve a diocesan model that respected proprietary interests. It is doubtful whether a bishop's authority over the territory within his diocese was ever absolute, as proprietor foundations were fundamental to the expansion of Christianity. Indeed, Bede describes secular authorities compelling clerics to accept lands or possessions to establish monasteries.[79] This forcible patronage by secular authorities recreated a social dynamic familiar from secular contexts. This was the operation of clientage over ecclesiastical establishments whereby the individual relationship between the heads of ecclesiastical centres and their secular patrons conditioned the extent of their authority. The familial status of

71 Ibid., pp 177–80. 72 *HE* V.23. 73 J. Blair, *The Church in Anglo-Saxon society* (2005), pp 100–8. 74 *CCH*, 'De provincia', Liber XX, cap. 2, p. 60. See R. Sharpe, 'Armagh and Rome in the seventh century' (1984), p. 67. 75 *HE* III.7. 76 T.M. Charles-Edwards, 'The church and settlement' (1984), p. 168. 77 Bede: *Epistola ad Ecgbertum episcopum*, ed. C Plummer (1896; repr. 1956), i, §14, pp 417–18. 78 *HE* IV.5. 79 *HE* III.26.

the clerical superiors had consequences for this relationship of dependency, should they be from ruling families as occurred in Ireland and Anglo-Saxon England. Patrick, born into a high-status family associated with an early British church, claimed that he sold out of his 'noble state for the sake of others'.[80] Proprietary churches could likewise be drawn in under the authority of an episcopal see dependent upon the clientage ties of its secular patron. In theory, a church could not assume sacramental privileges until a bishop permitted its establishment and personally consecrated the foundation.[81] As a result of this consecration, the bishop assumed the governance and spiritual correction over the church, effectively acting as its superior.[82] This may contradict Archbishop Theodore's ruling that 'no bishop shall interfere in any way with monasteries dedicated to God'.[83] It is likely, however, that Theodore's ruling was to prevent the alienation of monastic property and privileges by the local bishop. Benedict Biscop and his brother-abbot, Ceolfrid, gained papal dispensations and their king's endorsement to insure their foundations of Wearmouth and Jarrow against later property claims.[84] Patronage by the king would therefore be ideal and the king's ability to alienate land and estates in order to donate property to ecclesiastical establishments facilitated the expansion of his own territorial authority to the advantage of the church.

A distinction between monastic versus pastoral establishments does not appear to be sustainable for the early medieval period. Most of the episcopal sees in Northumbria were also monasteries and it is likely that the economic potential of monastic estates made them ideal episcopal headquarters with resident clerics to provide priestly services.[85] Bede informs us of Bishop Colmán's Sunday services, to which parishioners flocked in both churches and monasteries.[86] Colmán was also involved in pastoral outreach, with his priests and clerics touring villages to preach, baptize and visit the sick.[87] It is of interest that the Stowe Missal, produced in Ireland around the mid- to late eighth century, appears to have been used by a peripatetic cleric for pastoral services.[88] The Irish legal text *Bretha Nemed Toísech* stipulates that a church forfeited its rights when it failed to provide pastoral services.[89] That a reciprocal arrangement for pastoral services was a general expectation may be behind Bede's moral quandary over

80 'Epistola ad milites Corotici', *Libri epistolarum Sancti Patricii episcopi*, §10, pp 30–1. 81 'First synod of Patrick', *The Irish Penitentials*, §23–4, pp 56–9 [*Si quis presbiterorum aecclesiam aedificuaerit, non offerat antequam adducat suum pontificem ut eam consecret, quia sic decet*] [*Si quis aduena ingressus fuerit plebem non ante baptizat neque offerat nec consecret nec aeclessiam aedificet nec permissionem accipat ab episcopo*]. 82 *CCH*, 'De locis', Liber XLIII, pp 171–4. 83 *HE* IV.5. 84 Bede: *Lives of the abbots of Wearmouth and Jarrow*, ch. 15, pp 202–3. 85 *Venerabilis Baedae: Historiam ecclesiasticam gentis Anglorum*, ed. C. Plummer, 2 vols (1896; repr. 1956), 2, p. 384. 86 *HE* III.26. 87 Ibid. 88 S. Meeder, 'The early Irish Stowe Missal's destination and function' (2005), pp 182, 194; A. Breen, 'The text of the Constantinopolitan Creed in the Stowe Missal' (1990), pp 108–9. 89 *CIH* 2211.27–9; L. Breatnach, 'The first third of *Bretha Nemed Toísech*' (1989), § 6, pp 10–11.

extracting *tributum* from villagers who had not seen a priest.[90] According to Ian Cowan, Pictish episcopal territorial jurisdiction followed existing boundaries of lordship and were only formalized after the collection of church *teinds* (tithes) became regularized.[91] The reciprocal aspect of payment for pastoral care conforms to existing social customs that cemented a local church's authority over its community. Clancy proposes a gradual expansion of pastoral services in Pictland, over 'restricted territories' by a mother church or monastery leading to the establishment of small, local churches servicing community needs.[92] Therefore, the impetus to expand an ecclesiastical territory was the provision of pastoral care and the reciprocal payments from the communities. This would be contingent on there being a sufficient population in a region to warrant pastoral services. The Irish legal tract *Córus Béscnai* deals with the contractual obligations between church and laity and provides evidence that by the late seventh century churches were demanding 'tithes, first fruits and alms'.[93] It is unclear whether this was a general requirement or, as Etchingham and Charles-Edwards suggest, limited to tenants of church and monastic properties.[94] As Etchingham notes, however, the collection of church dues from the wider community probably required the agency of the local lord.[95] This was certainly the case for the implementation of *Cáin* laws, such as the *Cáin Adomnáin*, which required regnal authorization for its imposition. Once achieved, an entire population could be placed under its rulings, with the church and secular authorities profiting by the collection of fines for violations of the law. The institution of this law in Pictland would have promoted the expansion of the Pictish king Bredei filius Derelei's authority alongside that of the *familia Columbae*. This supports Bede's information that Iona had once held wide jurisdiction over Pictish foundations. The institution of *Cáin Adomnáin* and similar laws suggests that there were mutual fiscal opportunities and advantages for cooperative relations between church and magnate. Certainly, ecclesiastical establishments exercised property rights and accumulated wealth in a similar manner to secular lords.[96] The difference was that ecclesiastical establishments were able to accumulate and consolidate their wealth over generations, had extensive supra-regional support networks and, probably, a monopoly on scholarly training and rhetorical logic. This made them a valuable ally for a king with expansionary ambitions.

By the end of the seventh century, Christianity had become culturally embedded among the Insular polities, but it remains difficult to discern the extent or numbers of the clerical hierarchy. When Bede describes King

90 Bede: *Epistola ad Ecgbertum episcopum*, §7, p. 410. 91 I.B. Cowan, 'The post-Columban church' (1974), pp 255, 259. 92 Clancy, 'Deer and the early church in north-eastern Scotland' (2008), p. 392. 93 D. Ó Corráin, L. Breatnach and A. Breen, 'The laws of the Irish' (1984), p. 384. 94 C. Etchingham, 'The early Irish church' (1991); Charles-Edwards, 'The church and settlement', pp 172–4. 95 Etchingham, 'The early Irish church', pp 117–18. 96 S. Wood, *The proprietary church* (2006), pp 2–4.

Necthon's order to his clergy to comply with orthodox practices, he refers to them as *ministri altaris ac monachi*.[97] Clearly, Necthon could call on a range of ordained clerics as well as monastics in his territories, and probably members of Pictish ecclesiastical establishments in minor orders with lay members. A seven-level ecclesiastical hierarchy was itemized in the *Collectio Canonum Hibernensis* (influenced by Isidore's *De ecclesiasticis officiis* and fifth-century Gaulish tracts of the *Statuta*) of bishop, presbyter, deacon, subdeacon, lector, exorcist and doorkeeper.[98] There would have been modifications to this structure as a foundation grew, recruited and trained sufficient personnel to fulfil the required rituals.[99] Necessity could result in clerics assuming multiple roles. A number of early abbots were also bishops, being recruited from their monastic foundations after displaying keen administrative skills; such as Bishop Cedd who left his monastery in the care of his priors when he took up his pastoral duties.[1] It is also feasible that the possession of lucrative monastic foundations assisted the founder's promotion to bishop.

Early Irish advice literature as to the proper behaviour of bishops offers an insight into a role that appears to have expanded over the course of the seventh century.[2] According to Isidore, the etymology of 'bishop' is an overseer (*speculator*) or one who keeps watch over the behaviour of his people.[3] This explanation is expanded upon in the tenth grade of *De duodecim abusiuis saeculi*, which lists the pastoral requirements of a bishop as a watchman who announced the word of God, who watches out for sin in order to correct and, as God's elect, to be morally upright, sober, wise and hospitable.[4] Stephanus, quoting *Titus* I.7–9, describes a similar type of moral integrity required of a bishop who was to be an exemplar of the true Christian life.[5] In *De duodecim abusiuis saeculi*, particular attention is devoted to the lawful means of excommunication, described as the main executive function of a bishop. *Collectio Canonum Hibernensis* reiterates the bishop's position description from this tract, but adds detailed constitutional advice as to the bishop's election, his authority and the limitations to that authority. This text asserts a Roman orthodox public ordination by 'no fewer than three' other bishops, and preferably at a synod of clerics and lay people from throughout the provinces.[6] Compared to the description of a bishop in *De duodecim abusiuis saeculi* as a watchman, the Insular bishop's purview appears to have expanded over the course of the seventh century. There are some similarities with Archbishop Theodore's rulings from the Council of

97 *HE* V.27. 98 *CCH*, Liber I–IX, pp 3–27; R.E. Reynolds, 'Clerics in the early Middle Ages: hierarchies and functions' (1999), pp 22–6; R.E. Reynolds, 'The *De officiis VII graduum*' (1999), p. 121. 99 Reynolds, 'Clerics in the early Middle Ages: hierarchies and functions', p. 27. 1 *HE* III.23. 2 Pseudo-Cyprian: *De duodecim*, x episcopus negligens, pp 53–6. See also *CCH*, 'De episcopo', Liber I, pp 3–12. 3 S.A. Barney, W.J. Lewis et al., *The* Etymologies *of Isidore of Seville* (2006), VII.xii.8, pp 170–1. 4 Pseudo-Cyprian: *De duodecim*, ix rex iniquus, lines 9–13, p. 54 and lines 3–5, p. 56. 5 *VW* XI. 6 *CCH*, 'De espiscopo', Liber I, cap. 4–5, p. 4.

Hertford on preventing clerics from 'wandering' and bishops interfering with other dioceses and, according to the *Collectio Canonum Hibernensis*, bishops were able to have a wife.[7] This latter qualification is not unusual – although Gregory the Great had conceded that clerics in minor orders could marry if they must but not bishops – it may have led to inheritance claims by the offspring for their father's foundation and title.[8] Theodore's Council at Hertford attempted to establish clear directives for limiting the movement of clerics and bishops. Ruling five required clergy to be obedient to their bishop and clerics required a formal letter from the bishop to leave their diocese. These rulings asserted the paternal role of the bishop, placing him in a position of lordship over his clerics. The ruling limited the free mobility of clerics and attempted to restrain bishops to their own territories. In so doing, Theodore could maintain oversight of his bishops and their bishoprics to ensure orthodox teachings and control clerical movement and advancement. That Theodore's exercise of authority over his bishops was effective may be determined from Stephanus' animadversion that the archbishop expelled Wilfrid from his Northumbrian see.[9] There is a possibility that there were bishops without dioceses. This has been suggested for Egbert, renowned as a teacher, latterly among the 'monasteries of Columba'.[10] As Clancy observes, Bishop Fergus the Pict who visited Rome in 721 may have been another bishop lacking a diocese in order to maintain a peripatetic ministry.[11] These bishops may be the *Chorepiscopi* who were ordained by a single bishop and subsequently demoted to presbyter under the imposition of orthodox stipulations.

The advisory relationship between kings and bishops appears to have developed from an initial mode of top-down conversion. This resulted in the swift social integration of bishops and senior clerics into authoritative lordships, whose particular spiritual functions transcended but also competed with secular ones. According to Wood, the authority of bishops and kings can be expressed as 'outside lordship', or lordship imposed from outside direct possession.[12] Irish status and legal texts spell out the ambiguity of hierarchy that this dichotomy caused. *Críth Gablach* attempts to resolve this dilemma by placing the bishop's dignity above that of the king due to his religion while at the same time the bishop is required to acknowledge the superior secular authority of the king.[13] Similarly, the *Bretha Nemed* texts link the king and bishop into the highest grade (*sóer-nemed*) along with the *filid* (a *fili* is generally translated as a poet but their role is closer to a court advisor and intellectual).[14] Church councils from

7 *HE* IV.5; Pseudo-Cyprian: *De duodecim*, x episcopus negligens, lines 5–6, p. 55, cites Leviticus, 21.7 as to the type of wife that was unacceptable (but not from the Vulgate) and paraphrases 1 Timothy, 3.2, 7–9, 56; *CCH*, 'De espiscopo', Liber I, cap. 7, p. 5, directly cites the authority of Paul, also using 1 Timothy, 3.2. 8 *HE* I.27. 9 *VW* XXIV. 10 *HE* III.27, V.9, 10, 22. 11 Clancy, 'Deer and the early church in north-eastern Scotland', pp 379, 381. 12 Wood, *The proprietary church*, p. 190. 13 *Críth Gablach*, §48, p. 24. 14 *CIH* 1590–1618; 634–55; 2318–35.

Chalcedon (451) onwards gave bishops authority over all clerics in their territories and allowed them control over abbatial election and rights to arbitrate church property disputes.[15] The *Bretha Nemed* texts promote the direct involvement of bishops in the governance of the kingdom, not just arbitration rights over their own territories. In these texts, king, bishop and *fili* were accorded overarching jurisdictional authority.[16] The bishop, however, having inviolable integrity had the greatest legal capacity, as even a king could not overturn a bishop's evidence.[17] The presence of a bishop to legitimize sworn oaths became a necessary part of all legal proceedings, sometimes using a Mass or relics as well as cemeteries to validate contracts and agreements.[18] Oaths were the basis for all legal proceedings and contracts; scriptural metaphors likening an oath to God's covenant are prevalent in early Irish contract law.[19] The bishop, therefore, became integral to the operation of law and social and legal contracts, making his presence at political and legal assemblies fundamental to the operation of government. The prologue to the laws of King Wihtred of Kent similarly attests to the necessary presence of bishops at legal assemblies.[20] The bishops' and abbots' integrity made them ideal negotiators and diplomats with clerics, such as Adomnán of Iona, actively participating in diplomatic missions between kings.[21] As civil actors, bishops performed a key role in mediating heavenly knowledge: conduits safely connecting their people into a wider spiritual and temporal cosmology while interceding on their behalf to ensure divine good will. Ecclesiastical foundations similarly became the conduits for trade and learning. Indeed, excavations at Inchmarnock, in the Clyde Estuary, indicate the potential for even small monastic settlements to establish 'schools'.[22] In addition, bishops acted as close advisors to kings to provide the intellectual framework to reconstruct and legitimize royal executive functions.

The Pictish ecclesiastical presence

A symbiotic relationship developed between king and bishop that increased the geo-political authority of both offices. Bishop Wilfrid claimed episcopal jurisdiction over Northumbria and the Picts, 'as far as Oswiu's power extended'.[23] Nevertheless, Wilfrid was ultimately reliant on the Northumbrian king's goodwill in order to remain in authority over his vast diocese, which was divided soon after his removal from that office. Despite a bishop's claim to divine authority, Insular kings could, and did, exercise authority over them. It was politically expedient for both parties to form a mutual dependency. Signatory of the *Cáin Adomnáin*, Curetán of Rosemarkie was the bishop paired with Bredei

15 Wood, *The proprietary church*, pp 191–210; *CCH*, 'De locis', Liber XLIII, pp 171–4. 16 *CIH* 635.8. See Breatnach, 'Canon law and secular law in early Ireland'. 17 Kelly, *Early Irish law*, pp 199–200. 18 R. Chapman Stacey, *Dark speech* (2007), p. 47; Kelly, *Early Irish law*, pp 198–9. 19 N. McLeod, *Early Irish contract law* (1995), §51, pp 184–5. 20 *English historical documents*, §31, p. 362. 21 *HE* V.15. 22 C. Lowe, *Inchmarnock* (2008), p. 263. 23 *HE* IV.3.

filius Derelei to guarantee Pictish consent to the law.[24] His appearance on the guarantor list of the *Cáin Adomnáin*, as the only Pictish cleric, may imply that Curetán's episcopal jurisdiction was congruent with Bredei's own territorial authority.[25] It is therefore of interest that an obituary notice of 725 records a bishop 'Brec of Fortriu' whose title suggests that Pictish bishoprics, as in England, were defined by the political groups to whom they ministered.[26] Brec of Fortriu may have been Curetán's successor, ministering to the Fortriu dynasts. This is not to say that the see of Rosemarkie was the only bishopric with jurisdiction in Pictland but the status of its bishop may have been that of *primus inter pares* due to a close association with the reigning dynasty. Evidence for the presence of Pictish bishoprics, other than at Rosemarkie, is suggestive rather than definitive. It should not be overlooked that abbots of early Insular monasteries wielded significant political authority comparable to that of bishops. Clancy has made a convincing case for an early abbacy near Fetternear, Aberdeenshire.[27] Indeed, the chronicle record of its abbot at 623, followed by the obituary notice of a *Nectain Neir* in 679, implies a politically important foundation whose pastoral responsibilities may have corresponded to that of a bishopric.[28] Abernethy, Perthshire, may also have been operating in an episcopal capacity. Whether this was indeed the case, the long cist cemetery evidence at Hallow Hill by St Andrews is indicative of pastoral activity in the area since the sixth century. The early twelfth-century foundation legend of St Andrews attributes its foundation to the gift of lands, named Cennrígmonaid, by a King Hungus (Necthon's successor, Onuist) to St Regulus, and this may recall the formal recognition of a bishopric.[29] In addition, Fraser has suggested that Iona established a bishopric at Logierait, Perthshire, from which to exercise jurisdiction over Pictland.[30] The lack of documentary evidence makes it unlikely that any episcopal organization can be verified in Pictland prior to the eighth century. While a cohesive diocesan organization was unlikely, individualized foundations exercising local spiritual and territorial authority would certainly be consistent with later evidence. It is also likely that Pictish episcopal centres emerged in the same period as those in Northumbria, if not earlier.

Although their date remains contested, the material evidence of the Class II sculptured cross-slabs similarly points to the established presence of monastic centres and a variety of churches serving communities. These Class II sculptured cross-slabs, which include Pictish symbols, are indicative, as Fraser suggests, of patronage rather than major religious change or imposition.[31] The monastic centre of Portmahomack in the north of Scotland provides an

24 *CA*, §28 (22). 25 See B. Yorke, *The conversion of Britain* (2006), p. 154. 26 *AU* 725.7; Woolf, *From Pictland to Alba*, p. 56. 27 Clancy, 'Deer and the early church in north-eastern Scotland', pp 367–75. 28 *AU* 623.2; 679.4. 29 D. Broun, 'The church of St Andrews and its foundation legend' (2000). 30 *AU* 711.1; Fraser, 'Ministry mission and myth', pp 257–9. 31 Ibid., p. 218.

interesting case study for pre-eighth-century Pictish ecclesiastical activity and associated Class II cross-slabs. This site was established by the end of the sixth century near a natural harbour and the cemetery evidence confirms a male monastic establishment. By the end of the seventh century, extensive craft workshops were in operation and the multiple sculptural fragments on this site indicate a significant investment. Of particular interest is a number of newly broken Class II cross-slabs found under a destruction layer that has been radiocarbon dated to between 780 and 830.[32] This is an important determination from which it can be inferred that by this period churches and monasteries were making political statements of their presence through these elaborate and often sophisticated sculptural monuments. The erection and iconography of these sculptured cross-slabs at the earliest ecclesiastical foundations, including Rosemarkie, implies the assumption of control by the church with the consent of Christianized secular leaders.[33] What can be proposed is that bishops were necessary for parochial growth and, as mediators of the divine will of God, their superior status and wise counsels kept them in intimate contact with political authority. Through this relationship they were able to consolidate their presence over the social and political landscape and articulate this presence territorially through monumental display.

Itinerant rule

The endowment and patronage of new ecclesiastical establishments by the king had immediate political consequences. This was particularly the case when new foundations were established outside of a king's home provinces. This could announce the subjection of new territory by the king as his patronage of the foundation provided him with a venue on his regular *iter*, or circuit, of his kingdom. Kingship and rulership in the early medieval period was itinerant. The king's physical presence on his annual circuit made manifest his ideological and personal authority over the polities where he exacted tribute, as food render, for the maintenance of his retinue by right of lordship at the places he visited. Similarly, the king's participation in religious ceremonies at his new foundations reinforced his authority over the area while imbuing him with 'sacrality'. John Bernhardt emphasized that this 'sacrality', gained by the public expression of a king's Christian faith through building works and ceremonies, served to minimize opposition and legitimize the hierarchies.[34] It is therefore intriguing that later hagiographies record Bredei filius Derelei's (Dargart) property donation to St Serf of Culross in Strathearn, Perthshire.[35] While Restenneth, Angus, was reputedly given to St Boniface (Curetán) by Necthon filius

32 Carver, *Portmahomack*, p. 61. 33 S.T. Driscoll, 'Political discourse and the growth of Christian ceremonialism in Pictland' (1998), p. 173; I. Henderson, 'Early Christian monuments of Scotland' (1987), p. 48. 34 J.W. Bernhardt, *Itinerant kingship* (1993), pp 49–50. 35 Macquarrie, 'The kings of Strathclyde', p. 140.

Derelei.[36] These hagiographies are late and their value as evidence of early medieval donations is tenuous, resting on the preservation of the names of specific Pictish kings and older forms of place-names. Should these hagiographies retain a genuine record of the early endowment of Culross and Restenneth, by Bredei and Necthon respectively, it would suggest that these kings' territorial control extended south of the Mounth. These foundations, outside of the king's postulated home territories of Fortriu, could therefore be indicative of a king assuming royal prerogatives over new territories legitimized by his personal relationship with the saintly prelates. It may be significant that neither Restenneth nor Culross became bishops' sees as they may have been founded within existing dioceses. Nevertheless, these ecclesiastical endowments allowed the Pictish kings to extend their royal circuit southwards and exert their authority at assemblies along the journey.

Itinerant progressions displayed the concerted public power of the king and queen. The Life of St Wilfrid describes King Ecgfrid and his queen 'making their progress with worldly pomp and daily rejoicing and feasts through cities, fortresses and villages'.[37] Similarly, the Welsh *gwestfa* was a yearly progression by the rulers, and the Irish text *Críth Gablach* specifies a period for royal and noble visitations to their clients.[38] Bishops also regularly toured their *prouincia*, initiating preaching tours, resolving disputes and assuring communities of their bishop's spiritual oversight.[39] The regular circuit of a ruler's dependent territories was the means by which the ruler could govern and reaffirm his authority and status. This was particularly the case for the king whose itinerary needed to be adaptable to suit changing geo-political circumstances. As Fouracre has observed, the royal progression further justified the king's right to hold power.[40] In effect, the royal circuit was the means by which a king could exert his authority to restate and formalize both his and his provincial rulers' prerogatives. The public progress of the king among his subjects made a statement of his sovereignty and legitimacy, reinforced when his cavalcade drew to a temporary halt to hold an assembly.

GOVERNANCE AND THE ASSEMBLY

Welsh, Irish and Anglo-Saxon legal systems all required dispute settlement to be public (regular as well as ad-hoc) and the fora chosen were assemblies at fixed landmarks. As previously discussed, it is likely that in Pictland existing territorial divisions (units of lordship) maintained governance through the agency of

36 MacDonald, *Curadán, Boniface and the early church of Rosemarkie*, p. 16. 37 *VW* XXXIX; J. Campbell, 'Anglo-Saxon courts' (2003), p. 156. 38 *Críth Gablach*, §26, p. 15; Campbell, 'Anglo-Saxon courts', p. 157. 39 *HE* III.28. 40 P. Fouracre, 'Conflict, power and legitimation in Francia' (2004), p. 19.

assembly. These were the venues at which legal cases were heard, judgments were proclaimed, contracts could be made and celebrated, administrative matters negotiated and alliances ratified. The practice of assembly could be considered as enacting regular, institutionalized negotiation.[41] Assembly and the royal circuit were timed to coincide with the collection of food render as well as tribute, and the organization of labour for building works, agriculture and transport. As a communal forum, assemblies enhanced social unity, affirmed social hierarchies and identity and provided a venue for political participation wherein consensus could limit factionalism.[42] Notwithstanding this community-centred aspect of assembly, decision-making and adjudication of disputes was distinctly hierarchical. The assembly formed an ideal political platform for local governance but it worked effectively on a regional and 'national' level where people from across regions could meet safely to negotiate alliances. The evidence suggests that formal local and supra-regional assembly was practised by most Insular and northern European polities. In his examination of early English assembly practice, Woolf found close similarities to that of the ancient Norwegian kingdom of Trønder. This kingdom was divided into eight provinces that each had its own ruler and local assembly, with an annual assembly at which all the provinces came together to transact business.[43] A similar assembly structure operated among the kingdoms of Ireland with a regular 'national' assembly, known as the *Óenach*, occurring annually where high-kingship was validated by calling and presiding over the *Óenach Tailten*.[44] The poignant Welsh tale of Manawydan's execution of a mouse on the *Gorsedd Arberth* – a site used for political and judicial assembly which was located next the king's court – demonstrates the use of a hill to prosecute judgment and, in this case, access the legitimacy of the otherworld.[45] These were social venues where personal enmities were laid aside and ceremonial rituals could re-state normative social networks to provide the appearance of unity.[46] Assembly sites are usually associated with mounds: natural, purpose-built or Bronze-Age cairns were reused for assembly purposes across north-west Europe.[47] The assembly site is often adjacent to Neolithic, Bronze-Age or Iron-Age monuments, indicating that a deliberative and normative selection criterion existed for sites of assembly that endowed the ritual with a potent historic and sacred legitimacy.[48] According to Richard Hingley, ancient monuments appear to have been consciously appropriated and adapted in every period to redefine the past according to the political

41 M. Mann, 'The autonomous power of the state' (1984), p. 188. 42 P.S. Barnwell, 'Kings, nobles and assemblies' (2003), pp 21–4. 43 Woolf, 'Community, identity and kingship in early England', pp 102–6. 44 E. Bhreathnach, '*Termoria: Caput Scotorum*?' (1996), pp 75–6. 45 *The Mabinogian*, trans. J. Gantz (1976), p. 93; T.M. Charles-Edwards, 'Gorsedd, Dadl and Llys' (2004), p. 98. 46 S. Airlie, 'Talking heads' (2003), pp 39–40. 47 O'Grady, 'The setting and practice of open-air judicial assemblies', p. 376. 48 S. Semple, 'Locations of assembly in early Anglo-Saxon England' (2004); Driscoll, 'The early historic landscape of Strathearn', p. 326.

present.[49] The 'constructed' nature of these sites functioned to invest the action taking place within the locale with communal meaning and ritual.[50] The conflation of ancient monuments with current political agenda presents the appearance of continuity to reinforce local identification with the land and its rulers.

While there is little direct reference to assembly and its functions in early Insular documentary sources, P.S. Barnwell identified the practice of assembly as central to 'the political and administrative workings of earlier medieval units of governance'.[51] The habit of assembly appears to have been established long before the end of the seventh century and – while in practice ancient – the sites of assembly were socially dynamic political arenas where changes to political organization were physically manifested. As a case in point, the assembly mound at Scone, Perthshire, appears to have been deliberately created in the ninth century as a site of royal inauguration and assembly, to make manifest a new social identity and territorial focus for the kingdom of Alba.[52] Similarly, the Northumbrian assembly site at Yeavering, Ad Gefrin, fell out of use when the focus for royal power shifted to another site, possibly after the consolidation of Deira and Bernicia.[53] Bede's information on Yeavering provides a rare insight into how the assembly can concentrate regnal authority. From this assembly site King Edwin introduced and imposed a radical social and cultural change on his people: Christian conversion and baptism. Yeavering was also the site of a royal residence, visited by the king and queen on their annual circuit, and when later kings abandoned the site its use as an assembly also appears to have discontinued. Increasing territorial consolidation by a king would lead to both larger assemblies on traditional sites and the creation of new sites to provide a 'show-place for new royal power'.[54] This was particularly pertinent for the inauguration of a king. Newly endowed and established bishoprics also provided a focus for assembly and the visible manifestation of the king's authority. Indeed, where a king's authority expanded over several territories, at a local level the highest-status lord may have been the bishop. This would have impacted the location and maintenance of the local assembly. In a study on early Swedish assembly sites, Alex Sanmark found that provincial 'thing' sites (or hundred meeting places) could be relocated up to ten kilometres from older sites in order to meet shifting political requirements, including appropriation by a church.[55] Similarly, the erection of the Pillar of Eliseg in Powys, Wales, over a traditional assembly place has been interpreted by Nancy Edwards as 'the growing role of the church' in secular political ceremony.[56] Overarching control of assemblies constituted an important tool of legitimacy and authority for consolidated kingship.

49 R. Hingley, 'Ancestors and identity' (1996), p. 241. 50 C. Tilley, *A phenomenology of landscape* (1994), pp 17–23. 51 P.S. Barnwell, 'Political assemblies: an introduction' (2003), p. 1. 52 S.T. Driscoll, 'The archaeological context of assembly' (2004). 53 *HE* II.14. 54 Airlie, 'Talking heads', p. 34. 55 A. Sanmark, 'Administrative organization and state formation' (2009). 56 N. Edwards, 'Rethinking the Pillar of Eliseg' (2009), p. 169.

Political assemblies occurred at local, regional and supra-regional sites for the purpose of legislation, jurisdiction, celebration and the promulgation of socio-political agendas.[57] As sites of communal memory, they would probably have been regularized, possibly geographically fixed in relation to monumental remains. Regional and larger assemblies, however, were more prone to a shift in location dependent upon the affiliation and patronage of the political leadership. Wider territorial domination by a ruling dynasty led to the favouring of sites chosen by that dynasty and, as at Yeavering, the disuse of previously customary sites.[58] The supra-regional assembly, such as the Irish *Óenach Tailten*, required a fixed date to ensure participation and the king was required to initiate proceedings or risk his honour and sovereignty. The right to call an assembly and preside over them allowed the king to exercise his executive functions and this authoritative act made him king. Similarly, political franchise was directly related to a person's right to attend an assembly. An assembly of the polity could be required in response to specific circumstances; an example of this was outlined in *Críth Gablach* when a king needed to exert an autocratic decree in response to an emergency or new religious regulation.[59] Celebrations also occurred at relevant sites, such as a king's inauguration or the consecration of a new church, which were one-off events, but they were nevertheless important foci of communal participation. Similarly, assemblies for festivals such as Easter, Lammas and Beltaine included games, markets as well as the render of produce to the local lord, and could be performed at multiple sites around a parish.[60] The flexibility of assembly made it a supremely useful and responsive platform from which the political leadership made and enacted authoritative decisions with the appearance of consensus; most likely militating against the practice being hidebound by official and customary legislation.

THE SUPRA-REGIONAL POLITICAL ASSEMBLY

The localized meeting (or moot) sites functioned in a similar way to regional and national assembly sites, having certain topographic features that distinguished them as sites of ritual importance. These larger sites have been studied primarily for their role in inauguration ritual. Using Scone as the exemplar, Driscoll identified the typological traits of assembly sites: hills, usually flat-topped mounds with associated megalithic structures, nearby sacred trees and wells and occasionally symbolism indicating horseracing.[61] Other features included panoramic views and sites close to river confluences, while tribal affiliations in

57 Barnwell, 'Political assemblies: an introduction', p. 3. 58 Driscoll, 'The early historic landscape of Strathearn', p. 324. 59 *Críth Gablach*, §38, pp 20–1. 60 R.I.M. Black, 'Scottish fairs and fair-names' (1999). 61 Driscoll, 'The archaeological context of assembly', p. 83.

place-names of significant hills suggest regional foci.[62] The latter signifier prompted Driscoll's identification of Moncreiffe Hill, Perthshire, as a primary assembly site for the Tayside-Strathearn region, pre-dating the creation of Scone.[63] This significant site probably catered to a political community that included numerous territories of the Picts south of the Mounth. Assembly sites north of the Mounth have yet to be determined, although it is likely that a major assembly site was located in the vicinity of the fort of King Bridei filius Mailcon at Inverness and at other sites close to centres of northern political power. Supra-regional sites, where people from different territories could meet under terms of temporary treaty, would certainly have facilitated territorial consolidation. Ascertaining the existence of a Pictish supra-regional assembly site, analogous to the Irish *Óenach Tailten* or Northumbrian Yeavering, could answer a number of questions as to early medieval methods of territorial consolidation and inter-regional mobility. Irish and Anglo-Saxon assembly sites continue to receive scholarly attention, and those few that have been identified in Scotland have similarly provoked closer investigation. As the later centre of political power, southern Scottish sites such as Scone and Forteviot, Perthshire, have been scrutinized in reference to the operation of assembly and government. Interest in examining the north of Scotland to answer the same research questions has been limited. Nevertheless, by pinpointing sites of assembly in northern Pictish regions, questions may be answered as to the means by which northern and southern Pictland became consolidated.

Political assembly and Rhynie, Aberdeenshire

One such northern Pictish assembly site may be at Rhynie in Strathbogie; a village situated at a significant crossroads connecting the north with the south through the Mounth. Rhynie is around 35 kilometres north-west of Aberdeen, and a similar distance south-west of Elgin, Morayshire.[64] The concentration of Pictish symbol stones found in and around Rhynie has recently drawn archaeological attention to the site and the finds suggest high-status activity in the vicinity during the early medieval period. Now an unprepossessing village, Rhynie is overlooked by the impressive Tap o'Noth hill that is capped by the remains of a hillfort. At the foot of the Tap o'Noth, the modern village sits within a glen, cupped by the surrounding hills. The area has numerous prehistoric megalithic remains, including cairns and stone circles and Rhynie itself lies along an important glen pass.[65] The place-name is tantalizing, potentially including an early Celtic word for king. Documentary references are late, however, with one of the earliest appearances of the name in the Moray Register, which records the church of *Ryny* in 1222–42, the church of *Rynyn* in 1226 and

62 Ibid., pp 76–7. 63 Ibid., pp 90–1. 64 J. Robertson, *Illustrations of the topography and antiquities* (1847), 2, p. 178. 65 W.D. Simpson, 'Lesmoir Castle and the church of Essie' (1932), p. 87.

the lands of *Rynyn* in 1227.[66] In a charter dating to 1232 Rhynie is recorded three times as *Rynyn* and once as *Ryny*.[67] Bagimond's Roll of 1275 records the church of *Ryni*.[68] In 1553 it is recorded as (the prebend of) *Ryne*.[69] The place-name does not have the same derivation as *rinn* ('point'), which lies behind the Rhinns of Galloway, as this has a short vowel, compared to the long vowel in Rhynie. Watson's identification of Loch Ryan, Wigtownshire, with Ptolemy's *Rerigonion* (on the *Rerigonios* bay) may, however, point to a possible interpretation for Rhynie. According to Watson, *Rerigonion* as **re-rīg-on-ion* may be interpreted as 'very royal place', with **re* an intensifier, and *rīg-on* 'royal', similar to Welsh *rhion* 'lord, chief' and Old Irish *rí* 'king'; while the final *–ion* is a place-forming suffix.[70] In the case of Rhynie, the first syllable does appear to derive from **rīg* 'king' (as an adjective: 'royal'), with the final suffix appearing variously as *–yn/–in* (which develops to *–ie/–y* by about 1300) meaning something to the effect of 'place of' or 'settlement of'.[71] Given the lack of evidence for an intensifier, a possible reconstruction of Rhynie in early Celtic is **rīgonin* or **rīgonīn* meaning 'place of (*īn*) a great (*–on*) king (*rīg-*)'.[72] This interpretation of Rhynie may be augmented by the nearby place-name of (Mains of) Lesmoir, in the neighbouring parish of Essie, Aberdeenshire, which preserves a possible early name for a palace. A medieval castle was built on this site and traces of a motte survive.[73] In his discussion of this place-name, Aidan MacDonald suggested that Scottish sites containing **lis* names are P-Celtic and indicate centres of aristocratic administration sometimes associated with nearby assembly and ecclesiastical sites.[74] These place-names, Rhynie and Lesmoir, are suggestive of an early royal presence in the area. A royal presence would also suggest the occurrence of political assembly.

The parish of Rhynie is situated on the western edge of the shire of Aberdeen and was absorbed into the diocese of Moray by 1226 and later combined with Essie parish.[75] A church dedicated to the early medieval saint MoLuóc is situated on the bank of the River Bogie close to a recently excavated prehistoric ceremonial site. In relation to the place-name of Lesmoir in Essie parish, it is of interest that MoLuóc's sixth-century primary foundation was on the island of Lismore in Argyll. In Scotland, St MoLuóc's feast day was 25 June, an ideal date for a regular and large political assembly. The site has the potential to accommodate the muster of stock and men, markets, and various sports including horseracing and hunting. By the early medieval period, the hillfort may have

66 *Registrum episcopatus moraviensis*, no. 81, p. 91; no. 69, p. 73; no. 73, p. 79. **67** Ibid., no. 35, pp 28–9. **68** A.I. Dunlop, 'Bagimond's roll' (1939), p. 44. **69** *Registrum episcopatus moraviensis*, no. 473, p. 429. **70** *CPNS*, pp 34–5. **71** S. Taylor and G. Márkus, *The place-names of Fife*, 5 (2012), pp 407–12. **72** This derivation was developed with the expert advice of Simon Taylor over correspondence and discussions from 2006 to 2014. **73** *NSA*, 12, p. 1016; NMRS: NJ42NE 2. **74** A. MacDonald, 'Caiseal, Cathair, Dùn, Lios and Ràth in Scotland' (1987), pp 38, 51. **75** Robertson, *Illustrations of the topography and antiquities*, 2, pp 178–9, n. 1.

been symbolic rather than habitable, but it remains accessible by foot or on horseback via a processional path that curves around the Tap o'Noth. While a temporary camp could be laid out in the meadows below, the king and his immediate court may have been housed in an enclosed settlement at Lesmoir. What makes this site significant, however, is the number of Class I symbol stones located around the parish; these include symbols carved onto a prehistoric standing stone known as the Craw Stane. Excavations around the Craw Stane indicate that it was a focus for late Bronze-Age/Iron-Age and early medieval ceremonial activity.[76] Based on the prevalence of the eight Class I symbol stones around Rhynie, Isabel Henderson suggested that this site was a significant centre in the early medieval period.[77]

The uniformity of the small range of symbols used for Class I Pictish symbol stones points to a conscious cultural purpose instigated by a leadership to express unity and dominance.[78] Their distribution, which is predominantly in the north and south-east, is suggestive of a cultural and political continuum that may territorially define the Pictish *regnum*. The stones make visible statements of authority that, Meggen Gondek suggests, represent 'the culmination of a series of socially loaded processes' in their production and erection.[79] The deliberate investment of Class I symbol stones into a site already endowed with a range of megaliths and ancient topography suggests that Rhynie was 'remade' as an important focus of early medieval ceremonial activity. Moreover, the creation and erection of Class I symbol stones around Rhynie implies that the site was deliberately used for a political purpose, possibly as early as the sixth century and may have continued into the eighth century as a site of ritual authority. In the same way that megaliths and cairns dotted the landscape and left a lasting memorial of their putative ancestors, so too the erection of Class I symbol stones at this site may have been intended to draw together the landscape and the people under the authority of the king. This may have been the intent in the deliberate reworking of the Craw Stane, where Pictish symbols were inscribed onto the megalith at the centre of earlier ceremonial activity. In effect, they were creating a site that was 'multi-temporal, simultaneously drawing from the obsolete, the contemporary and the futuristic' to perpetuate a dominant political authority.[80] Overall, the site is inward looking and self-contained, having room for large assemblies and their associated activities. Its location on a crossroad expedited the participation of a wide political community from northern Pictland, and potentially participants from the south and Orkney. Excavation around the Craw

76 M. Gondek and G. Noble, 'Landscape with symbols' (2006). See also Noble and Gondek, 'Symbol stones in context'. 77 I. Henderson, 'The origin centre of the Pictish symbol stones' (1957–8), p. 48. 78 Ibid., 57. Also I. Henderson, 'The meaning of the Pictish symbol stones' (1971), p. 65; I. Henderson, 'The monuments of the Picts' (1975), p. 10. 79 M. Gondek, 'Investing in sculpture' (2006), p. 107. 80 M. Serres and B. Latour, *Conversations on science, culture and time* (1990), p. 60.

Stane has uncovered evidence of a defensive palisade and post-setting as well as an assemblage of luxury continental imports dating from the fifth to sixth century.[81] While this fortification, concentrated at the Craw Stane, appears to have been destroyed in the sixth century, this does not suggest the total abandonment of the area. The evidence from this investigation suggests that Rhynie was an important centre of political power from the fifth to the ninth century, with links to western trade routes and multi-period activity.[82] Potentially, Rhynie constitutes an important place of ancient assembly that endorsed the territorial authority of the Fortriu kings, enhanced by a numinous landscape. Rhynie was ideally located for a northern king to expand his authority into southern Pictland. Provincial and national assembly sites established regular foci for the reception and patronage of the king during his yearly circuit of the kingdom with his nobles: through this ritual, the authority of the king was made visible, thus asserting his lordship over territory and people.[83] Moreover, these were sites of active governance in which the personnel who facilitated the operation of government can be identified.

Functionaries of assembly

According to early Irish documentary evidence, the king's role in assembly was clear. The king was the guarantor of correct and just proceedings. The king could call an irregular meeting or muster but he must play host to both regular and irregular assemblies, ensuring that all business was conducted according to consensual law and custom. For the irregular or emergency assembly, it is likely that the king's messengers announced the summons to assemble throughout the provinces concerned, and probably disseminated information on key decisions and alliances made at the regular assemblies to distant rulers and the general populace.[84] As all economic activities and relationships compacted during seasonal assemblies and gatherings were framed as public legal contracts, it was necessary that a number of functionaries were present to ensure legal compliance. Likewise, for those seeking the king's justice, judges and legal experts on a range of laws and various skill levels were required. Ancillary functionaries included: historians and record keepers who verified and reinterpreted past procedures and events affecting a case; stewards and guards to ensure each plaintiff received a hearing, witnesses were called and present, sureties collected and the sanctuary of the assembly was upheld; and personnel to carry out the judgment.[85] A bishop, and his personal retinue, was present in order to witness oaths, provide counsel to the king and determine judgment on cases that were considered to cross into the spiritual. Many of these officials were permanent

81 Noble and Gondek, 'Symbol stones in context', pp 317–21. 82 C. Catling, 'Village of the Pictish symbol stones' (2012) pp 8–9; G. Noble and M. Gondek, '"A very royal place" Rhynie and the Picts' (2012). 83 Foster, 'Before Alba', pp 20–1. 84 Barnwell, 'Kings, nobles and assemblies', p. 27. 85 Kelly, *Early Irish law*, pp 193–6.

members of the king's own court, travelling with him on circuit. The larger the assembly, the more functionaries were required and the king's retinue was similarly expanded with his personal household, counsellors, judges, bishop and bodyguard. Bards publicly rehearsed sagas and tales that provided key political messages or warnings, as well as celebrating the deeds and repute of the king, his faithful nobles and the posterity of his dynasty.[86] Other court members, such as his nobles, foster children, kin, allies, hostages, as well as his queen and her retinue, were a visible statement of the king's authority. The display of wealth as an adjunct to power was an important aspect of the assembly, for the king's subjects as well as visiting envoys and diplomats. At the same time, the king's demonstration of largesse ensured the fealty of provincial lords and his leading magnates.[87] The display of authority was not limited to the assembly but, as Barnwell has proposed, was demonstrated by the large retinues of great men and women passing through the countryside to and from the assembly in apparent unity of purpose.[88]

Few Insular sources make explicit statements about early medieval governance and the functionaries that expedited a king's political aims. It is therefore of interest that the Irish status tract *Uraicecht Becc* does appear to outline a political constitution and a complex society of political functionaries.[89] This 'primer' identifies those persons with inherent power and endows them with rights over judicial regulation.[90] According to this tract, and the associated *Bretha Nemed* corpus, certain legal privileges were accorded to those referred to as *nemed*; such as rights of judgment, immunity from certain contractual requirements, sick-maintenance and refectory allowances, and the ability to cross territories while maintaining status and legal prerogatives.[91] *Uraicecht Becc* defines two social groups within the *nemed*; they were the *sóer-nemed* (free/noble *nemed*) and the *dóer-nemed* (subject *nemed*).[92] The *sóer-nemed* include the *flaith* 'rulers/kings', *eclais* 'church[men]' and *filid* 'poets', all of whom held active political duties in the secular and ecclesiastical spheres.[93] According to *Uraicecht Becc*, the *sóer-nemed* established, maintained and enacted the law through their exercise of judgment, making this group foundational to governance and comprising the legislature.[94] The word *nemed* appears in Old Irish texts as an abstract noun meaning 'sacredness, privilege', as well as in relation to a place, animals or trees.[95] Something of this 'sacred' meaning has been attributed to the *sóer-* and *dóer-nemed*, which has been taken to imply that they were imbued with a residual religious or metaphysical quality.[96] An examination of the roles of those

86 Pseudo-Cyprian: *De duodecim*, ix rex iniquus, lines 13–14, p. 51, distinctly warns against actors, and the bards would have been under contract to ensure no damaging satire of the king. 87 Barnwell, 'Kings, nobles and assemblies', pp 25–6. 88 Ibid., p. 27. 89 *CIH* 634–55; MacNéill, 'Ancient Irish law', pp 272–81. 90 See Gardner, *Law as a leap of faith*, pp 103–4. 91 J. Grigg, 'The Nemed, *Uraicecht Becc* and early Irish governance' (2013). 92 *CIH* 636.22–7. 93 *CIH* 1593.5–6. 94 *CIH* 1592.8–17. 95 *Bechbretha*, pp 107–9. 96 Kelly, *Early Irish law*, p. 9; N.B. Aitchison, 'Kingship, society and sacrality' (1994), p. 72.

categorized as *nemed*, however, could suggest that the designation related to their public persona as functionaries of governance. The key may be in the functions of the *dóer-nemed*, who included such persons as doctors, lawyers, poets, metalworkers, woodworkers, fishermen and professionals deemed to have achieved their status through their *dán* (art).[97] These professionals are accorded some rights over judgment and David Dumville has suggested that this group represents an organizational paradigm from a 'common Celtic antiquity'.[98] Indeed, while the administration of justice by the *dóer-nemed* was restricted to their own professions, extant legal standards attest to strict and well-established manufacturing codes that protected their trades.[99]

The roles of both 'free' and 'subject' *nemed* were socially and culturally valuable. The common thread linking persons of art and those who rule was their direct participation in the creation and maintenance of civilizing society by physical and metaphysical means. The *sóer-nemed* had a key performative role in the assembly, directing and controlling social action, by which they governed and administered justice. The *dóer-nemed*, in their turn, supported the authority of these civil actors by the provision of high-status items (such as the penannular brooch) and the promulgation of cultural tenets in support of the hierarchies. Patronage was fundamental to a *dóer-nemed* person as their status and profession relied directly on the endorsement of a *sóer-nemed* patron.[1] These groups, therefore, were tied into a relationship of functional reliance and mutual support. The members of the *nemed* practised specialist skills and knowledge that were accorded cultural primacy. It is of interest, therefore, that Helms identified master artisans, from a range of ethnographic sources, as having socio-political influence through their ability to transform matter (physical and metaphysical), to create 'cultural order' and to manifest 'social order'.[2] On the face of it, their social value relates to their functional skills and Douglas MacLean, in his analysis of the stone sculptor, suggests that specialists such as the chief artisans should also be considered 'king's architects'.[3] This connects the artisan to the political arena in a culturally transformative role. Similarly, their ability to travel and work outside their home territories without loss of legal franchise – fundamental for a fisherman – suggests that these professionals could make ideal conduits for establishing long-distance trade and diplomatic networks on behalf of the rulers. Old Irish literary sources also suggest that members of the *dóer-nemed* attended the king's council to provide advice and their presence was necessary at assemblies. Muirchú describes a pagan assembly at Tara to which all kings, leaders, nobles, druids and 'inventors and teachers of every craft and every skill' were summoned.[4] The Irish *nemed* grades, therefore, appear to embody a

97 *CIH* 1612.4–9, 1616.22–27. 98 *CIH* 1613.26–26; D.N. Dumville, 'Kingship, genealogies and regnal lists' (1977; repr. 1979), pp 102–3. 99 N. McLeod, 'The metalworking tradition in medieval Irish law' (2004). 1 *CIH* 637.1–3. 2 Helms, *Craft and the kingly ideal*, p. 25. 3 D. MacLean, 'The status of the sculptor in Old-Irish law' (1995), p. 134. 4 *The Patrician texts in*

codification of those functioning members who engineered and maintained social order, the assembly being the means through which social transformation and political consolidation was achieved. For this reason, the *nemed* category appears to constitute a paradigm for early medieval functional government.

The agency of assembly

Regular assemblies were the primary means of promoting and expanding social networks. They were the locus of political power from which to enforce social order and cohesiveness. Economic pressures further stimulated competition at a local level, which led to the increased presence of the resource-rich at a supra-regional assembly, in turn facilitating their access to social networks and support.[5] Attendance at a supra-regional assembly was most likely reserved for those in an economic and social position to attend, which had ramifications for personal as well as social identity. The mobility explicitly extended to the early Irish *nemed* grades suggests that there were restrictions on trans-territorial movement and the concomitant political franchise. Upward transfer of wealth and authority was ensured by the 'resource-rich' personages having personal access to the king at assemblies, allowing them to consolidate their social standing, with the corollary effect of decreasing the lower ranks' access to authority and limiting their political presence. Real and effective power was thus restricted at both regional and local level. This would assist the increased accrual of authority by the king who dealt with, and dominated, a smaller corpus of leading lords who had control over wider territories. *Críth Gablach* voiced a concern that the king and the leading nobles could make major political decisions without public consensus. It warned that the king was not to make binding promises on behalf of his *túath* at an assembly attended only by his nobles.[6] The Irish law tract, *Di Astud Chor*, reiterated this concern declaring 'that which the assembly of the kingdom does not confirm is not an accepted practice'.[7] Of course, in reality meetings such as the Irish *rígdál* – an assembly of kings and leading nobles to negotiate treaties – could not involve every free member of the various kingdoms. As Barnwell has observed, if carefully controlled and ritually managed the public nature of assembly could ensure the appearance of consensus and repress dissent.[8]

The physical presence of the king at an assembly provided a visible reminder of his authority, particularly during the exercise of judgment. At the same time, ideally the king was required to substantiate his right to that authority through the 'just' administration of law.[9] The king could also control future social

the Book of Armagh, 'A. Muirchú', §I.15 (14) (2), pp 84–5 [*et omnis artis omnisque doni iuentoribus doctoribusue uocatis ad Loigaireum*]. 5 Woolf, 'Community, identity and kingship in early England', p. 106. 6 *Críth Gablach*, §35, p. 20. 7 McLeod, *Early Irish contract law*, §52, pp 186–7. 8 Barnwell, 'Political assemblies: an introduction', pp 6–7. 9 *Audacht Morainn*, §23–52, pp 8–15.

mobility by displays of royal favour. Social contacts engendered by the assembly at both regional and supra-regional levels meant that participation in this shared ritual allowed for a greater identification of the self within the culture: that culture being a result of shared law, language and the perception of a shared origin.[10] As assemblies were also the venues at which diplomatic and business transactions, marriages, fosterage and apprenticeships were negotiated; they facilitated the greater mobility of familial and social relationships across territories. The assembly was an ideal vehicle for the creation of collective identity and the expansion of governmental authority. One of the most important functions of an assembly was the dissemination of political propaganda, dressed as bardic verse or official legislative acts. Supra-regional assemblies enforced the authority and legitimacy of the king, ensuring the suppression of competing dynasties while at the same time endorsing the hierarchy of nobles through ties of clientage. In terms of centralization, assemblies offered a mechanism by which to enact political cohesion and promulgate 'nation-building' ideologies. They were venues of collective political activity that encouraged communal identification with a single ruler over a single kingdom.

CONSTRUCTING THE STATE

The evidence from annals points to Bredei filius Bili consolidating Pictish provinces under his leadership. These chronicle entries imply that this king won the allegiance of disparate Pictish provinces through successful military campaigns that culminated in the Battle of Nechtansmere. It is likely that the ruling dynasties in the south of Pictland had been repressed during Northumbria's overlordship of the region. If so, the potential power vacuum in the south, after the Northumbrian defeat, offered Bredei an opportunity to assist the instatement of his favoured rulers from among the southern dynasties for mutual advantage. In addition, new groups allied with Bredei may have moved into territory abandoned after Northumbrian withdrawal. This is a situation that his successor may have capitalized on, given the late hagiographical record of Bredei filius Derelei's land grant to St Serf at Culross in Strathearn, Perthshire.[11] What is uncertain is the degree to which Bredei filius Bili's reign was hegemonic.

The concept of hegemony in this setting, defined as the coercive political, military or cultural domination by a group or leader, is limiting. It is certainly a serviceable term but falls short of illuminating the political conditions and processes behind the consolidation of early medieval Insular political authority. It is apparent that Bredei filius Bili did have the military capability to coerce

10 A. Tyrrell, 'Early medieval bodies and the corporeal identity' (2000), p. 154. 11 A. Macquarrie, '*Vita Sancti Servani*' (1993), pp 133, 140.

alliance for the distinct purpose of removing Northumbrian overlordship. It is the way that he maintained his leadership that makes it clear that Bredei's *regnum* worked within existing social customs and systems, not against them. Bredei's subjugation of Orkney is a case in point. The comprehensive attack implied by the term *deletae* in the chronicle entry suggested to Foster that Bredei placed his loyal agent at Birsay to ensure Orkney's political compliance.[12] Yet, this type of institutional arrangement – of agents of the king planted into regional power bases to effect administrative and political control – appears precipitate for the close of the seventh century. There is certainly an example from Anglo-Saxon sources in which Oswiu placed his own ealdormen over Mercia, although this policy failed as it fomented rebellion.[13] Rather than a direct replacement of regional rule by faithful retainers of the king, Adomnán's description of the Orkney ruler at the court of the *rex potentissimus* Bridei filius Mailcon suggests that he was not an imposed agent. This is made clear by Columba's request to Bridei that he used his Orkney hostages to demand immunity for clergy venturing into Orkney.[14] Hostages were an effective means by which authority could be enacted over distant and competing territories; compliance could be enforced, fealty demanded and alliances negotiated. The Irish dynastic polity of the Uí Néill traced their line back to *Niall Noígiallach* (Neil of the nine hostages), whose hostages expressed his political dominance.[15] *Críth Gablach* places 'forfeited hostages in fetters' to the north-east of the presiding king when he appeared in public, clearly implying that this was an accepted practice, augmenting his authority and political standing.[16] Comparisons with later Carolingian texts indicate that hostages (*obsedes*) were not a simple surety transaction but a unilateral grant.[17] The practice appears to have been extensive with males from leading political opponents being usual – future rulers, such as Theodoric, could serve time as a hostage – and their placement in 'foreign' households provided an opportunity for their acculturation.[18] Indeed, during his youth, King Ecgfrid was a hostage in the household of the Mercian queen Cynwise.[19] In the case of the Orkney ruler, Bridei filius Mailcon's possession of Orkney hostages is indicative of political submission after military subjugation. This was clearly a procedure to ensure public obedience to the Pictish king, rather than a private legal transaction. While the possession of hostages was initially coercive, their status as members of rival dynasties allowed Bridei the opportunity to foster social ties with the next generation of leaders. Rather than sustained, coercive military dominance, the taking of hostages promoted political alliance and adherence in the future. This was one of the fundamental mechanisms through which regional control was exerted and the king's power

12 S.M. Foster, 'Brochs: domestic architecture and changing social configurations' (1993), p. 464. 13 *HE* III.24. 14 *VC* II.42. 15 F.J. Byrne, *Irish kings and high-kings* (2001), pp 70–1. 16 *Críth Gablach*, §46, p. 23. 17 A.J. Kosto, 'Hostages in the Carolingian world' (2002). 18 P. Kershaw, *Peaceful kings* (2011), pp 18–21. 19 *HE* III.24.

actualized. Clientage and fosterage were similarly tied into the creation of dependent relations that ensured social obedience to the political aims of a dominant leadership.[20]

Hostage, clientage and fosterage all relied on a personal contractual relationship with an authoritative leader. Maintaining these relationships was a delicate balancing act and required conceptual frameworks that encouraged willing participation in order to limit expenditure on military coercion. The main material evidence that attests to emerging Pictish political cohesiveness is the Class I Pictish symbol stones. Their distribution, predominantly in the north, including Orkney, and southwards into Fife (they are notably absent from Atholl) appears to reflect the territorial extent of Pictish rule at a time of cultural and political unity.[21] Their dating remains contested, although some archaeological evidence suggests a period in the late seventh to eighth century.[22] Driscoll has argued that the sets of incised symbols, which form a discrete coherent group, bear a close resemblance to writing and their context implies an active social role.[23] Furthermore, citing Danish examples of carved stones acting as charters, Driscoll suggested that Class I symbol stones had a similar purpose and acted as 'ideological reinforcement' of new social structures.[24] The use of charters elsewhere during the early medieval period promoted (or provided the appearance of) hereditary tenure.[25] Class I symbol stones may have similarly articulated a permanent claim over the landscape in a period of increasing physical mobility. The distribution of the Class I stones also narrates a centralized initiative, most likely royal, expressing political authority and unity. The placement of these symbol stones, which articulate a desire for longevity and legitimacy, provide the closest indication of willing regional participation in an emerging territorially defined kingdom and political community.

DEFINING THE STATE

In presenting the evidence for Pictish political amalgamation it is necessary for clarity to employ modern political terminology in order to describe political phenomena of the early medieval period. This does raise significant problems in reconciling earlier systems of governance against modern ones. When early medieval writers such as Abbot Aldhelm do refer to a state-like apparatus, using Classical terms such as the payment of tax (*tributum*) to the *res publica*, it remains difficult to estimate Aldhelm's own notion of the comparative degree of bureau-

20 Kosto, 'Hostages in the Carolingian world', p. 137. **21** Driscoll, 'Political discourse and the growth of Christian ceremonialism in Pictland', p. 224; Henderson, 'The monuments of the Picts', p. 10. **22** Close-Brooks, 'Excavations in the Dairy Park', p. 332. **23** Driscoll, 'Political discourse and the growth of Christian ceremonialism in Pictland', pp 224–6. **24** Ibid., pp 228–9. **25** G. Halsall, *Settlement and social organization* (1995), pp 47–8.

cratic sophistication of his 'state' to that of Classical Rome.[26] Yet, as Susan Reynolds has pointed out, medieval writers were deeply concerned with issues of law and governance, issues that could be considered ones of 'state and its sovereignty'.[27] The existence of customary law is a prerequisite of a governing constitution; one which identifies, imposes and empowers legislative and judicial rights on governing officials.[28] Texts such as *Uraicecht Becc* are inherently concerned with such constitutional operations in much the same way as this is framed within the operations of a modern state, an organization or a medieval kingdom. Here, the concept of the kingdom as a territory under the political governance of a king and leading nobles, with the agreement of a community with shared customs, is applicable to the early medieval situation.[29] Although, as with hegemony, the term kingdom provides limited insight into the political processes that underpin the cultural and political consolidation of Insular polities in this period. Whereas the use of 'nation', to describe a people united by a shared sense of identity and culture, does correspond with the concept of a kingdom and appears to confer a unified political distinction in keeping with the contemporary Latin Christian term *natio*.[30] The nation as a construct, as Benedict Anderson has asserted, fits with the overall contention of this study; that political unification in Pictland was directed and deliberate.[31] Likewise, the employment of 'centralized government' to describe power concentrated in a central authority to which local and regional polities are subject, attempts to outline a less coercive regime than the definition of 'state' usually allows. Indeed, the 'state' is a particularly difficult fit within a medieval context, although it certainly needs to be considered in terms of developing administrative authority.

Framing the Pictish *regnum* towards the end of the seventh century in geopolitical terminology is therefore problematic. The emergence of an organized and legitimate political elite indicates the beginning of a process where society moved from an institution based on kinship to one that was politically and territorially ordered under a form of sovereign control; whether this control presided in an individual or an institution. Until recently, the attribution of statehood to any sizable politically cohesive group was accepted, but this definition has since undergone revision.[32] According to Michael Mann, a society that is organized around kin groupings rather than one based on a circumscribed territory exhibits a 'pre-state' condition.[33] Further, Mann observed that the state evolved from the need to control social relations by institutionalizing the overlapping

26 M. Lapidge and M. Herren, *Aldhelm: the prose works* (1979), pp 41–2; *Aldhelmi opera*, ed. R. Ehwald (1961), p. 71 [*quasi quoddam rei publicae victigal et fiscale tributum*]. 27 S. Reynolds, 'The historiography of the medieval state' (1997), p. 112. 28 Gardner, *Law as a leap of faith*, pp 89–94. 29 S. Reynolds, 'The idea of the nation as a political community' (2005), pp 56–7. 30 H. Tsurushima, 'What do we mean by "nations" in early medieval Britain' (2010), p. 3; Scales and Zimmer, 'Introduction', p. 7. 31 B. Anderson, *Imagined communities* (1983). 32 For instance, N.K. Chadwick, *Celtic Britain* (1963), p. 63. 33 M. Mann, *The sources of social power* (1986), pp 26–7.

spheres of economic, ideological, military and political power and, consequently, territory would become institutionalized.[34] As Rhys Jones has noted, however, economic, military and ideological control can be exercised through social relationships, such as the kin-group or through clientage, in both pre-states and states.[35] Returning to Mann's theoretical definition, his unambiguous precondition for a society to be considered a state is the presence of a centralized authority with a unified territorial reach over defined physical boundaries.[36] This is summed up in his emphatic claim that 'there are no complex, civilized societies without any centre of binding rule-making authority'.[37] Gledhill, however, takes a more reductionist stance when he views a state as bureaucratic, imposing a centralizing hierarchy over 'previously autonomous local units' and appropriating much of their organizational functions.[38] This transition is noted by Driscoll, who maintains that the 'construction of administrative networks with increasing disregard for kinship relations as characteristic of the development of states'.[39] A simpler definition of statehood, defined by Susan Reynolds, is 'an organization of society in which the ruler or governing body more or less successfully controls the legitimate use of physical force'.[40] This definition is not predicated on a reductionist requirement of individual sovereign control, coinage or institutional law and complex bureaucracies: social differentiation and a formally located control of coercive power can make an autonomous polity a state.[41] The absence of strong, impersonal bureaucracies in this period does not mean an absence of effective power, instead power appears to be located in familial and clientage networks through which the king and his council could act. As Jane Tibbetts Schulenburg has observed, with no distinction between the private and public sphere the king's hall and his household became the locus of power.[42] The king's household was not only the centre of public power but defined its governance through images of patriarchal concern for the welfare of the kingdom as an extension of that household. This form of protective paternalism is characterized in Bede's description of King Edwin's rule.[43] This may offer a means for identifying early medieval statehood through centralized patriarchal control, evidenced in the maintenance of customary law and the imposition of kingdom-wide legal or religious reforms, rather than through formalized bureaucracies. The exercise of authority under this type of patriarchal governance remained – in appearance at least – communally negotiated rather than autocratic. Despite this simple model, there has been limited consensus on the qualifications required for early medieval statehood.[44]

34 Ibid., pp 14–15. 35 Jones, 'Mann and men in a medieval state', p. 68. 36 Mann, 'The autonomous power of the state', pp 198–201. 37 Ibid., p. 195. 38 J. Gledhill, 'Introduction: the comparative analysis of social and political transitions' (1988), p. 5. 39 S.T. Driscoll, 'The archaeology of state formation in Scotland' (1991), p. 108. 40 Reynolds, 'The historiography of the medieval state', p. 120. 41 Ibid., p. 122. 42 J. Tibbetts Schulenburg, 'Female sanctity' (1988), p. 105. 43 *HE* II.16. 44 For instance, in the same volume, see A. Thacker, '*Peculiaris*

The processes by which societies achieve statehood are varied and rarely conform to theoretical concepts of state formation. Those that exhibit signs of emerging centralization do not always become states or retain their statehood; systems of governance are, after all, never static. According to Henri Claessen and Jarich Oosten, a state emerges after a long evolution of its socio-political systems, rather than a conflict-ridden sudden manifestation.[45] In the case of Pictland, conflict does appear to have stimulated political cohesion but this was against easily identified outsiders and existing social institutions supported the extension and upward transfer of authority. This is not to say that state formation does not cause conflict between local versus centralizing administrations. The process of state formation requires the incorporation of non-homogenous societies, which may be interpreted through records of conflict and the creation of ethnic identifiers.[46] Richard Hodges recognized three distinct pre-state horizons whereby small tribal territories were swallowed into larger kingdoms by inter-polity competition. These were further merged into an even larger kingdom under the sway of individualized leadership, itself leading to dynastic power.[47] While Hodges' developmental theory does appear to correspond to early medieval patterns, his classification of what constitutes a 'pre-state' condition appears unnecessarily reductionist. Certainly, conflict and military coercion appear to be an unsustainable method by which to maintain and extend political centralization. A shared language, legal and social system where communal agreement and hierarchical control is established could certainly expedite political coherence. This combination conforms to the definition of a nation, having a collective bond and political aspiration.[48] In Pictland, while the uniting factor was initially coercive, the influence of Christianity added a new dynamic to the perceptions of identity and leadership. If a definition is appropriate to this period of political organization then the term *emergent state* may be applicable. This would encompass the way in which existing institutional systems promoted political consolidation while a self-aware leadership actively constructed a collective identity. Political transition occurred within existing social institutions but the process by which political consolidation was consciously engineered displays a state-building agenda.

Patronus Noster' (2000), p. 3; Maddicott's chapter is entitled 'Two frontier states'. **45** H.J.M. Claessen and J.G. Oosten, 'Introduction' (1996), pp 4–7. **46** Thurston, *Landscapes of power, landscapes of conflict*, p. 11; C. Ward Gailey and T.C. Patterson, 'State formation and uneven development' (1988), p. 76. **47** Hodges, 'Peer polity interaction', p. 76. **48** L.E. Cederman, *Emergent actors in world politics* (1997), pp 17–19.

CONCLUSION

A transition in the exercise of Pictish kingship, attested to in the documentary record, coincides with the career of King Bredei filius Bili. Arguably, it was his success at the Battle of Nechtansmere which empowered Bredei with considerable psychological and material advantage. He gained dependent alliances by sword and treaty, additional militia and equipment as well as plunder to 'fuel the cycle of gift-exchange'.[49] Access to wealth could ensure the continuance of dependent allies thereby increasing the king's ability to exercise political authority over wider territories. His operation of lordship over these territories was made simpler by the existing territorial organization, although that control was yet to be geographically consolidated. Clientage similarly transferred local lordship rights into the hands of regional rulers and upwards to the king. The custom of hostage sureties enabled the king to exercise authority more effectively over distant dissenting groups and lessened the requirement for a costly military presence. Foundational to the operation of authority, the assembly was the agency of government through which social controls could be effected and at which the physical presence of the king reinforced his authority. Existing social institutions therefore provided the king with real power over the economic and political direction of his kingdom. In addition, the king's patronage of ecclesiastical establishments augmented the consolidation of his authority over distant territories. Clerical networks throughout Britain and Ireland, if not beyond, linked the political leadership into trade opportunities and access to new technologies and intellectual developments. Among the latter were western Christian ideologies promoting political consolidation and a behavioural framework that legitimated and expanded kingship. The increasing integration of Christianity into all levels of social life resulted in bishops and senior clerics taking a fundamental role in the operation of governance, which, in turn, formalized the rights of the king over legislature. Royal investment in statements of power – such as personal ornaments like the penannular brooch and signifiers of cultural alliance like the Class I symbol stones – express the widening territorial authority of the Fortriu kings. For the emergent Fortriu dynasty, power was no longer a transient exercise by a ruling group whereby control equated to the depletion of resources. Instead, with economic and personal mobility came an increase in social networks and political groups were able to identify themselves within a wider cultural dynamic through their mutual fealty to a single king.

49 Moreland, 'Concepts of the early medieval economy', p. 16.

3

The king's prerogative

The emergence of national identity in Britain during the early medieval period, it could be argued, was a naturally evolving process in which kin-relations, inherent social traditions and language together laid the foundation for the gradual territorial cohesion of a collective polity. This is suggested by Bede's tidy division of four ethnic groups separated by their vernacular languages yet joined by their use of Latin.[1] The archaeological evidence demonstrates increased social contacts and alliances across regions of Pictland from the sixth century, with administration potentially occurring at regional and national assemblies. The gradual coalescing of social networks – through community attendance at assemblies, kinship, social alliances and the pervasive clientage system – manifested a sense of shared cultural identity.[2] There are, however, indications that a new vision of national identity was being self-consciously promulgated in Pictland towards the end of the seventh century with the appearance of an origin myth and a dynastic king list. In addition, western Christian political theories on government, transmitted through clerical channels, offered a new and enlarged role for kingship, one that promoted ideas of national cohesion and identity. As a result, Pictish kingship underwent a transformation during this phase of territorial consolidation where an assertive clergy actively promoted a vision of Christian theocratic monarchy.

Early medieval Insular kingship continues to engage scholarly interest and recent research is challenging long-held notions on the exercise of regnal authority among the polities. Perceived differences between Irish kings as having limited constitutional powers and Anglo-Saxon kings as widely autocratic have been largely revised.[3] Indeed, by the end of the seventh century the influence of Christian ideas on kingship had permeated the polities and Insular kings displayed similar prerogatives over their increasingly identifiable political communities. It is clear from the sources that these Insular polities interacted and influenced each other. By recognizing the clerical influence in constituting kingship alongside a comparative analysis of kingship functions Pictish kingship can be brought into communion with their neighbouring kings as active leaders of their kingdoms political direction. Of course, dynastic succession conditions

1 *HE* I.1. 2 Roymans, *Tribal societies in northern Gaul*, pp 39–45. 3 P. Wormald, 'Celtic and Anglo-Saxon kingship' (1986); M. Gerriets, 'The king as judge in early Ireland' (1988); R. Chapman Stacey, 'Law and order in the very old west' (1991); J. Campbell, 'Archipelagic thoughts' (2009); Charles-Edwards, 'Celtic kings: "priestly vegetables"?'.

across the Insular polities did vary, with the occasional weak king and interregnal competition destabilizing political cohesion. Nevertheless, successful dynastic succession with supportive kin alliances led to expanding territorial control and the gradual centralizing of that control. The accrual of a king's authority was expedited by clerical ideals of theocratic kingship that empowered the office with sacred legitimacy, endorsing the expansion of the king's prerogatives over his subjects.

SUCCESSION AND GENEALOGICAL ASPIRATIONS

Dynamic political consolidation transformed Insular polities during the seventh century. Among the neighbours of the Picts, the Irish Southern and Northern Uí Néill promoted themselves as high-kings of Ireland in the late seventh century.[4] With the support of the legal and ecclesiastical establishments, they created a mythic dynasty by which to legitimize their claims to overlordship as kings of Tara.[5] This family of aggressive territorial consolidators had some influential clergy among their members (such as St Columba and successive abbots of Iona), who were in an ideal position to create an imagined past for the dynasty and mediate an image of God-ordained destiny.[6] Likewise, the territorial ambitions of the Munster Eóganacht king, Cathal mac Finguine (721–42), appear to have encouraged a new, intellectual vision for expansionary kingship as *righ ruirech* (king of kings).[7] This king is noted in the records for the wasting of Mag Breg in 721, a territory associated with the symbolic assembly of Tara that was also linked to the possession of high-kingship.[8] The generation of genealogies and origin myths among the Irish and Anglo-Saxon kingdoms in the seventh century defined a 'common mythical past to promote a common sense of belonging'.[9] According to Yorke, the Anglo-Saxon origin myths provided legitimization of property claims by the king, a key step in defining territorial overlordship.[10] The Irish and Anglo-Saxon genealogies asserted mythic origins for the leaders and kings of their polities, expressing their status as historical and pre-ordained in both success and failure. Origin myths likewise provided an authoritative, cohesive vision of political unity and destiny. The appearance of genealogies and origin myths reveal the dominant contemporary political agenda and alliances that are framed by an awareness of a distinct identity.[11] This

4 T.M. Charles-Edwards, 'The Uí Néill, 695–743' (2002); N.B. Aitchison, *Armagh and the royal centres* (1994), pp 200–1; K. Hughes, *The Church in early Irish society* (1966), pp 111–20. 5 D. Bray, 'The myth of Tara' (2003), pp 288–90. 6 B. Lacey, *Cenél Conaill and the Donegal kingdoms* (2006), pp 29–47. 7 Breatnach, 'Canon law and secular law in early Ireland', p. 444. 8 *AU* 721.6. 9 Moreland, 'Ethnicity, power and the English', pp 50–1. 10 B. Yorke, *Political and ethnic identity* (2000), p. 78. 11 Dumville, 'Kingship, genealogies and regnal lists', p. 77; P.J. Geary, *Women at the beginning* (2006).

evidence indicates that the neighbours of the Picts were developing the apparatus of state, with a pre-eminent king and an emergent administration that was self-consciously adopting the propaganda of belonging. Bede confirms that the Picts had also developed an origin myth. This myth legitimized the Picts' presence in northern Britain as 'ethnically' separate from other Brythonic speaking groups and the Gaels, and ruled over by a single dynasty of prominent kings.[12]

The Picts, like their neighbours, were moving towards a more cohesive sense of their identity with its advantages of self-determinism and the consolidation of territories. It is likely that the Picts had an existing form of government at a regional level with a common language and legal system throughout the provinces.[13] A transition in the Picts' political consolidation appears to coincide with the reigns of the three early medieval kings of the Picts: Bredei filius Bili, Bredei filius Derelei and his brother Necthon filius Derelei. These kings capitalized on dynastic successes to exercise coercive and ideological authority in order to construct a distinct political identity in Pictland.

Pictish succession and paternal alliance

There are indications that the brothers Bredei and Necthon were kin to Bredei filius Bili; their mother, Derelei, was possibly a daughter of Bredei filius Bili. Clancy, who interpreted Derelei as a female name, has convincingly argued that the father of the sons of Derelei was a Gael named Dargart of the Cenél Comgaill of Dál Riata.[14] Dargart may have claimed descent from the Dál Riatan ruler Conall mac Comgaill whom St Columba of Iona reputedly met upon his arrival in Britain.[15] During this meeting, Columba revealed to Conall the outcome of a battle in Ireland in which adherents of the Northern Uí Néill, including a cousin of Columba, defeated the Irish Cruithin.[16] Adomnán's description of the conference implies ancient political links between this Dál Riatan ruler, progenitor of the Cenél Comgaill, and the dominant Irish Cenél Conaill to whom Columba and Adomnán both belonged.[17] Fraser, however, has raised doubts about such a simple reading of diplomatic conditions, as during the late seventh century the Cenél Comgaill may have aligned themselves with the Strathclyde Britons, from whom Bredei filius Bili owed his own patrimony.[18] Nevertheless, Adomnán does appear to provide the Cenél Comgaill with genealogical rights to regnal aspirations.

Aedán mac Gabrán succeeded his cousin Conall mac Comgaill to the kingship and it was his descendents, the Cenél nGabráin, who dominated in Dál Riata until the end of the seventh century. The Cenél Comgaill are first mentioned in

12 *HE* I.1. 13 S.M. Foster, 'The state of Pictland in the age of Sutton Hoo' (1992), pp 217–34; M. Miller, 'Matriliny by treaty' (1982), p. 158. 14 *Clancy*, 'Philosopher-king', pp 128–33, n. 29, p. 135. 15 *VC* I.7. 16 Sharpe, *Adomnán of Iona*, pp 267–8, n. 278, 280. 17 M. Herbert, *Iona, Kells and Derry* (1988), p. 12. 18 Fraser, 'Strangers on the Clyde', p. 109.

Irish chronicle entries from 709, in relation to the killing of Necthon's sons.[19] Bannerman suggested that this group had gained political equality among the septs of the Dál Riata around 700 as a result of the fading fortunes of the Cenél nGabráin.[20] A Dál Riatan genealogical tract, dated by Dumville to pre-719, describes four competing cenéla in this period: the cenéla nGabráin, Loairn, Oengus and Comgaill.[21] It is probably not by chance that the political prominence of the Cenél Comgaill waxed after the successful reign of Bredei filius Bili. It has been argued that a branch of this Cenél moved into newly acquired territory around Clackmannan, Clackmannanshire; a defensive buffer zone against Northumbrian expansionary ambitions.[22] The emergence of the Cenél Comgaill in chronicle records of this period is suggestive of a military alliance with Bredei filius Bili, rewarded and maintained by a marriage into a dominant Pictish noble house. In linking the progenitor of the Cenél Comgaill with St Columba, Adomnán formally recognizes the political identity of this cenél. Political alliances between northern British groups, and some Irish polities, were complex and fluctuating.[23] Throughout this period Iona retained dominant links to the Irish Cenél Conaill (who supplied the high-kings of Ireland) but also nursed their connections in the north of Britain, as Adomnán's personal connection with Bredei filius Derelei attests. Alliance with the Cenél Comgaill, however, would have ensured the offspring of Derelei with an influential patrimony and connections to the Gaels of Dál Riata and dominant political groups in Ireland. The influence of the *familia Columbae* under Adomnán may also have dominated the ecclesiastical direction of Pictish churches due to the apparent personal and ascendant relationship between the abbot of Iona and Bredei filius Derelei.

The marriage of a Pictish 'princess' to a member of the Gaelic elite appears to have constituted a treaty whereby each side were obliged to muster forces to protect their mutual interests. Indeed, the patronymics of Pictish kings offer an insight into the rise and fall of dominant political groups and alliances throughout this period. It is not until after Necthon's reign that the patronymics of Pictish kings suggest internal matrimonial alliances. The mixed parentage of the sons of Derelei had interesting ramifications for their authority in Pictland, particularly if Clancy is correct in placing Dargart and his kin within the vicinity of Clackmannanshire and Stirlingshire.[24] This region formed a strategic buffer between the Northumbrians, Britons and Southern Picts. Later hagiographical evidence indicates a Pictish king's proprietary interest in this region. Bredei filius Derelei, with the patronymic Dargart (Brude filius Dargart), is identified in the Life of St Serf as donating the lands of Culross – which comprise parts

19 *AU* 709.4. 20 Bannerman, *Studies in the history of the Dalriada*, pp 78–80, 109–10. 21 D. Dumville, '*Cethri Prímchenéla Dáil Riata*' (2000). 22 Clancy, 'Philosopher-king', pp 138–42. 23 Fraser, 'Strangers on the Clyde', pp 109–11; Herbert, *Iona, Kells and Derry*, p. 55. 24 Clancy, 'Philosopher-king', pp 138–42.

of the old British region of Manaw – to the saint, with the endorsement of Adomnán. This donation appears to link the Pictish king intimately with Adomnán and, by extension, the *familia Columbae*. While the Life of St Serf is undoubtedly late, it may nevertheless preserve a cultural memory that this area was considered to be within Bredei's gift or that of his paternal kin.[25] Place-name evidence, while problematic, suggests that this was very much a Pictish foundation as this region lacks the typical Gaelic ecclesiastical toponyms (such as '*cill*').[26] Instead, Taylor found a preponderance of the place-name '*bod*' or '*both*' associated with early churches in west Fife and in central and eastern Scotland.[27] While the '*both*' element is cognate with Welsh '*bod*' meaning a 'dwelling' or 'residence', and in Irish *both* translates as 'hut' or 'cabin', its ecclesiastical association appears to be a specifically Pictish development.[28] The use of Bredei's patronymic in the land donation to St Serf suggests that Dargart's kin moved into the area that may have been vacated by Northumbrian settlers after Ecgfrid's defeat made Anglo-Saxon settlement in the area untenable. This kin-group, however, did not impose a Gaelic ecclesiastical presence but appears to have retained Pictish descriptive religious nomenclature for the foundations. This may suggest that this putative Gaelic group identified more closely with Pictish political agendas than those of the Dál Riata. The donation of strategic and economically rewarding estates to a prominent cleric, like St Serf or his followers, ensured the spiritual and material oversight of the region by a group loyal to the donor. Suppression of the surviving Pictish rulers in the area may have been necessary. Certainly, the evidence of the *Amra Choluimb Chille* suggests there was a powerful political presence around the Tay that, possibly until the Northumbrian domination, may have encouraged a political division between north and south of the Mounth.[29] This division may support Bede's binary vision of Christian conversion of Pictland. The establishment of ecclesiastical houses in new-won territory was a distinctly political act whereby the king extended his authority through the benevolent arm of a church, itself in a position of clientage to the king for the land donation. The utility of ecclesiastical donations in extending the real and political presence of kings was a key strategy in territorialization.

The Pictish king lists create the impression of a centralized office of ancient antecedence, and may have been in circulation by the mid-seventh century.[30] With no obvious pattern of succession, short reigns are a feature in the lists representing a highly competitive system probably reliant on birth, popularity, wealth, and diplomatic and military proficiency. The king lists, as they have survived, describe a single dynasty's 'historic' right to the office of over-king and

25 Macquarrie, '*Vita Sancti Servani*', pp 125–6, text at p. 140. **26** Taylor, 'Place-names and the early Church', p. 101. **27** Ibid., pp 96–8. **28** Ibid., p. 98. **29** Clancy and Márkus, *Iona: the earliest poetry of a Celtic monastery*, pp 104, 112; *HE* III.4. **30** Anderson, *Kings and kingship*, pp 88, 240–91; N. Evans, 'Royal succession and kingship' (2008), p. 6.

authenticates their authority and leadership functions.[31] These lists represent a conscious decision to articulate, in writing, the legitimacy of the Fortriu dynasty's kingship. The decision to construct an 'archive' for the pedigree of Pictish kings going further back than the 'historical horizon' was, according to Molly Miller, deliberate.[32] As a corollary to the invention of ancient Pictish dynastic kingship, evidenced by the king lists, the authority of regional rulers underwent a transformation that potentially diminished their status. In describing the presence of the 'subject-king' of Orkney in Bridei's court, Adomnán refers to him as *regulus* as opposed to Bridei's *rex*.[33] The significance of this terminological differentiation is inconclusive as neither Adomnán nor Bede appears to be consistent in their descriptions of rule. Contemporary Irish vernacular texts suggest that new terms for provincial or subject rulers had yet to be fully developed to reflect the changing political conditions.[34] There is evidence that Irish scholars were considering how to define the emerging political reality. It is notable that *Críth Gablach* describes a *rechtga*[e] *ríg* 'king's government' over other kings 'such as the government of the king of Cashel in Munster'.[35] This appears to be a type of over-king that is outlined in the contemporary status tract *Míadslechta* as a *triath*, 'mighty king', who 'penetrates Erinn's lands from wave to wave'.[36] In addition, a statement in *Bretha Nemed Toísech* connects the right to hold assembly at Tara and the binding of kings into clientage as characterizing a king of kings (*righ ruirech*).[37] Early Irish scholars were seeking to define a form of territorially expansive kingship while retaining normative hierarchical nomenclature. Nevertheless, whether there were terminological changes or a semantic shift in titles designating rule, regional leaders who supported the new political direction of theocratic kingship were likely to have had their authority over their domains legitimated; and, while narrowed, their effective local authority may have been increased.

A number of entries in the Pictish king lists indicate that a king was succeeded by his brother. In these cases, some form of dynastic kingship was being asserted. A reigning king's brother would receive military or other secular responsibilities, along with fiscal returns, that increased his potential to succeed his brother. The right to rule would require a range of political machinations. Provincial leaders and the nobility would provide support to a claimant for whom they were clients or kin. Alternatively, the selection would be ideologically and economically expedient. Bredei filius Bili reigned between twenty and twenty-one years and it is unlikely that he remained in his position purely because of continual military success.[38] His ability to remain king of an extensive Pictish *regnum* was a result of administrative controls. These controls are

31 Geary, *Women at the beginning*, p. 64. 32 M. Miller, 'Royal pedigrees of the insular Dark Ages' (1980), p. 213. 33 *VC* II.42. 34 J. Campbell, *Bede's Reges and Principes* (1979), pp 3–4. 35 *Críth Gablach*, §38, p. 20. 36 *CIH* 583.7–12. 37 *CIH* 2219.39–40. 38 Anderson, *Kings and kingship*, p. 262, n. 217.

likely to have been similar to other Insular kings and included convening assemblies; dispensing justice at assemblies; a visible itinerant court; dispensing favours and property; collection of render and tribute; and personal oaths of fealty from the nobility supported by hostages. Bredei's success in battle provided a powerful legitimacy for his right to rule. His victories endowed him and the next generation with the 'justification for the holding of power'.[39] At the same time his military success appears to have ushered in a period of peace. This suggests that Bredei effectively subjugated internal opposition to present a united front to neighbouring polities. He achieved this state through the same mechanisms as Kershaw has noted for other early medieval kings, through 'oath swearing and the giving up or exchange of hostages', which were fundamental elements of the peacemaking process.[40] According to the ninth abuse of *De duodecim abusiuis saeculi*, peace was the sign of a just king by which he ensured fecundity for his people and, as a consequence, cosmological harmony.[41] However the previous systems of succession and kingly prerogatives were constituted, the influence of clerical advice, which transmitted western political theories on rulership and government, added a new vision of consolidated kingship and one that was God-ordained.

CONSTRUCTING THE ROLE OF A CHRISTIAN THEOCRATIC MONARCH

Extant prose and verse texts from the sixth century reveal the increasing influence of Christianity on Insular kingship. Initially, these texts express the inherent conflict between earthly power and leading a good Christian life, taking a pessimistic stance towards the office of kingship. This is clear in the, putative, sixth-century Columban Irish *Altus Prosator*, which laments:

> The momentary glory of the kings of the present world,
> fleeting and tyrannical, is cast down at God's whim.[42]

Similar sentiments are expressed in the *Elegy for Gwallawg*, a northern Britonnic ruler:

> To the onlooker, heavy-hearted are kings
> While they live, wealth's not theirs in the grave:
> They can take no pride in their way of life;
> Harder the torment to which they may go.[43]

39 Fouracre, 'Conflict, power and legitimation in Francia', p. 15. 40 Kershaw, *Peaceful kings*, p. 17. 41 Pseudo-Cyprian: *De duodecim*, ix rex iniquus, lines 10–19, p. 52. 42 Clancy and Márkus, *Iona: the earliest poetry of a Celtic monastery*, §10, K, p. 47. 43 Clancy, *The Triumph Tree*, p. 92.

Despite this melancholy outlook, clerics in the west were beginning to define the correct manner by which a king should rule according to Christian principles. After all, a king like any other sinner could be redeemed from the evils inherent in positions of secular power. The Insular author Gildas in his *De Excidio Britonum* uses an extensive range of scriptural references to represent the antithesis of good kingship in order to highlight new concepts of Christian monarchy.[44] A century later, the ninth abuse of *De duodecim abusiuis saeculi* similarly warns the Christian king, that 'since he is set up on the throne as the first of all men, if he fails to act justly, in the same way he inhabits the first place of punishment'.[45] These *contradictio in adiecto* texts were not a dialogue between familiars but display a distance between church and secular authority. Once direct correspondence between clerics and kings is established, a paternal and affectionate dialogue emerges. Towards the end of the seventh century, personalized advice from clerics to kings on the proper manner in which to rule become more prevalent; indicative of the keen interest taken by clerics in the government of the secular realm.[46] Around the same period, Merovingian texts emphasize scriptural comparisons and themes in order to describe rulership.[47] A detailed definition of the moral obligations of Christian kingship had been widely promulgated by Isidore of Seville at the fourth Council of Toledo (633), and his influence can be detected on Insular *speculum principum* literature.[48] Isidore's *Etymologies* were clearly the source for the reference to a king as corrector of his subjects in the ninth abuse of *De duodecim abusiuis saeculi.*[49] Clerics tied themselves closer to the concerns of rulers by assuming the role of advisors. Aldhelm's letter to King Aldfrid includes secular ideas and vocabulary to describe his relationship with the king. Aldhelm refers to the king as joined to him in 'bonds of spiritual clientship'.[50] He further asserts that in the past he 'acquired the name of "father" and that you received the appellations of your adoptive station'.[51] According to Richard Martin, the *topos* of foster-father instructing the future king was a feature of a Classical tradition.[52] This same tradition is evident, with slight variation, in the advisory tone of the prologue to *Audacht Morainn*.[53] This advisory position is formalized in the *c.*eighth-century *Ríagail Pátraic* text which, in describing the duties required of a bishop, demands that a primary duty of a chief bishop was to act as spiritual advisor to rulers.[54] Perhaps the most significant model of a paternal voice providing advice

44 Gildas: *De excidio Britonum*, §27. 45 Pseudo-Cyprian: *De duodecim*, ix rex iniquus, lines 11–13, p. 53. 46 See J. Grigg, 'The just king and *De Duodecim Abusiuis Saeculi*' (2010). 47 Hen, 'The uses of the Bible', pp 283–4. 48 Sancti Isidori: *Collectio Canonum*, ed. J.P. Migne (1850), 84, cap. LXXV, col. 385; A. Breen, '*De XII Abusiuis*: text and transmission' (2002), p. 84. 49 Barney, Lewis et al., *The* Etymologies *of Isidore of Seville*, IX.iii.4, p. 200. 50 Lapidge and Herren, *Aldhelm: the prose works*, p. 34. *Aldhelmi opera*, p. 61 [*mihique iam dudum spiritalis clientelae catenis conexo*]. 51 Ibid., p. 62 [*paternum memini me nomen adeptum teque adoptivae dignitatus vocabula*]. 52 R.P. Martin, 'Hesiod, Odysseus and the instruction of princes' (1984), pp 33–4, n. 11. 53 *Audacht Morainn*, §4, pp 4–5. 54 J.G. O'Keeffe, 'The Rule of Patrick'

to a king was that of David who, in *Proverbs* 1.8, exhorted 'Listen, my son, to your father's instruction'.

Aldhelm clearly asserts a paternal claim over King Aldfrid. By the end of the seventh century the advisory position of clerics towards kings was an accepted function and clerics took a more proactive approach to their moral and spiritual rights over secular matters. In turn, clerics shared in a range of western Christian ideas on the constitution of theocratic kingship transmitted by writers such as Isidore of Seville.[55] Indeed, the Old Testament provided ideal *exempla* for the behaviour of kings, and Isidore refers to the virtuous king exercising his authority in due humility after the example of the Israelite King David, while actively instituting and delighting in justice as the corrector of his people.[56] By expressing the role of a Christian king as a God-given office, whereby he was required to be 'just' and the 'corrector' of his people, the king gained the moral legitimacy to extend his authority over the public and private behaviour of his people. Clerics encouraged a closer management of the populace by the king, urging his participation in justice and emphasizing his responsibility for his people's spiritual welfare. This is clearly stated in *De duodecim abusiuis saeculi*, which demands the moral rectitude of the king as corrector of his subjects.[57] The Irish status text *Críth Gablach* asks 'king [*Rí*], why is he so called?' and answers because he 'exerts [*riges*] the power of correction [*chun(d)rig*] over the members of his *túath*'.[58] On the other hand, his kingship would be violated should he display 'falsity or violence or overmight'.[59] Clerics also promoted the use of physical punishment as an appropriate corrective measure by the king.[60] This is attested to in *Collectio Canonum Hibernensis*, which declares that the 'word of the king is a sword for beheading, a rope for hanging'.[61] Punitive measures were not necessarily fully adopted as the legal mechanisms in place to avert retributive retaliation offered more flexibility through compensatory measures. Clerics, however, encouraged a greater exercise of physical authority by the king, framed in Irish law as 'coercive power to prevent every evil', which legitimized autocratic action and justified it on the grounds of Christian correction.[62] The expectation of increased physical correction, through the direct intercession of the king's justice, implies a corresponding increase in the executive functions of the king over the *minutiae* of public and private life. This type of protective paternalism is exemplified in Bede's description of Edwin's rule.[63]

(1904), p. 218 [*fri hanmchairdes do flaithib*]. **55** J.N. Hillgarth, 'Ireland and Spain in the seventh century' (1984), p. 9. **56** Sancti Isidori: *Sententiae*, ed. J.P Migne (1862), 83, cap. XLIX, cols 720–4, 721–2, 724. **57** Pseudo-Cyprian: *De duodecim*, ix rex iniquus, lines 7–8, p. 51; *Audacht Morainn*, §12–17, pp 6–7. **58** *Críth Gablach*, §31, p. 18. See Grigg, 'The just king and *De duodecim abusiuis saeculi*', p. 40. **59** *Críth Gablach*, §39, p. 21. **60** Ó Corráin, Breatnach and Breen, 'The laws of the Irish', pp 382–438. **61** *CCH*, 'De regno', Liber XXV, cap. 17, pp 81–2. **62** *CIH* 340.28; Ó Corráin, Breatnach and Breen, 'The laws of the Irish', p. 387. **63** *HE* II.16.

Rex dei gratia

Biblical precedents and the example of papal government also encouraged secular ideas of centralized power embodied in an authoritative and paternalistic leader; one who is ordained by God and through dynastic succession.[64] Continental parallels for the development of Christian kingship indicate an enlarged role for the king as leader of his people in war and their protector in times of peace.[65] Irish and Anglo-Saxon clerical leaders were often from the dominant dynasties and regnal influence was of particular importance to clerical advancement. The advantage and disadvantage of royal favour can be seen in the career of Bishop Wilfrid of Northumbria. During King Oswy's reign Wilfrid claimed authority over all churches within the king's dominions, yet a quarrel with Oswy's successor lost him his diocese and, despite direct papal appeals, the king retained effective power over church offices denying Wilfrid's reinstatement.[66] Eventually Archbishop Theodore, who had conspired in the removal of Wilfrid from his vast diocese in 677, negotiated Wilfrid's restoration to the diocese of York after it was subdivided.[67] Archbishop Theodore's own spiritual responsibility covered more territory than any contemporary Anglo-Saxon king and his yearly convocation of bishops ensured orthodoxy and underscored his position as head of the English ecclesiastics.[68] Not only did Theodore's scholarship attract large numbers of local and foreign students to Canterbury, he also ensured unanimity of orthodox Catholic practice and an increase in dioceses, allowing a closer clerical scrutiny over a community's behaviour.[69] Theodore's example of centralized authority would have provided an interesting lesson to Insular kings.

Evidence from Ireland reveals cooperative action between Insular kings and clerics, which impacted on the role of kingship. The emergence of centralizing kingship in Ireland towards the end of seventh century, under the northern and southern branches of the Uí Néill, coincided with an increase in secular and ecclesiastic Irish writing and the rise in clerical claims to authority over spiritual and temporal life.[70] Texts such as *Críth Gablach*, which attempt to explain and circumscribe Irish social and political structures, betray an attempt to reconcile a new constitutional framework with the polity.[71] This is even more overt in the *Bretha Nemed* tracts, which integrate clerical and secular hierarchies along with hierarchies of skilled practitioners; which Aitchison describes as 'a more ambitious rationalization of social order' than *Críth Gablach*.[72] Similarly,

64 J. Canning, *A history of medieval political thought* (1996), pp 29–31. 65 J.M. Wallace-Hadrill, *Early Germanic kingship*, p. 54. 66 *HE* IV.3, 12; *VW* XI, XV, XXI. 67 M. Lapidge, 'The career of Archbishop Theodore' (1995), pp 26–7. 68 *HE* IV.4, 17. 69 Lapidge, 'The career of Archbishop Theodore', pp 26–7. 70 F.J. Byrne, 'Tribes and tribalism in early Ireland' (1971), p. 153; P. Ó Néill, 'Irish transmission of late antique learning' (2002), p. 71. 71 T.M. Charles-Edwards, 'A contract between king and people' (1994). 72 Aitchison, 'Kingship, society and sacrality', p. 56.

Adomnán and his affiliates' conscious literary creation of inauguration rituals gave 'historical' precedents to new political developments in the role and reach of the king.[73] Irish clerics bestowed new histories of godly ordination and selection on the ancestors of the dominant Uí Néill kings, while Bede's history presents an 'authorized' version of Anglo-Saxon dynastic rights. In the same period, Armagh aspired to be the ecclesiastical alter ego of this new centralizing and expansionary high-kingship, its *Liber Angeli* claiming archiepiscopal status for the bishop of Armagh as the earliest foundation of St Patrick.[74] As Bart Jaski observed, 'political propaganda focuses on the past rather than the present or future' to legitimize contemporary political agendas.[75] Notwithstanding these textual claims, high-kingship in Ireland rested on individual authority, which may have limited the potential for sustained political centralization.

How far clerics inspired ideas of centralizing kingship is difficult to ascertain. They certainly provided an idealized model of Christian theocratic monarchy to which a king was encouraged to conform in order to retain his legitimacy and clerical support; resulting in the king's moral obligation to his clerics. The polities, indoctrinated into Christian concepts of God's omnipotence and justice, were presented with advice literature exemplifying correct moral behaviour and new legislation and ritual that supported the authority of a theocratic monarch.[76] *Críth Gablach*, however, indicates that ordination by God was not the only authority a king required in order to rule, as public consensus was framed as a constitutional requirement. Following a description on levels of kingship, *Críth Gablach* asks 'who is higher in dignity the king or his *túath*?'[77] The answer to the question is in the next line of text; that the king was higher because his *túath* raised him to his position, but this was conditional on his protection of the rights of his *túath*.[78] Charles-Edwards gives a translation of this response with due attention to its paradox: 'for it is the people which ordains a king, it is not a king which ordains a people'.[79] The king's exercise of power was therefore understood to be reliant on the tacit approval of the populace, without which his authority and dynastic prospects was severely limited. Expressions of public benevolence were therefore key to the king's image as patriarch. Exemplifying this benevolence, the king's patronage of ecclesiastical establishments gave him useful moral capital. Not only would the spiritual benefits of regular prayers on his behalf augment his image and spiritual consequence, but his patronage provided him access to intellectual capital in the form of sophisticated

73 M.J. Enright, *Iona, Tara and Soissons* (1985), pp 6, 24. 74 *The Patrician texts in the Book of Armagh*, 'E. Liber Angeli', §21, pp 188–9 [*Item omnis aeclessia libera et ciuitas ab episcopali gradu* <*quae*> *uidetur esse fundata in tota Scotorum insola ... iuxta uerbam angueli in speciali societate Patricii pontificis atque heredis | cathedrae eius Aird Machae esse debuerat, quia donauit illi Deus totam insolam, ut supra diximus*]. 75 B. Jaski, 'Early medieval Irish kingship and the Old Testament' (1998), p. 331. 76 Hen, 'The uses of the Bible', pp 281–2. 77 *Críth Gablach*, §35, p. 19. 78 *Críth Gablach*, §§35–6, pp 19–20. 79 Charles-Edwards, 'A contract between king and people', p. 110.

theological debate and education that was disseminated from the scriptoria. Through these venues, the king could access the wider culture of Christendom to pursue knowledge and participate in new ideas and technologies. Moreover, he could exploit the extensive clerical trade networks for economic as well as ideological benefits.

Support for centralizing high-kingship in Ireland was of mutual benefit to the success of the *familia Patraic*; and of the *familia Columbae*, particularly during the lifetime of Adomnán.[80] According to modern scholarship, Adomnán belonged to an Irish clerical reform group, given the appellation of *Romani* due to their Roman orthodox aspirations. Aidan Breen discerned that these *Romani* intellectuals produced *De duodecim abusiuis saeculi*, and the later *Collectio Canonum Hibernensis* with their *speculum principum* advice.[81] Adomnán's apparent links with the Pictish *regnum* suggest that similar theories of theocratic kingship were promoted in Pictland. Clerics appear to have been pursuing a conscious programme to rework the executive functions of Insular kings in order to align them more closely with contemporary western Christian political ideas. In turn, the influence of clerics over royal behaviour and politics assisted the increasing authority of favoured churchmen within society. Land donations to ecclesiastical foundations by those wishing to obtain diplomatic advantage followed; approved by the king who also ensured the rollout of specific social and political agendas, such as the *Cáin Adomnáin* that raised revenue for king and the *familia Columbae*. Clerics endorsed and legitimized their kings by quasi-historical and legal precedents and, potentially, new consecration rites that endowed them with the unquestionable favour of God.

A contemporary of Adomnán, Muirchú, wrote a Life of St Patrick that emphasized the dominance and historical legitimacy of the Uí Néill claim to high-kingship as a pre-Christian *imperator barbarorum*.[82] Armagh's patrons were from the Southern Uí Néill dynasty of the midlands, and were politically more powerful from 654 to 695 than their northern counterparts, who held Columba as their patron saint.[83] It is therefore of interest that Adomnán refers to the Northern Uí Néill king and Columba's contemporary, Diormit son of Cerbaill, as ordained 'by God's will, as the ruler of all Ireland'.[84] Elsewhere in the Life of St Columba, Adomnán applies the idea of God's ordination legitimizing a more expansive and centralizing type of kingship. He employs the biblical anointing *topos* of Samuel and Saul in the angelically inspired choice of Áedán mac Gabráin to the kingship, using Columba as the conduit.[85] In addition, Columba also promises that the youngest son of Áedán would inherit the kingship, a move

80 Enright, *Iona, Tara and Soissons*, p. 2. 81 Breen, '*De XII Abusiuis*: text and transmission', p. 84. 82 *The Patrician texts in the Book of Armagh*, 'A. Muirchú', §I.10 (9), pp 74–5. 83 Charles-Edwards, 'The Uí Néill, 695–743', pp 412–13. 84 *VC* I.36. 85 *VC* III.5; Enright, *Iona, Tara and Soissons*. See Charles-Edwards, 'A contract between king and people', p. 109, n. 9, p. 118.

to direct dynastic inheritance that sits curiously within the usual Gaelic tanistry rights.[86] Written up as the prophet of kings, Columba provides a post-mortem miracle by ensuring victory for King Oswald of Northumbria over King Cadwallon, with the extraordinary result that Oswald was thereby 'ordained by God as emperor of all Britain'.[87] The veracity of these accounts is questionable, but the aim of Adomnán in pitching his founding father as determining the outcome of battle and legitimizing the succession of kings was to establish the *familia Columbae* as kingmakers, with a historical precedent. As Michael Enright suggests, 'Adomnan was bidding for a role in their selection and in the determination of their policies'.[88]

The Life of St Columba defines Oswald's overlordship of Britain as *imperator*. While in his history Bede refuses such outright Classical allusion, he nevertheless indicates that King Oswald's rule was achieved directly through God.[89] Adomnán displays more than a passing interest in kings outside Ireland. In the case of Pictland, the Life of St Columba is less overt in bestowing godly ordination on the Picts. In Columba's confrontations with King Bridei filius Mailcon there is one particular event that may suggest the validation of the king as a theocratic monarch. This is Columba's recitation of Psalm 44 (Psalm 45 in modern versions) at Vespers celebration outside the king's fortress.[90] This psalm appears an unusual choice for the office of Vespers, as its use is unattested in traditional liturgies of the period.[91] There also appears to be a discrepancy between the words of the psalm and Adomnán's use of the story to emphasize the dramatic effectiveness of Columba's uplifted voice on a terrified Pictish court. The psalm is a laudation poem to a king on his marriage. Augustine of Hippo devoted a chapter to exploring this psalm as an allegory of Christ and the church as his bride.[92] The psalm is also incorporated into the Life of St Wilfrid to describe the church of Ripon as a bridal chamber.[93] This exposition, however, is difficult to reconcile with the drama of Adomnán's vignette. Gilbert Márkus suggested that Columba selects the psalm as a promise of future blessing should King Bridei and his people establish ties with Iona.[94] While Fraser points to the Davidian imagery of the psalm, which, he suggested, was intended for Bredei filius Derelei.[95] An early eighth-century Irish/Northumbrian manuscript *glossa* on the psalms includes a suggestive gloss in the heading to Psalm 44 that explains *id est de regno iusti*.[96] This gloss accords with the pervasive ecclesiastical political concept of the 'just king' found in the ninth grade of *De duodecim abusiuis saeculi*

86 *VC* I.9. 87 *VC* I.1. 88 M.J. Enright, 'Royal succession and abbatial prerogative' (1985), p. 102. 89 *HE* III.6. 90 *VC* I.37. 91 See J. Black, 'The Divine Office and private devotion in the Latin West' (2001), pp 57–8; *Sancti Columbani Opera*, ed. G.S.M. Walker, vol. 2 (1957, repr. 1970), 2, rule VII: of the choir office, lines 20–7, pp 130–1; M. Curran, *The Antiphonary of Bangor* (1984), pp 169–73. 92 St Augustine: *City of God*, trans. H. Bettenson (1972, rev. 2003), bk XVII.16. 93 *VW* XVII. 94 G. Márkus, 'Iona: monks, pastors and missionaries' (1999), p. 135. 95 Fraser, *From Caledonia to Pictland*, pp 360–1. 96 M. McNamara, *Glossa in Psalmos* (1986), p. 36.

and in the Irish vernacular *tecosca* text, *Audacht Morainn. Collectio Canonum Hibernensis* reiterates the idea of a 'just king' that is encapsulated in a saying attributed to Gregorius Nazianzenus, that a short reign of a just king is better than the long reign of an unjust one.[97]

Adomnán sets the drama outside the fortress of King Bridei filius Mailcon, among threats of magicians and heathens, at the liminal moment of sunset. Vespers was celebrated at sunset and this Office was intended as a communal act prior to the evening meal, as was enjoined on the king in *De duodecim abusiuis saeculi.*[98] According to the *First Synod of Patrick*, clerics were required to attend Matins and Vespers or risk excommunication.[99] The idea of everyone in the kingdom from king to the lowest born freeman simultaneously participating in the evening Office, then breaking bread in temporal unity, provided a potent sense of sacred unity. Returning to Adomnán's drama, Columba with his small band of brethren proceeds with the Office of Vespers. Beginning with Psalm 44, after attempts by the magicians to prevent 'the sound of divine praise', Columba's mighty voice rings like a peal of thunder and 'both the king and the people were filled with intolerable dread'. It could be assumed that the terrified reaction of the king and his people reflects heathen awe, but it also resembles one of proper Christian trembling before the authority of God. Rather than a miracle that terrifies the king into conversion, the response of terror bears comparison to Columbanus' direction to his brethren that perfect fear and the practice of humility was pleasing to God.[1] As Fraser has observed, there was 'little suggestion that Columba moved among a non-Christian population when he visited "Brude"'.[2] Psalm 44 certainly reads as an exhortation to a king walking in God's favour and the unique inter-textual reference to this psalm in the Life of St Columba appears deliberate. Verses five and eight of the psalm are particularly evocative of the overall theme of the ninth abuse in *De duodecim abusiuis saeculi*.

44.5: With your splendour and your excellence extended, proceed prosperously, and reign for the sake of truth and meekness and justice; and so will your right hand lead you wondrously.
44.8: You have loved justice and hated iniquity. Because of this, God, your God, has anointed you, before your companions, with the oil of gladness.[3]

97 *CCH*, 'De regno', Liber XXV, cap. 7, pp 76–82. 98 Pseudo-Cyprian: *De duodecim*, ix rex iniquus, lines 5–6, p. 52. 99 'First synod of Patrick', *The Irish Penitentials*, §7, pp 54–5 [*Quicumque clericus ussus neglegentiae causa ad collectas mane uel uespere non occurrerit alienus habeatur nisi forte iugo seruitutis sit detentus*]. 1 *Sancti Columbani Opera*, lines 16–18, 32–3. 2 J.E. Fraser, 'Adomnán, Cumméne Ailbe and the Picts' (2003–4), p. 187. 3 All scriptural references are to the Clementine version of *Biblia Sacra Vulgata*. [Psalms 44.5: *Specie tua et pulchritudine tua intende, prospere procede, et regna, propter veritatem et mansuetudinem, et iusitiam: et deducet te mirabiliter dextera tua.* 44.8: *Dilexisti iustitiam, et odisti iniquitatem: propterea unxit te Deus, Deus tuus oleo laetitiae prae consortibus tuis.*]

This scriptural allusion to the anointing of the king to his position by God links the Pictish king to King Oswald and the ascendant Uí Néill in that they, allegedly, possessed divine authority for their rule. The Life of St Columba expresses a contemporary political agenda and the Pictish king linked in textual sources with Adomnán was Bredei filius Derelei. Bredei's name appears on the guarantor list of the *Cáin Adomnáin*, promulgated in the same year as Bredei gained the kingship, and both appear together in a later Life of St Serf.[4] In addition, the problematic tenth-century *Betha Adamnáin* includes two elegiac quatrains to King Bredei filius Bili who was famous for removing Northumbrian control over southern Pictland in 685.[5] Fraser has suggested that Adomnán, during the compilation of his Life of St Columba from Cumméne's earlier work, deliberately transferred Columba's mission to Pictland from the Tay to Inverness, thereby bypassing another king contemporary with Columba, Cennalath 'the great king of the Tay'.[6] This enabled Adomnán to credit Bredei's dynastic antecedent and namesake, 'Brude', with the saintly visitation. According to Geary, the reuse of significant names within a family endowed a form of 'immaterial inheritance' that often bequeathed the status and material destiny to the recipient.[7] It has been suggested by Nicholas Evans that the name Bredei was one of a handful of names preserved for the ruling dynasty of Fortriu and given to any child that had the qualifications to succeed to the kingship.[8] Psalm 44, therefore, appears to have been deliberately included in the Life of St Columba as a laudation for Bredei filius Derelei. This not only provides the king with the apparent divine ordination of his dynasty, acknowledged by Columba, but illustrates the affection and political support held for the present king by Adomnán and the *familia Columbae*. As the quasi-historical Pictish king Bridei filius Mailcon was already provided with a pagan foster-father as primary counsellor, his ordination was direct from God, thereby bypassing the old order to institute a new one. Likewise, Adomnán did not claim that Columba converted the king but visited him on a diplomatic mission. It appears that in this drama Columba (and by extension Adomnán) was not claiming proprietorial rights over the direction of Pictish kingship.[9] Instead, the relationship was more subtle: the dynasty had a moral obligation to the *familia Columbae* for their recognition of the Fortriu dynasty's claim to ordained kingship matched by a relationship between king and abbot of spiritual and temporal advice. Nevertheless, a king could not rule without a duly constituted polity and another strategic approach to this issue may have been taken by the Fortriu dynasts. A Pictish origin myth appears in this period that identifies a distinct Pictish nation

4 Ní Dhonnchadha, 'The guarantor list of the Cáin Adomnáin', p. 214; Macquarrie, '*Vita Sancti Servani*', p. 140. 5 *Betha Adamnáin*, p. 32, §14, pp 58–9. 6 Fraser, 'Adomnán, Cumméne Ailbe and the Picts', pp 191–2. 7 P.J. Geary, *Living with the dead* (1994), pp 88–9. 8 Evans, 'Royal succession and kingship', p. 25. 9 Fraser, 'Adomnán, Cumméne Ailbe and the Picts', p. 197.

and welds the political communities together under a new vision of a shared ancient heritage.

POLITICAL IDENTITY AND THE ORIGO GENTIS PICTORUM

The role of the Pictish king appears to have undergone a transformation in favour of contemporary political ideas on Christian theocratic kingship – whereby the king's executive authority increased and was defined by his exercise of Christian virtues. At the same time, the political community was being consolidated and their identity conceptualized. This is evident from the Pictish origin myth, which made manifest a new proposition for Pictish identity and political consolidation. The earliest version, recorded by Bede, has been responsible for raising confusion among scholars with regard to the vexed question of Pictish matrilineal inheritance.[10] The pertinent line comes at the end of the myth: that 'in all cases of doubt, they should elect their kings from the female royal line rather than the male; and it is well known that the custom has been observed among the Picts to this day'.[11] This final clause indicates an occasional innovation rather than a regular practice of cognatic succession through the maternal line.

According to Anglo-Saxon and Irish concepts of kingship succession, inheritance through the maternal line was not permissible, although this may not have been such a hard and fast rule among the Britons. Woolf drew attention to a number of Welsh kings who succeeded through the female line, which indicates that the practice was permissible, but not customary, among other Brythonic-speaking people.[12] The evidence of the Irish *Banshenchas* may also suggest that a genealogical list of the mother's of the kings of Tara was necessary to underscore the king's legitimacy, particularly during a period of 'shifting political loyalties'.[13] Neither can it be strictly ruled out as a contributing factor in the claims of King Oswald, who added the kingdom of Deira to his inheritance of Bernicia on the basis of his mother's royal Deiran bloodline.[14] Oswald's brother Oswy, however, had to remove a rival king of the Deiran line and then bolster his claim to a united Northumbria through marriage.[15] The realities of succession must have meant using as many routes as were available to legitimize a claim to kingship. Certainly, the Irish and Anglo-Saxon genealogies indicate that, at times, rather circuitous methods were employed to justify succession.[16] It appears likely that having a royal mother would enhance eligibility but a, rather dubious, link to a distant kingly ancestor was preferable when recording his

10 A. Ross, 'Pictish matriliny?' (1999). **11** *HE* I.1. **12** A. Woolf, 'Pictish matriliny reconsidered' (1998), pp 151–2. **13** A. Connon 'The *Bannshenchas*' (2000), p. 108. **14** B. Yorke, *Kings and kingdoms in early Anglo-Saxon England* (1990; repr. 2005), p. 172; *HE* III.14 and 15. **15** *HE* III. 15. **16** Woolf, 'Pictish matriliny reconsidered', pp 151–2.

posterity. As Miller pointed out, our extant documents came from scriptoria upholding the *status quo* who selected 'those memories useful for retention'.[17] Notwithstanding the arguably unique caveat to the election of Pictish kings, the *origo gentis Pictorum* describes an apparently new constitutional framework for succession. This was undoubtedly in the interests of protecting the rights of the Fortriu dynasty and limiting the grounds for legitimate competition by other ruling families.

The important lines from the final sentence of the legend are 'in all cases of doubt' and 'the custom has been observed among the Picts to this day'. As Clancy notes, it was during Bede's career that both Bredei and Necthon gained their kingship through their mother's line.[18] This would make cognatic inheritance through the maternal line a contemporaneous political feature, possibly specific to the Fortriu dynasty, rather than an ancient regular practice. This was not necessarily an innovation as the myth needed to be acceptable within the social norms of the Pictish polity.[19] What is interesting is the manner in which the myth legitimizes female participation in the kingship succession. It suggests that a degree of female political authority existed among the Picts. According to Geary, the role of women in dynastic histories and origin myths was circumscribed by being a masculine discourse, betraying 'a tension between transmission and suppression'. This was particularly evident in the, apparently, passive Gaelic brides of the Pictish origin myth who, nevertheless, were the foundation of a new Pictish 'social structure and political power'.[20] Significantly, the origin legend indicates its versatility by making a newly manifested social order appear to have historical antecedents.[21]

Female political participation

The Pictish origin myth hints at the political participation of their founding mothers, revealing the concern of noble women in actively propagating the myth to promote the success of their own dynasty.[22] Yet, constructing a case for early medieval female agency from the paucity of sources is a significant problem. As John Barrett pointed out, 'the methodological question of visibility' hinders gender identification, making it difficult to pursue a more integrated historical analysis.[23] As a consequence, female participation in terms of political development tends to revolve on concepts of their interiority.[24] This is behind Matthew Innes' suggestion that royal women did have a crucial role in facilitating Pictish succession and unifying polities.[25] Although it should be considered whether

17 M. Miller, 'The last century of Pictish succession' (1979), p. 57. **18** Clancy, 'Philosopher-king', p. 146. **19** Evans, 'Royal succession and kingship', p. 24. **20** Geary, *Women at the beginning*, pp 23–5, 44, 76. **21** E. Hobsbawm, 'Introduction: inventing traditions' (1983), p. 1. **22** Geary, *Women at the beginning,* pp 23–4. **23** J.C. Barrett, 'Fields of discourse' (1988), p. 12. **24** Erler and Kowaleski, 'Introduction: a new economy of power relations'. **25** M. Innes, *Introduction to early medieval Western Europe* (2007), p. 346.

royal women's roles were less circumscribed than the provision of marital alliances and dynastic longevity. After all, the three sculptural representations of penannular brooches on Pictish cross-slabs are worn by women. Their images dominate the Class II crosses: Hilton of Cadboll, Monifieth and Wester Denoon.[26] Interpreting these images as cultural expressions of gendered agency is, however, problematic. For instance, identifying the Wester Denoon figure as a woman, given the lack of head and stylized nature of the robes, may be incorrect; likewise, there have been suggestions that the Hilton of Cadboll figure is not wearing a brooch.[27] The worn nature of surviving cross-slabs makes it difficult to assess whether there are any male figures also depicted wearing penannular brooches or whether their position on the body is gender specific in a Pictish context. A general survey of the corpus suggests that male figures are usually depicted in profile. The occasional exceptions appear to be those of religious figures, which are depicted front on. This is the case with the two clerics on the Invergowrie cross-slab who may be wearing stylized disc brooches on each shoulder; but they may also be angels.[28] It is therefore notable that the female figures are depicted looking straight at the viewer. The Hilton of Cadboll figure, while not taking an active part in the represented hunt scenario, is central to the action. Her hair is unbound, unlike the woman on the Monifieth sculpture, which may represent an abbess. The Monifieth sculpture's proximity to Abernethy, with its dedication to St Brigit and commemorations to nine virgins, suggests that if Abernethy was not a double-house it had a female foundation nearby.[29] The Wester Denoon figure holds a similarly dominant position on the cross. Whatever their social function, the figurative representation of women on sculpture implies a degree of visible female political and economic participation. Whether Pictish female agency is recoverable from this limited evidence is doubtful, but compared with Irish and Anglo-Saxon sculpture, where representative female figures are primarily Marian, the Pictish female figures on Hilton of Cadboll and Monifieth cross-slabs are unusually dynamic. It may be inferred that aristocratic Pictish women were more than facilitators of Pictish succession through marital alliances which increased their family's political mobility.

For non-royal Pictish women it is likely that independent female action was circumscribed by status and that there were similar limits on their legal capacity to those expressed in early Irish law, which ensured legal dependency on her husband or male kin.[30] Widows, however, appear to have enjoyed some rights of usufruct and where a woman married beneath her status she was able to preserve more of her properties. Whether the legislative aims of Adomnán's *Cáin*

26 Allen and Anderson, *The early Christian monuments of Scotland*, ii, pp 61–3, 229–30. The Wester Denoon cross fragment was found in 1994: see NMRS: NO34SE 16. **27** E. Sutherland, *In search of the Picts* (1994), p. 187. **28** Henderson and Henderson, *The art of the Picts*, p. 57. **29** MacKinlay, *Ancient church dedications in Scotland: non-scriptural* (1914), pp 16, 129–30. **30** Kelly, *Early Irish law*, pp 68–78.

Adomnáin did indeed offer greater protections for females, it did re-assert their social role as passive. Theoretically, this law was guaranteed by the king who stood as protector of the defenceless; a role promulgated in the ninth abuse of *De duodecim abusiuis saeculi* as 'defender of strangers and orphans and widows'.[31] The intent of the *Cáin Adomnáin* may have been protection but its aim appears more compensatory than preventative. In adopting a protective role over the safety of his 'innocent' subjects, the king expanded his ideological rights but also restated the dependency of women to a patriarch. Bede's claim of Edwin's reign instituting such a degree of peace that a woman with her new-born child could cross the country unmolested stands as a motif for his protection of the most defenceless in society.[32] According to Kershaw, this story imagines the ruler as a head of a household, patriarch of his subjects.[33] It would follow that the ruler's consort was also conceptualized as mother and chatelaine of this enlarged household. While it is likely that social and economic activities in Pictland were gendered, there is some evidence that a few professions were available to women through which they could achieve economic independence. Early Irish law enumerates the female satirist, wright, physician, 'hostage ruler', 'one who holds back the tides of war', 'a woman revered by the territory' and a female mystic as having a special legal capacity.[34] Females practising these skills were classed as *nemed*, accruing some level of legal independence. In addition, there was one strictly gendered activity, according to Irish law, which was recognized as a skilled profession. This was an embroiderer, and it is worth considering the possibilities of this economic activity for female involvement in political action; as the law tract *Bretha im Fuillema Gell* claims 'a woman who embroiders earns more profit even than queens'.[35] According to the Martyrology of Oengus, the nun Ercnat was St Columba's chief robe-maker and embroiderer, while St Patrick employed three embroiderers to enhance his image.[36] Not only would this have been a profitable activity, but it provided impressive visual enhancement to rituals and high-status persons as well as a canvas for disseminating visual metaphor in support of authoritative political concepts. As a skilled professional, the embroiderer participated in the promotion of the dominant socio-cultural ideology. These were artists who created the images of power.

Royal women had an enlarged sphere of action compared with their lower-status sisters. Their marriage alliances introduced significant cultural changes and their presence in political ceremonies created community and re-enacted hierarchy.[37] Bede's record of the royal assembly site of Yeavering, at which a mass baptism occurred, describes King Edwin and Queen Ethelberga jointly

31 Pseudo-Cyprian: *De duodecim*, ix rex iniquus, lines 11, 15, p. 52. 32 *HE* II.16. 33 Kershaw, *Peaceful kings*, p. 35. 34 *Bretha Crólige* in Kelly, *Early Irish law*, pp 350–1. 35 *CIH* 464.2–3; Kelly, *Early Irish law*, p. 78. 36 *Félire Óengusso Céli De: The Martyrology of Oengus, the Culdee*, ed. and trans. W. Stokes (1905; repr. Dublin, 1984), Jan. 8, p. 43; W. Stokes, *The Tripartite Life of Patrick* (1887), 1, pp 266–7. 37 Kershaw, *Peaceful kings*, p. 20.

participating in the royal circuit.[38] Significantly, Queen Ethelberga is credited with introducing Christianity into the Northumbrian court and a papal letter, recorded by Bede, urges the queen to play an active role in the conversion of her husband and his people.[39] Edwin is converted, but apparently by an earlier heavenly intervention when another queen privately counsels her king, Raedwald, not to betray his oaths by casting Edwin to his enemies.[40] This appears to be more than 'pillow-talk' and her counsel, which serves to preserve her husband's honour and status, represents an important aspect of female intervention into masculine politics; conforming to a woman's perceived peacemaking role and potentially circumscribed public voice.[41] Bede ascribes significant political power to royal women in his history, with Queen Eanfled able to sponsor Wilfrid in his climb to the status of bishop.[42] That she does so through familial connections is unsurprising as these networks were at the heart of male and female political agency.[43]

Bede's attitude to secular female power may appear surprising when his description of Wilfrid's life is set against the official hagiography composed by Wilfrid's biographer Stephanus. Bede recalls Wilfrid's initial sponsorship by the queen; Queen Bathild's summary order to kill Bishop Dalfin sends Wilfrid back to Britain; and a vision of the Virgin Mary heals the bishop and promises restitution and peace.[44] Wilfrid's hagiographer, Stephanus, was less inclined to credit any female intervention in the bishop's successful career. With a single-line mention of Queen Etheldreda's property donation of Hexham, he bitterly ascribes the cause of Wilfrid's exile to Ecgfrid's second queen, Iurimburg.[45] This is an interesting case in point, as Bede blames this exile squarely on a dispute between King Ecgfrid and the bishop.[46] Wilfrid's encouragement of Ecgfrid's first wife Etheldreda in refusing to consummate their marriage, and her eventual retirement to the convent of Coldingham, may not have eased relations.[47] Stephanus barely alludes to this episode, merely stating that the royal couple were 'obedient to Bishop Wilfrid in all things'.[48] Bede, however, appears to have asked Wilfrid directly about the queen's continuing virginity and was advised that it was indeed the case, despite King Ecgfrid's attempts to suborn Wilfrid through promises of estates if he would persuade the queen to consummate their marriage.[49] While Bede enumerates Etheldreda's virtues as abbess, Wilfrid's counsel of chastity to the queen could be interpreted as anarchic in denying Ecgfrid dynastic continuity and a public expression of his virility in a masculinized socio-political realm. Whether Stephanus was following contemporary social norms by expunging powerful female intervention from the *Vita* or Bede was unusually sympathetic, the difference between these two clerical attitudes to female agency is intriguing. Observing distinct differences between

38 *HE* II.14. 39 *HE* II.11. 40 *HE* II.12. 41 Kershaw, *Peaceful kings*, p. 20. 42 *HE* V.19. 43 J.A. McNamara, 'Women and power through the family revisited' (2003), pp 18–21. 44 Ibid. 45 *VW* XXII, XXIV. 46 *HE* IV.12. 47 *HE* IV.19. 48 *VW* XIX. 49 *HE* IV.19.

the two, Walter Goffart suggested that Bede used his history to deliberately refute aspects of Stephanus' *Vita*.[50] Indeed, Stephanus' polemical description of Iurimburg as 'the weaker vessel, the woman, by whom he [the devil] has constantly defiled the whole world', 'jezebel', 'she-wolf' and 'sorceress' may suggest a personal attitude his bishop never expressed. The language and allusions to Eve, in binary opposition to Mary to whom Wilfrid dedicates a chapel, are nevertheless familiar from patristic writings and later clerical attitudes.[51] Stephanus' claim that after the death of Ecgfrid his queen became 'a lamb of God, a perfect abbess and an excellent mother to the community' suggests that he saw secular female power as dangerous and something to be mediated through religious confinement. It would indicate that Anglo-Saxon noble women were able to exercise real political power whether in the secular realm granting estates or in the church exploiting and enlarging their own estates.

Royal female patronage of Christian foundations significantly encouraged the adoption and expansion of ecclesiastical authority. Christianity was a powerful political and supernatural tool that offered kings a means to publically enact their influence over their people and establish new forms of obligation through conversion of their fellow rulers.[52] The Merovingian queen Brunhild was influential in Gregory of Tours gaining his bishopric and Bede links the faith and good counsel of queens to initiating conversion and correcting religious practices.[53] Abbess Hild's foundations, like Chelles where she had once yearned to go, had extensive scriptoria and libraries and her own wisdom was of such renown that kings and princes consulted her for advice.[54] There was no ban on Anglo-Saxon ecclesiastical women being scholars due to their gender. Whether Pictish royal and ecclesiastical women were patrons or leaders of ecclesiastical establishments remains unproven. The presence of female religious houses in Ireland and Northumbria in the seventh and eighth centuries, including double-houses such as Kildare and Whitby, makes it likely that similar foundations were established in Pictland. When St Patrick proselytized in Ireland, his converts included high-ranking women, widows and virgins.[55] As Christina Harrington has shown, Patrick's encouragement of female conversion stemmed from an established western Christian tradition that understood the potential of women as social agents; which would have been familiar from his British background.[56] The Pictish origin myth may restate that female political power was mediated by their ability to give birth to rulers, yet it does credit this role as fundamental to the creation and maintenance of the nation of Pictland.

50 W. Goffart, *The narrators of Barbarian history* (1988), pp 235–328. 51 T. Reed, *Shadows of Mary* (2003). 52 *HE* III.22; J. Lynch, *Christianizing kinship* (1998). 53 P. Stafford, *Queens, concubines and dowagers* (1983), p. 13. 54 *HE* IV.23. 55 'Confessio', *Liber epistolarum Sancti Patricii episcopi*, §42, pp 80–1. 56 C. Harrington, *Women in a Celtic church* (2002), p. 31.

The assumption of 'difference'

The origin legend is also suggestive of special legal pleading. If the inheritance of kingship through a maternal line were a fully legitimate practice, it follows that Bredei filius Derelei succeeded uncontested to his kingship. The Irish chronicles are clear that he did not. Rather, he achieved his position by the forcible expulsion of his predecessor (Taran filius Entifidich, *c.*693–7).[57] Bredei filius Derelei was next noted as *rí Cruithintuathi* and guarantor for the Abbot Adomnán of Iona's *Cáin Adomnáin* in the same year, 697; although these titles were added to the guarantor list at a later date.[58]

Despite ousting the previous king, Bredei filius Derelei's Gaelic patrimony may have been an issue in his claim to the kingship. Perhaps this presented difficulties for him to retain hold of a kingdom confederated under his heroic predecessor, Bredei filius Bili. While Bredei's own paternity appears British, the myth's allusion to Gaelic support suggests that the *origo gentis* myth, as Bede presents it, was not current for his reign. New kings needed to renew treaties with their Pictish provincial leaders in order to maintain authority, even if Bredei filius Derelei was able to call on the support of his Dál Riatan relatives. King Taran, after all, had probably been endorsed as Bredei filius Bili's heir by a circuit of the Pictish provinces whereby he gained the approval of the leading nobles and regional leaders. Bredei filius Derelei required another way to legitimize his claim to kingship over a wide-ranging polity, and this may have been why the origin myth took this particular form. Despite extant Irish texts recounting divergent traditions of the myth, Bede's account has the advantage of geographic and temporal propinquity which suggests a Pictish source.[59] Given the connections between Bredei filius Derelei and Adomnán, Máire Herbert has proposed that the Pictish origin myth was a product of Columban circles in Pictland.[60] According to Woolf, the Pictish origin myth was a doctored version of the Irish sons of Míl origin myth, augmented by matrilineal succession and ancient Scythian ancestry.[61] For Fraser, however, the most likely source of the Pictish origin myth was the Dál nAraidi of Ulster, who were designated Cruithni, or Irish Picts.[62] While authorship is impossible to verify, the myth appears to have received approval, if not patronage, from the Pictish leadership. There have been many historical precedents for a new tradition to be dressed up with a 'factitious' historic past to provide a sense of credence and antiquity.[63] This deliberate manufacture of the past has been recognized as a means to announce political allegiance and overlordship as well as the idea of distinct ethnic affiliation.[64] The Pictish leadership could be seen as consciously creating

57 *AU* 697.1; 699.3. 58 *CA* §28; *AU* 697.3. 59 G. Mac Eoin, 'On the Irish legend of the origin of the Picts' (1964). 60 M. Herbert, 'The legacy of Columba' (1999), p. 4. 61 Woolf, 'Pictish matriliny reconsidered', pp 147–8, 150. 62 Fraser, 'Ministry mission and myth', pp 187, 190, n. 127. 63 Hobsbawm, 'Introduction: inventing traditions', p. 2. 64 Dumville, 'Kingship, genealogies and regnal lists', p. 77.

an 'imagined community' in which its members could participate in a wider communion and identify themselves within an ascendant political culture.[65] This would be particularly effective if the 'ethnic' identifier 'Pict' had gained widespread currency, as appears likely.

A striking aspect of the Pictish origin myth is the way it separates the Picts from the native British with different countries of origin. According to Bede, the Picts were from Scythia while the Britons were from Armorica.[66] The myth also makes clear that the Picts settled in unclaimed territory, which Miller perceived as a legal statement in that the Britons could make 'no anterior claim to Pictland'.[67] A hundred years later, the *Historia Brittonum* has a different and hostile view of the Picts' legal entitlement to the north of Britain.[68] In direct contradiction to Bede's information, the *Historia Brittonum* claims that all of Britain belonged to the Britons, before the Picts, some eight centuries later, arrived in Orkney and proceeded to lay claim to what became Pictland.[69] The *Historia Brittonum* similarly perceives an ethnic difference between Pict and Briton. The Pictish origin myth may also represent an emphatic claim to the territory most recently abandoned by the Northumbrians. The Picts may have learnt a lesson in political consolidation from Oswiu and Oswald; although, as the myth appears to corroborate, the ascendant relationship during the reign of Bredei filius Derelei was with the Gaels.

If the role of the native Britons in the Pictish origin myth is negligible then the link with the Gaels and their support for the establishment of the Picts is clear. The origin myth promises the Picts Gaelic military assistance to gain their new homeland, a marital treaty that appears to reflect contemporary political alliances between the Gaels and the Picts. Power networks built from aristocratic marriages outside of the kin-group were a typical early medieval practice.[70] Nor is there any reason to presume that the postulated marriage alliance between Derelei and Dargart removed Derelei from the Pictish political orbit. As she possessed a higher status than her husband, Dargart may have entered the royal Pictish household rather than Derelei being married 'out'.[71] In addition, Geary noted that when a daughter from a 'higher-status family' is married to someone of lower status it may be indicative of 'a reward for past support as well as a guarantee of support in the future'.[72] The benefits for the family of Dargart were an increased political presence, evident in the continued appearance of the Cenél Comgaill in the chronicles, and cooperative interest in south-eastern territories during Bredei filius Derelei's reign.

Overall, the Pictish origin legend informs its contemporaries that the Picts

65 Anderson, *Imagined communities*, pp 15–20. 66 *HE* I.1. 67 Miller, 'Matriliny by treaty', p. 134. 68 Ibid., 135 n. 133, 156. 69 *Historia Brittonum*, ed. and trans. D.N. Dumville (1985), §24, p. 89; Miller, 'Matriliny by treaty', p. 135. 70 A. Wareham, *Lords and communities* (2005), p. 3. 71 Yorke, *Kings and kingdoms in early Anglo-Saxon England*, p. 172. 72 Geary, *Women at the beginning*, p. 51.

identified themselves as a separate people. They were allying themselves politically with the Gaels and attempting to prove ancient tenure of the north of Britain. With a new legendary ancestry they were not only constructing a myth of inclusiveness and exclusiveness but one pre-ordained to cohesive nationhood. This 'imagined community' was a deliberate construction that not only endorsed a cohesive communal identity but tied it fundamentally to the creation and election of a king under a new but legitimated constitutional framework. Foundation myths as well as a king list provided a sense of popularly perceived continuity with the past that, nevertheless, legitimized contemporary social and political transformations, particularly territorialization.[73] The Pictish origin myth legitimizes the role of a national king as a constitutional norm, endorsing the assumption of theocratic authority. The transformation of Pictish kingship through the imposition of centralizing myths and God-given legitimacy expanded the potential for authoritative action. Whether the king was able to enact real authority over his newly constituted and 'imagined' political community is another matter.

THE KING'S EXECUTIVE FUNCTIONS

New definitions of Christian kingship enhanced the role of kingship into one of patriarchal authority. This type of authority legitimized autocratic action as paternal correction to demand adherence to the will of the king. Nevertheless, local and regional leaders were the agents through which centralizing policies were enacted over the people and the complicity of these leaders and their subjects in empowering kingship was pivotal.[74] The itinerant nature of kingship required some devolvement of political power onto those regional leaders, who were tied into a personal relationship of fluctuating dependency to the king. Not all leaders identified with the emerging Pictish political *regnum* and ties of kinship and hostage coerced adherence in some instances. The king's territorial oversight therefore relied on the collaboration of regional leaders. Without this, the king had limited means of exercising his authority over a region other than through military coercion and treaty. Regional leaders did profit by identifying with a national king, not just because of the threat of the king's military resources, but because his annual circuit reaffirmed their own positions and promoted advantageous trade and fiscal opportunities. The king's exercise of justice at regional assemblies could further legitimize these leaders and repress internal dispute by having an apparently bi-partisan figure issuing a communally negotiated decision.

73 D.C. Harvey and R. Jones, 'Custom and Habit(us)' (1999), p. 230. 74 Innes, *State and society in the early Middle Ages*, p. 165.

Justice

Bredei filius Derelei could have used his Cenél Comgaill heritage – possibly by the treaty of assistance implied in the Pictish origin legend – in quashing any rebellion against his rule, but he also had the support of the *familia Columbae*. It appears deliberative that in the same year that Bredei filius Derelei usurped the kingship, he appears as a guarantor for the *Cáin Adomnáin*.[75] As guarantor, Bredei placed himself in the company of the most influential clerics and kings of Ireland and Dál Riata. Complying with this law was a legitimating act of kingship that was an important strategy in reinforcing his position in the eyes of neighbouring rulers. Bredei's appearance on this list as a non-Gaelic ruler of a significant *regnum* may also have been a political coup for Adomnán. As guarantor of the *Cáin Adomnáin*, Bredei was promising to implement the law in his kingdom and allow the *familia Columbae* unusual liberty to collect fines and prosecute justice according to the code.[76] The threat of maledictions may have compelled Bredei to enact the law, but the fiscal reward was an added inducement, as he would receive a portion of every compensation claim. The benefits also included diplomatic ties with other guarantors, a new fiscal levy as well as the potential reduction in warfare and civil disobedience. Ideologically, in order to be considered a 'just' ruler a king was required to be protector of the innocents. As the *Cáin Adomnáin* was directly concerned with the protection of women, children and clerics, it could be considered that Bredei was morally obliged to ratify the protective legislation or risk impugning his office. In addition, the *Cáin Adomnáin* also covered church property, which in effect made the king guarantor for the protection of churches in his kingdom.[77] Bredei's apparent agreement to implement the legislation within his kingdom also implies the existence of a similar compensatory legal system, through which the law was instituted, to that found in Ireland and Wales and among the Anglo-Saxons. Shared systems of control, through legal recourse to compensation, must have eased mobility between the polities.

As a promulgator of law, Bredei filius Derelei fulfilled a legitimizing act of kingship.[78] Alongside ecclesiastic support of kingship, Wormald detected an increasing involvement by Insular kings in legislation over the course of the seventh century.[79] Legislation that emphasized justice and promoted the protection of the marginalized also bolstered the moral right of the king to rule.[80] Clerics drew parallels between their kings dispensing justice and Old Testament kings, such as David and Solomon, exhibiting and delivering wise judgment.[81] *Críth Gablach* refers to a king as having *fír flathemon* ('ruler's truth/justice')

75 *CA*, §28. *AU* 697.1, 3; Ní Dhonnchadha, 'The guarantor list of the Cáin Adomnáin', p. 214. 76 *CA*, §37. 77 *CA*, §36. 78 Dumville, 'Kingship, genealogies and regnal lists', p. 74; McCone, *Pagan past and Christian present*, p. 108. 79 Wormald, 'Celtic and Anglo-Saxon kingship', pp 163–4. 80 Fouracre, 'Conflict, power and legitimation in Francia', p. 20. 81 Jaski, 'Early medieval Irish kingship and the Old Testament', pp 343–4.

when he ensured the safety of his people in peace and war, legally and physically; and adds that a king must 'be a man of all sides, full of right [*lándligid* – full of law]; let him be a man inquiring after knowledge'.[82] Knowledge and wisdom were an expectation of kingship, through personal study or by appointing just men to oversee the kingdom's affairs and by having counsellors who were 'old men and wise men and sober men'.[83] In theory, the exercise of justice was not limited to correct judgment but was a wider function, predicated upon the king's moral behaviour: virtue, honour and his capacity for compassion and generosity.

Until recently, it was assumed that the existence of professional judges and lawyers militated against the Irish king, in contrast to Anglo-Saxon kings, having any judicial role.[84] As Wormald has pointed out, however, Irish sources indicate that the king's executive functions did include judicial and legislative powers.[85] Many of the *tecosca* works and law tracts emphasize the function of the king in maintaining social order, underlining his general responsibility for justice. Insular kingship, in general, used the exercise of justice to preserve the status quo. An old Irish alliterative verse in the *Corpus Iurus Hibernici* expected the king to be fully conversant with a range of legal topics.[86] Knowledge of the law was necessary because the king was required to approve a judge's suitability to his profession.[87] The king held the right of final judgment, according to *Uraicecht Becc*, but in collaboration with a range of professional judges, wise men and clerics.[88] These professional ranks, while dependent upon the king for the maintenance of their roles within society, also held expert knowledge that allowed a concurrent ascendant relationship with the king. Irish legal tracts also provide a description of a legal court (*airecht*), with the king presiding over all procedures accompanied by a bishop and legal experts.[89] The king may appear to have a relatively inactive role within the court but his physical presence ratified the rulings. In evaluating the quasi-legal text *Gúbretha Caratniad*, Stacey found that the apparently false judgments of Caratnia required the mediation of a king in order to make them just.[90] Furthermore, the tale may represent a move towards the 'consolidation of justice under royal authority' with the riddle formula highlighting a transformation in the performative role of the king in judicial verdicts.[91]

The exercise of justice by the king maintained and promoted a Christian normative society, which strengthened the position of theocratic kingship. Conflict between the secular and religious relating to the right to judge legal

82 *Críth Gablach*, §39, p. 21. 83 Pseudo-Cyprian: *De duodecim*, ix rex iniquus, lines 16–17, p. 51. 84 For instance: C.E. Stancliffe, 'Kings and conversion' (1980). 85 Wormald, 'Celtic and Anglo-Saxon kingship', pp 168–70; Gerriets, 'The king as judge in early Ireland'. Also see Stacey, *Dark speech*. 86 *CIH* 570.34–5; Kelly, *Early Irish law*, pp 356–7. 87 *Audacht Morainn*, §23, pp 8–9. 88 *CIH* 635.32; Stacey, *Dark speech*, pp 163–7. 89 *CIH* 601.20–33; F. Kelly, 'An Old Irish text on court procedure' (1986); Kelly, *Early Irish law*, 354–5; *Críth Gablach*, §40, p. 21. 90 R. Chapman Stacey, 'Speaking in riddles' (2002). 91 Ibid., 248.

cases during the foundation of Christianity became a less separatist issue during the seventh century; although clerics continued their attempts to extend their privileges over judgment.[92] In the *Liber Angeli*, the church of Armagh claimed the right to judge legal cases that could not be resolved by a secular court.[93] There was a general trend in this period towards clerical claims to jurisdiction in Ireland and the evidence suggests that they colluded in the creation of written legal tracts.[94] Among the Anglo-Saxons, the preface to the *Law code of Ine* mentions the collaboration of bishops Haedde and Eorcenwald, and Yorke suggests that Aldhelm contributed to the development of law codes.[95] Furthermore, Bede describes Theodore of Tarsus, that great church reformer, applying and endorsing traditional Anglo-Saxon compensatory legislation to settle a potential blood-feud between kings Ecgfrid and Æthelred.[96] The support of the church in bolstering the king's position as judge, describing the king's justice and inventing new laws for the king's ratification, is particularly apparent in Insular sources. Clerics, such as Theodore of Tarsus and Adomnán, accrued both economic and moral capital by supporting dispute settlement legislation and promulgating their own protection of innocents.

The late seventh-century Irish legal text *Córus Béscnai* places the onus on the king to ensure the proper maintenance of contracts and treaties among his people, or risk the disorder of the world with plague and floods of war.[97] This made the king personally responsible for the continuance of social institutions, guaranteeing a just process even when not present, at the risk of cosmological failure and deposition. A list of the king's constitutional powers in *Críth Gablach* appears to indicate an attempt to negotiate and define the new claims of kingship. With his people's acceptance, a king was made responsible for the enactment and maintenance of common law; foreign affairs; calling a duly constituted assembly at which a hosting may be called for expelling invaders; special measures for harvest and plagues, and the ratification of new religious legislation (such as the *Cáin Adomnáin*).[98] The king's potential for autocratic action was confined by his role as protector and the recognition that he ruled consensually. The kings of Fortriu appear to have conformed to the expectations of a 'just ruler', promoting religious legislation and reform, which legitimized their positions and authoritative actions.

The king's right to call a muster in cases of invasion, stipulated in *Críth*

92 'First synod of Patrick', *The Irish Penitentials*, §21, p. 57 [*Christianus cui dereliquerit aliquis et prouocat eum in iudicium et non in ecclesiam ut ibi examinetur causa, qui sic fecerit alienus sit*]. 93 *The Patrician texts in the Book of Armagh*, 'E. Liber Angeli', §28, pp 188–9 [*Item quaecumque causa ualde difficilis exorta fuerit atque ignota cunctis Scotorum gentium iudicibus, ad cathedram archiepiscopi Hibernensium, id est Patricii, atque huius antestitis examinationem recte referenda*]. 94 Stacey, *Dark speech*, pp 203–4. 95 Yorke, *The conversion of Britain*, p. 235. 96 *HE* IV.21. 97 *CIH* 522.28–35; Ó Corráin, Breatnach and Breen, 'The laws of the Irish', p. 384. 98 *Críth Gablach*, §38, pp 20–1.

Gablach, suggests an attempt to regulate a form of military service. As the example given in the text was the invasion of Saxons, the ruling was a response to exceptional circumstances.[99] In the seventh-century poem, the *Goddodin*, the Saxons were the enemy that drew large contingents of British war bands into temporary alliance.[1] War leaders brought their own bands of fully mounted and outfitted warriors on the promise of plunder and a year's refectory. Some Anglo-Saxon leaders also participated on the British side, which could be put down to the opportunism of war but reveals the fluid nature of identity and alliance. Nevertheless, the Saxons were the enemy of Bredei filius Bili who may have legitimized a countrywide military muster with reference to the heroic cause expressed in the *Gododdin*. In order to understand early medieval political organization, Innes insists that it is pivotal to examine the way in which military service was organized.[2] Without charter or documentary evidence, Pictish military organization remains opaque, although the limited contemporary references indicate that most Insular polities shared a similar approach to forming responsive militia. These militia were fundamental to a king's exercise and maintenance of coercive control.

The retinue surrounding the king similarly played an important role in ensuring the continuance of political control and the king's ability to acquire skilled professional warriors was reliant on wealth, alliances and opportunity. Adomnán describes Bridei filius Mailcon in the midst of his council, which Richard Sharpe understood to refer to his nobles and their war bands.[3] The king's court attracted young nobles from among his allies who could be fostered and trained in military skills. Having a retinue of young skilled nobles increased the king's prestige but also his safety. By tying young nobles into the service of a king a potentially divisive social element was harnessed to the prevailing political institution, valorized by saga tales of warriors and battles.[4] Benedict Biscop's early military career demonstrates the advantages that a young warrior could receive in service to his king. As a leader (*thegn*) and warrior in the king's retinue, until the age of twenty-five, Benedict received a grant of land equivalent to his rank from his king.[5] Felix's Life of St Guthlac describes the saint as a leader of a *comitatus* until the age of twenty-five when he renounced the world.[6] This suggests that the life of an Anglo-Saxon nobleman included full-time service to the king or lord until the age of twenty-five at which time he could receive land in recognition of his service. A nobleman's participation in this type of service had ramifications for his family's prestige and continuing participation in the dominant political leadership.

Outside the plunder collected in war, the granting of land befitting rank was

99 Ibid. 1 Clancy, *The Triumph Tree*, pp 46–77. 2 Innes, *State and society in the early Middle Ages*, p. 143. 3 *VC* II.33. Sharpe, *Adomnán of Iona*, p. 337, n. 301. 4 McCone, *Pagan past and Christian present*, p. 213. 5 Bede: *Lives of the abbots of Wearmouth and Jarrow*, ch. 1, p. 187. 6 *Felix's Life of Saint Guthlac*, ed. and trans. B. Colgrave (1956), chs XVI, XIX.

an important incentive to join the ranks of a king's *comitatus*. Possession of land brought with it the potential to raise a family, attain noble rank without waiting for inherited dues, and operate actively within society.[7] Military service to the king was also important for the maintenance of status and the honour of the warrior's kin group. It is likely that loyal warriors in Pictland received land awards and other gifts, certainly the Anglo-Saxon nobles exiled among the Picts and Irish would have joined the kings' service with the expectation of reward.[8] According to Charles-Edwards, a nobleman could join the service of a foreign king to win land and status although there would be continuing obligations to the foreign king for this gift.[9] The same would be true for warriors serving a king in their native kingdom. Bede's letter to Bishop Ecgbert decries the parlous state of his times where insufficient land was available for veteran soldiers to receive an estate, forcing the sons of nobles to fight in other countries.[10] Land gifted for service in the *comitatus* was held in stewardship for the lifetime of the noble or the king, with render and services still expected by the king.[11] Ultimately, the prestige associated with service to the king and the military and hunting skills learnt in his *comitatus* defined noble status, encouraging long-term fealty to the leading dynasty.

In his *Vita*, St Columba meets and baptizes an elderly Pictish man, Artbranán, who is described as a chief commander of the *Geon* warband (*decrepitus senex, Geonae primarius cohortis*).[12] Despite being past his prime, this leader appears to have retained his rank, which indicates that *primarius cohortis* was a lifetime sinecure. Drawing a comparison with the later Welsh *penteulu* (head of a ruler's personal retinue), Dumville proposed that Artbranán was the war band leader and possible kin to a ruler named Geon.[13] This position correlates with the later (Gaelic) *Toisech* who appears, as head of a kin-group, to be a military leader in charge of his local militia.[14] The difficulty remains in squaring the description of the man as *decrepitus senex* to his leading a war-band. Taking Dumville's reading of the role, the responsibilities appear to have been the maintenance and mustering of a permanent body of warriors. The training and equipping of a war-band was the responsibility of the ruling nobility, on behalf of the king or their regional lord.[15] Military strength was one of the most important requirements for a successful reign and it is likely that regional leaders organized their own permanent war-bands. As King Edwin recognized, a display of military might underpinned a peaceful realm.[16] For his warriors, the right to

7 T.M. Charles-Edwards, 'The distinction between land and moveable wealth' (1976), p. 183. 8 *HE* III.1, 27. 9 Charles-Edwards, 'The distinction between land and moveable wealth', p. 181. 10 Bede: *Epistola ad Ecgbertum episcopum*, §11, pp 414–15. 11 Charles-Edwards, 'The distinction between land and moveable wealth', p. 184. 12 *VC* I.33. 13 D. Dumville, '"Primarius Cohortis" in Adomnán's Life of Columba' (1978). 14 Skene, *Celtic Scotland*, 3, p. 214. 15 N.B. Aitchison, *The Picts and the Scots at war* (2003), p. 40. 16 *HE* II.16; Kershaw, *Peaceful kings*, pp 37–8.

bear arms was a requisite of their status.[17] Outside of professional warriors, prescribed military service was organized regionally alongside a mandatory render of provisions for their sustenance. The late seventh-century core of the *Míniugud Senchasa Fher nAlban* formalizes the requirement of these levies from Dál Riata territory.[18] These levies were to man naval vessels: the Irish chronicle reference to the loss of 150 Pictish ships off *Ross Cuissine*, even if the numbers are inflated, implies that the Picts were also able to organize substantial naval contingents.[19] Returning to *Críth Gablach*, the conditional privilege of the king to call a hosting for the defence of the homeland operated in tandem with an assembly. This was an ideal venue for the king's allies and dependents to respond to his call to arms. Failure to respond in such a public forum had serious ramifications.

The king required a ready and continual supply of material wealth in order to fund military expeditions, maintain his retinue and clients, and provide the appearance of authority through public works and generosity.[20] Wealth was a means by which kingly power could be legitimated and enacted.[21] Large-scale building works, both infrastructural and defensive, were also funded by a regularized service and render requirement on local lords and their people. Logistical administration of this type of work required specialist oversight that may have been supplied by the king's own master craftsmen.[22] Warfare and the imposition of tribute contributed to the king's wealth as well as more regularized services and goods through which he consolidated his authority. Nevertheless, the cost of waging war and keeping an active military presence was a drain on resources. This would have encouraged alternative methods of political control through treaties and hostages. In addition, the enactment of law provided the king with a portion of fines levied against litigants when they appeared in his court, encouraging a king to control and maintain regular legal procedures. An old Irish legal tract stipulates that 'he is not king who does not have hostages in fetters, and to whom no royal tribute is rendered, and to whom no fines for breach of promulgated law are paid'.[23] An Insular king was therefore able to extract wealth and establish a royal *fisc*, apart from the traditional render expected of his subjects. It is possible that the expansion of the king's *fisc*, through breach of law and the regular extraction of tribute, encouraged the development of administrative centralization and functionaries to ensure collection.

In this period, it is difficult to detect any difference between a king's public and private revenue. Some form of private *fisc* may be implied by Adomnán's reference to a royal treasury in the household of King Bridei filius Mailcon.[24]

17 Charles-Thomas, *Early Christian Ireland*, p. 69. 18 Bannerman, *Studies in the history of the Dalriada*, pp 41–9. 19 *AT* 729.2. 20 Wormald, 'Celtic and Anglo-Saxon kingship', p. 167. 21 Fouracre, 'Conflict, power and legitimation in Francia', p. 10. 22 MacLean, 'The status of the sculptor in Old-Irish law', p. 134. 23 *CIH* 219.5; Kelly, *Early Irish law*, p. 19. 24 *VC*

This treasury included the pebble blessed by St Columba, a relic that shows how temporal wealth was understood to encompass objects endowed with spiritual significance and alleged magical efficacy. Gifts from clients, diplomats and neighbouring kings seeking royal favour also increased royal wealth. These gifts may have provided useful cultural capital to enhance the king's image as a ruler able to access new technologies and luxury goods. For instance, Adomnán's gift of his *De Locis Sanctis* to King Aldfrid allowed the king to create a network of obligation through its loan to specially favoured clerics and monasteries. Evidence from Irish law tracts and Anglo-Saxon law codes indicate that the king took a keen interest in the protection of merchants and traders, making it likely that the king also profited from trade revenue.[25] Control of trade and trade routes played an important part in discouraging competition and ensuring primacy. A king over a coercively confederated kingdom could extract tribute as moveable wealth from those peripheral areas subdued or sworn to fealty. Some hint as to the fiscal arrangements in Northumbria can be gleaned from Aldhelm's allusion to prayer resembling a regular taxation in his letter to king Aldfrid: 'without cease, we fulfil the obligations of prayer – as though a kind of tax to the state and fiscal payment – revolve and rotate according to a heptadic interval between assemblies'.[26] Aldhelm's equation of a Roman bureaucratic state 'taxation' with an Insular local secular administration may be a leap, but the church was attempting to impose a regularized payment from their parishioners.[27] As Aldhelm implies, regular assemblies created an ideal opportunity for the extraction of regular render and tribute. Any exchange of property and goods that occurred at this venue required the oversight of the king who would have exacted a fee. The king's rights over property distribution were fundamental to the exercise of his power by which he profited economically and ideologically.

The king's ability to donate and alienate property in this period was a means by which he could display regnal generosity and public strength.[28] This assumes that the king held prerogatives over territorial distribution. Analysis of Welsh charter evidence suggested to Davies that during the late seventh century there was a significant alteration in property rights. Between *c.*660 and *c.*770 Welsh religious establishments received property grants through the agency of the king.[29] There were also non-royal donations of property to the church which, significantly, required the purchase of property directly from the king.[30] Davies' concluded that the right of the Welsh king to alienate property to religious houses was a hangover of the Roman *imperium* and its micro-management of

II.33. **25** Stacey, 'Law and order in the very old west', p. 44. **26** Lapidge and Herren, *Aldhelm the prose works*, pp 41–2; *Aldhelmi Opera*, p. 71 [*quasi quoddam rei publicae victigal et fiscale tributum, orationum officia persolvimus, septena sinaxeos intercapidine revolute rotantur*]. **27** Bede: *Epistola ad Ecgbertum episcopum*, §7, p. 410. **28** Davies and Fouracre, 'Introduction', p. 7. **29** W. Davies, 'Land and power in early medieval Wales' (1978), p. 11. **30** Ibid.

land transactions.[31] Charles Doherty, however, found that in Ireland during the same period, where there had been no Roman *imperium*, the king's consent was also required for property grants and sales.[32] The *additamenta* in the Book of Armagh support Doherty's contention, as the recorded land donations to a religious institution stipulate the requirement of the king's approval.[33] Bede's letter to Bishop Ecgbert describes Northumbrian kings 'selling' large estates and small land units for the creation of ecclesiastical establishments.[34] Wilfrid reinforces the possession of his ecclesiastical estates in a synod where 'in the presence of the kings' he 'read out clearly a list of the lands which the kings, for the good of their souls, had ... presented to him, with the agreement and over the signatures of the bishops, and all the chief men'.[35] Unless specified, the donation of property for ecclesiastical use did not necessarily exempt the new clerical landlords from customary obligations of render, tribute, participation in muster and local building works. By donating property in this way, the king retained the right to extract customary obligations and ensure an ascendant position as benefactor and protector, gaining wider political and spiritual support from the ecclesiastic brethren. The king could increase his prestige further by offering specific exemptions from some of the customary obligations.[36] When King Oswy donated land to the monastery of Hartlepool, where his daughter was an oblate, the gift specified the absence of military obligations.[37] Similarly, Irish evidence suggests that some churches achieved exempt status.[38] This form of property donation appears similar to the properties bestowed for military service but must have been perceived as a distinct ideological act of alienation where a king would be unable to grant the property away from the ecclesiastical tenants. A later analogy may be with the property records in the Book of Deer where a donor 'extinguished' their rights to exact lay dues from church lands.[39] Nevertheless, some doubt as to the perpetual nature of donated lands appears to have prompted Benedict Biscop to gain assurances from the papal court and his king to ensure his monastery remained free from future secular claims.

Land donation was a key aspect of regnal power, which was dependent upon the king's ability to claim new estates and administer those in his purview. In Wales and Ireland the size of the kingdoms could have resulted in a higher ratio of land held by the kings in their home territories. Within these territories they controlled the right to alienate property in order to endow estates on religious institutions. Anglo-Saxon kings appear to have possessed a number of 'royal'

31 Ibid., pp 21–2. 32 C. Doherty, 'Some aspects of hagiography' (1984), pp 309, 313. 33 For instance: *The Patrician texts in the Book of Armagh*, 'Additamenta', §8 (1), pp 172–3 [*et postquam babtitzauit obtulerunt filius Cairthin et Caichan quintam partem Caichain Deo et Patricio, et liberauit rex Deo et Patricio*]; Kelly, *Early Irish farming*, 411, n. 476. 34 Bede: *Epistola ad Ecgbertum episcopum*, §12, p. 415. 35 *VW* XVII. 36 Wormald, 'Celtic and Anglo-Saxon kingship', p. 167; Fouracre, 'Conflict, power and legitimation in Francia', p. 10. 37 *HE* III.24. 38 *CCH*, 'De furto', Liber XXIX, cap. 6, p. 101; J.T. McNeill and H.M. Gamer, *Medieval hand-books of penance* (1965), pp 140–1. 39 Broun, 'The property records in the Book of Deer', pp 332–49.

estates in their kingdom. Similarly, in Ireland the king retained estates in each *túath* over which he exercised his lordship and these properties could be granted into the stewardship of a favoured retainer.[40] Recent analysis by Charles-Edwards has also drawn out Irish evidence for the king's rights over the estates of his client kings.[41] This would certainly facilitate an over-king's authority within client kingdoms, particularly if the client kingdom reneged on the alliance allowing the over-king to legitimize his appropriation of demesnes. Alienation of land for the endowment of religious houses seems to have increased from the late seventh to the early eighth century. Furthermore, the evidence from Wales, Ireland and Northumbria suggests that the king's consent was mandatory in property transactions. Indeed, the king's ability to alienate property relates directly to the territorialization of his authority; whereby the king's client required the king's approval in any property exchange. By extension, the king's authority over regional lords ensured the king's jurisdiction over their regions, and probably included his approval of property transactions. This was not a mere formality but a strategic and economic transaction that kings were quick to commandeer.

The later lives of the Pictish saints Serf and Boniface make reference to their foundations, of Culross and Restenneth, respectively granted by Bredei filius Derelei (Dargart) and Necthon filius Derelei.[42] While late, these lives do appear to retain a cultural memory of important religious property transactions by these kings. Fouracre noted a similar occurrence in the Carolingian period where many of the saints' lives display direct contact with royal authority, emphasizing the centrality of royal power.[43] Bredei and Necthon were also enacting pious benevolence by their putative donation of estates to the followers of Serf and Boniface. Serf's property at Culross was in a region that had been under Northumbrian domination until 685, suggesting that Bredei gave the saint, or his followers, sword-land. In the case of Boniface, the alleged donation of Restenneth in Angus may be indicative of Necthon's consolidation of authority over the region's nobles; who may have included the future king of the Picts, Oniuist filius Urguist. Property grants to ecclesiastical foundations were politically expedient and allowed the king to swiftly realign the balance of regional authority to his advantage. Moreover, exemptions and additional bequests to favoured foundations could extinguish older ties of patronage and veneration to establish the political agenda of a new benefactor.

The appearance of new architecture or decorative wealth at an ecclesiastical foundation would therefore indicate the interest of a high-status benefactor aligned to the dominant rulership. The proliferation of Class II cross-slabs, invariably co-located with an early church foundation, does demonstrate

40 Kelly, *Early Irish law*, p. 101. 41 Charles-Edwards, 'Celtic kings: "priestly vegetables"?', pp 72–6. 42 Macquarrie, '*Vita Sancti Servani*'; MacDonald, *Curadán, Boniface and the early church of Rosemarkie*. 43 Fouracre, 'Conflict, power and legitimation in Francia', p. 4.

significant material investment. Both Henderson and Graham-Campbell have proposed that the Class II cross-slabs, ornamented with a combination of Pictish and Christian symbols, were being carved and erected by the early eighth century.[44] The sculptural cross-slab form is a prevalent feature of early Pictish ecclesiastical sites representing a distinct cultural fashion. The virtuosity and artistry of these sculptured crosses points to a vibrant, creative approach to religious participation. The physical and economic investment required for the sculpture and erection of these crosses infers patronage at the highest level of the social scale.[45] It has been suggested that the Class II cross-slabs represent early charters of land donation or immunities to the church, as well as marking ecclesiastic territory.[46] Martin Carver has argued that the placement of Class II cross-slabs across the Tarbat Peninsula, in Ross and Cromarty, denote the monastic territory.[47] In this case, they declare a proprietary investment in the territory on behalf of the monastery at Portmahomack. The cross-slabs also make a statement of the monastery's wealth and favoured political position. Many of the slabs display energetic hunt scenes on the west face, reminiscent of the Carolingian institutional use of a hunt to complete and confirm an agreement. Hunting played a significant part in external and internal diplomacy throughout the medieval period.[48] It was an elite activity, with hunting grounds set aside for the sport, and provided the opportunity for leaders to display their prowess and virility outside of battle. One such hunting ground near St Andrews – *muckros* (the swine's promontory) – was in King Onuist's gift, and it is tempting to similarly attribute the royal forest/moor at Alyth, Perthshire, with early royal patronage.[49] For royalty, hunting and ecclesiastic donations do not appear to be a strictly gendered activity. If the reading of the Class II cross-slabs as land charters is correct, then the hunt may very well represent the formal binding of an agreement with a benefactor of the church. The prevalence of these cross-slabs may represent a new administrative system being established over ecclesiastical land tenure, instigated by a central authority that encouraged statements of authentication through sculptural display.

Assembly and the royal circuit

Dissemination of propaganda in support of the king's policies as well as the visible appearance of power, wealth and the king's justice were manifested through the assembly and royal circuit. Rituals at assembly, dedicatory ceremonies of newly endowed foundations, and the retinue that surrounded the king and his queen endorsed his prestige and allowed a greater exercise of the

44 I. Henderson, *The art and function of Rosemarkie's Pictish monuments* (1990), p. 10; Graham-Campbell, *Pictish silver: status and symbol*, pp 34–8. 45 Gondek, 'Investing in sculpture', pp 105–42. 46 S.T. Driscoll, 'Power and authority in early historic Scotland' (1988). 47 Carver, 'Sculpture in action', pp 13–36. 48 Campbell, 'Anglo-Saxon courts', p. 163. 49 *CPNS*, p. 397; RCAHMS, *North-east Perth* (1990), p. 6.

king's authority in judgment. As Campbell has pointed out, the current dual meaning of 'court' as the 'sovereign and his councillors and retinue' and the 'court of judicature, of law, or of administration' were combined in early medieval kingship.[50] Itinerant kingship prevailed over the medieval polities. This was true for Ireland but was also the case for the courts of Charlemagne to Otto III, which are perceived as having significantly more complex administrative systems. These latter examples serve as a reminder of the way in which an itinerant court could effect long-term constitutional change as well as reactive rule. Early medieval government resided in the body of the king rather than a fixed physical site. Symbolic capitals such as Charlemagne's Aachen, and the later use of Scone in Scotland, represent strategic places from which to enact political decisions and sacred ceremonies, but real power rested with the physical presence of the king and his mobile court.[51] The assembly, therefore, offered the king a venue to assert a progressive performative role and disseminate his political programme, which could be publicly debated and legitimized.[52] The king's control of the assembly and its proceedings provided a strategic venue for his display of superior wealth and strength that physically reasserted his hierarchy over his leading magnates and, increasingly wealthy and influential, bishops and abbots.[53] The magnates, by allowing the devolvement of their authority onto their king, acceded to the king's rights over land transfer, marital contracts and hosting; at the same time, the magnates' local power expanded to reflect the new ideological construct of rule. Contracts were announced publicly at the assembly, validating the real and effective power of the king and ensuring the tactical political alliance of future generations. While the Fortriu kings may have held dynastic territories, their success rested on their ability to tap into the mechanisms of itinerant governance. In this way, the creation of a Pictish origin myth, the erection of institutional symbols and the consolidation of communal identity under theocratic kingship were a strategic means by which the dynasty could expand their territorial purview and individual power.

CONCLUSION

The construction of a national identity in Pictland was not a linear, organic journey. Instead, the identity of the kingdom as a coherent nation was ideologically constructed allowing an expansion in the executive functions of authoritative kingship. Christian models for kingship as being God-ordained and God's viceroy on earth redefined the role of the Insular king.[54] This endowed

50 Campbell, 'Anglo-Saxon courts', p. 167. 51 J.L. Nelson, 'Aachen as a place of power' (2001). 52 I. Alfonso, 'Judicial rhetoric and political legitimation' (2004), p. 51. 53 Fouracre, 'Conflict, power and legitimation in Francia', p. 10. 54 Canning, *A history of medieval political thought*, pp 4, 17.

the king with moral legitimacy for a greater exercise of his authority over larger territories and accompanying economic prerogatives. Clerics successfully advocated theocratic kingship and, as a result, land donations to favoured clerics multiplied as the power networks between them became increasingly horizontal. Kings may have asserted their authority by the sword and careful coalitions, but they were also conversant with the utility of nation-building ideologies to support the construction of a cohesive identity. The Pictish origin myth and king lists are a clear indication that a centralized authority was creating a new vision of identity. Moreover, the myth symbolically promotes a united Pictish polity to which communities could subscribe. The dynastic heritage of their kings was therefore legitimized through the king lists and through their military might and regular royal circuits of their kingdom. Clerical machinations endorsed the right by which the Fortriu dynasty held the Pictish kingship, but it was the exercise of their prerogatives that won the kingdom. The theocratic exercise of Pictish kingship flourished under the reign of Necthon filius Derelei, whose political acumen saw the expansion and consolidation of his kingdom, and is the subject of the following chapters. Necthon was active in politicizing his kingdom's differences by authorizing new church practices and this was just part of a wider centralizing strategy. In identifying the king as patriarch of his people, clerics bestowed on the king all the rights of a father to chastize and correct his people, protect and support them and expect love and obedience from them in return. The Fortriu kings courted ecclesiastical support to bolster their positions, define their political agenda and legitimize their legacies for posterity as *reges potentissimi*.

PART II

4

Necthon the scholar king

The successive reigns of the Pictish kings Bredei filius Bili and Bredei filius Derelei instituted a new political direction for their people. Beginning with conquest, by the close of the seventh century a vision of consolidated Pictish identity had transformed a loose confederacy of provinces into a kingdom. Bredei filius Bili, arguably from a base at Inverness, had forcefully brought the polities of northern Pictland under his leadership and won back southern territories from the Northumbrians. His successor, Bredei filius Derelei, appears to have built on this success by endorsing legislation, promoting an origin myth and, potentially, founding ecclesiastical foundations in Strathearn. Complete territorial control over southern Pictish polities remained tenuous; particularly in Atholl, a province whose rulers' relationship with the Fortriu dynasts appears ambiguous and, at times, competitive. Nevertheless, when Necthon filius Derelei succeeded his brother the idea of a Pictish kingdom with a single ruler appears to have become normalized. It is in Necthon's reign that pro-state strategies come to the fore and the authority of theocratic kingship becomes actualized.

Necthon's reign affords an opportunity to witness the manner in which these strategies may have been put into practice. The following two chapters interpret Necthon's political activities in light of his centralizing agenda. In order to do so, recent conjectural analyses will be incorporated to construct a picture of political momentum. Necthon was most famous for his institution of liturgical reform. His ability to enforce religious change on his people suggests that his reign was significantly authoritative. It is notable that the Insular political climate at the onset of Necthon's reign was one of transition, as prominent dynasties and ecclesiastical foundations lost dynamic leaders, causing a shift in the balance of power. This shift is evident in the numerous conflicts recorded in the chronicles that occurred in the early years of Necthon's reign. Intersecting with these notices of military engagements, the *familia Columbae* were a tangible presence, one that appears to have forced Necthon to consider religious reform. Overall, Necthon's political strategy was diplomatic rather than militaristic and, as a 'philosopher' king, he appears to have successfully negotiated peaceful relations to promote unified government.

Necthon filius Derelei gained the kingship of a united Pictish kingdom after the death of his brother Bredei in AD706.[1] No direct notification of his rule

1 *AU* 706.2.

occurs until 713, in the context of Necthon's apparent revenge imprisonment of Tolarg filius Drostain, where he is afforded neither principality nor patronymic.[2] This has led to a cautious suggestion by Clancy that Necthon may not have come into the kingship until this event.[3] This proposition may have some value, although given the potential disruption on Iona after the death of Abbot Adomnán in 704 the Irish chronicle records reflect a general lack of information on external political conditions until monastic government apparently stabilized.[4] It is more likely, as Marjorie Anderson has pointed out, that the annal entries – being contemporaneous – did not need to specify the title of kings except where clarity was required: references to successors are rarely provided in kings' obituary entries.[5] It appears unlikely that an alternate succession after Bredei could be suppressed so thoroughly from the documentary record at this period. Likewise, there is no evidence for a dismantling of Pictish political consolidation that may have occurred from an interregnum. It appears justified, therefore, to accept the evidence of the Pictish king lists *D*, *F*, *I* and *K*, which estimate a reign length of eighteen years for Necthon: and, in the case of list *I*, an additional nine-month period between 728 and 729.[6] An argument could also be made for a longer reign, as Bede does not mention any other reigning Pictish monarch. Bede, after all, completed his history in 731 and Necthon's death is recorded at 732.[7]

POLITICS IN NORTHERN BRITAIN IN THE EARLY EIGHTH CENTURY

Prior to Necthon's ascension to the Pictish kingship, a number of leading political figures in northern Britain and Ireland had died. This potentially had a significant impact on the balance of power among the Insular polities. Abbot Adomnán, after a long career that straddled religion and politics across the north of Britain and in Ireland, passed away in 704. From this point, the influence of Iona and the *familia Columbae* in northern Britain ebbed. Whether due to internal divisions within the Iona hierarchy, or the abbatial responsibilities being reformed and devolved, the succession list of the Iona abbacy in the years following Adomnán's death is confused.[8] Any existing confidential relationship between Iona and the Fortriu dynasty may have similarly ceased, leaving Necthon to look elsewhere for spiritual guidance. In the previous year, Adomnán's cousin and titular king of Ireland Loingsech mac Oengusa and three of his sons fell in battle. The swift transfer of this king's office to his first cousin Congal Cenn Magair (fellow guarantor to the *Cáin Adomnáin*) appears to have

2 *AU* 713.7. 3 Clancy, 'Philosopher-king', pp 125, 137. 4 *AU* 704.2. 5 Anderson, *Kings and kingship*, p. 173. 6 Ibid., pp 265–89. 7 *AT* 732.7; see A. Woolf, 'AU 729.2 and the last years of Nechtan mac Der-Ilei' (2006). 8 Herbert, *Iona, Kells and Derry*, pp 57–62; Fraser, *From Caledonia to Pictland*, pp 260–2.

been prepared in advance, suggesting a peaceful transition of authority.[9] Nevertheless, continued political pressure from their opponents during the early eighth century destabilized this dynastic line.[10] This would certainly have had an influence on the *familia Columbae* whose abbots were predominantly recruited from the leading Cenél Conaill and the dissipation of this dynasty's influence left the way open for an increase in Armagh's authority.

Returning to the chronicle entries for 704, the first laconic entry relays the information that the Dál Riata were destroyed in Srath Limnae: the collective noun implying that their opponents were a different political group.[11] Fraser, following Watson, identified the battle site as the glen of the River Leven where it debouches from Loch Lomond. Its geographic proximity to Dumbarton points to the protagonists being Strathclyde Britons.[12] A decade previously, the chronicles note the death of the king of Strathclyde, Dyfnal map Owain, and he appears to have been succeeded by the Beli map Elfin whose obituary is noted at 722.[13] If the Strathclyde king list is accurate, Beli's reign was long and saw the expansion of Northumbrian interests into Whithorn and, potentially, a fluctuating alliance with the Cenél Comgaill.[14] There is limited information on the political situation in Strathclyde Britain, but their putative success against the Dál Riata in 704 suggests successful political consolidation; as does their continued presence as a recognized kingdom between an expansionary Dál Riata and Northumbria. The Dál Riata of Argyll and the Western Isles had also experienced a hard-fought transfer of power from the Cenél nGabráin to the Cenél Loairn. It remains uncertain whether the Dál Riatan political structure corresponded to the Irish situation of small kingships over which an over-king could gain coercive authority, but the indications of conflict between the leading cenéla suggests that a form of expansionary kingship was at stake. From at least 697 the annals note the escalating conflict between these two groups, as well as increasing aggression between factions within Cenél Loairn until, around 701, Selbach mac Ferchair took the kingship of the Dál Riata.[15] In the latter years of their reigns, Necthon's career follows a strikingly similar trajectory to that of Selbach and this could be indicative of a close connection between these two major leaders of northern Britain.

The chronicle record of Adomnán's peaceful death in 704 is followed by the obituary notice of his putative pupil, the Northumbrian king Aldfrid.[16] Both figures had made a significant rapprochement between Gaelic and Northumbrian political and religious interests after King Ecgfrid's military aggression. As the Picts' nearest neighbour, political developments in the

9 *AU* 703.2. 10 Lacey, *Cenél Conaill and the Donegal kingdoms*, pp 254–7. 11 *AU* 704.1. 12 Fraser, 'Strangers on the Clyde', p. 104, n. 5; *CPNS*, p. 119. 13 *AU* 694.6, 722.3. 14 Macquarrie, 'The kings of Strathclyde', pp 18–19; Fraser, 'Strangers on the Clyde', pp 107–8. 15 Bannerman, *Studies in the history of the Dalriada*, p. 112; Fraser, 'Strangers on the Clyde', p. 103. 16 *AU* 704.3; *ASC* 705.

kingdom of Northumbria affected relations between these kingdoms during Necthon's reign. After Aldfrid's death, Eadwulf succeeded and, whether legitimately or not, the Life of St Wilfrid claims that this king failed to observe the wishes of his predecessor to reappoint Wilfrid to his diocese; for which Eadwulf's sudden deposition in 705 may be read as a fitting judgment.[17] After this coup, Aldfrid's eight-year-old son Osred was installed in the kingship, in an exceptional application of primogeniture.[18] This appears to have been an act of political expediency by the remaining members of Aldfrid's dynasty. Indeed, Wilfrid may not have helped Eadwulf's cause, as Wilfrid had custody of Eadwulf's son when he petitioned the king to return his diocese. Despite this leverage, Wilfrid was summarily dismissed.[19] It is likely that this rejection motivated Wilfrid to join the camp of his past detractors (including Oswy's daughter the abbess Aelffled of Whitby) in order to oust the 'pretender' in favour of Osred.[20] There can be no doubt that the minority rule of Osred required plenty of political manoeuvring by the Northumbrian secular and ecclesiastical leadership in order to minimize factionalism and external threats. Benedict Biscop, due to his 'innate wisdom and mature counsel', had been a close confidante of Ecgfrid and the retirement of Ceolfrid in the same year that Osred was killed (716) strongly suggests that the abbots of Wearmouth and Jarrow had continued a close alliance with Oswy's dynasty, including support of Osred's candidacy.[21] Fraser has suggested that Osred's minority rule signifies a well-developed institutional kingship able to delegate authority, although the political skill of Osred's powerful relatives and their supporters was more likely the true source of authority.[22] The grim warning from Ecclesiastes (10:16) 'woe to the land whose king is a child', repeated in *De duodecim abusiuis saeculi*, would have been difficult to dismiss.[23] Bishop Wilfrid's declared affection for Osred saw the cleric regain his bishopric at what appears to have been a hastily called synod capitalizing on Osred's succession; Wilfrid died four years later in 709.[24] The death of the cleric Aldhelm in the same year as Wilfrid removed two very public ecclesiastical figures from their influence over northern politics.[25] Osred survived in his kingship for eleven years and was killed in 716, possibly by his successor Coenred.[26] Osred, understandably, appears to have been poorly prepared for the kingship and the real authority of the Northumbrian sceptre was shared among the surviving leaders of Oswy's dynasty and 'a nobleman, second in rank only to the king', Beorhtfrith, who led an attack against the Picts in 711.[27] Coenred was from a collateral dynastic line and was replaced by Osric,

17 *VW* LIX. **18** Goffart, *The narrators of Barbarian history*, p. 271. **19** *VW* LIX. **20** Ibid.; Goffart, *The narrators of Barbarian history*, p. 271, n. 166. **21** *The anonymous history of Abbot Ceolfrith*, ed. and trans. D.H. Farmer and J.F. Webb (1965, repr. 1998), §12, p. 217. **22** Fraser, *From Caledonia to Pictland*, pp 265–7. **23** Pseudo-Cyprian: *De duodecim*, ix rex iniquus, lines 6–7, p. 52. **24** *HE* V.19. **25** *ASC* 709. **26** *HE* V.18, 24; *ASC*, Peterborough MS, 716. **27** *VW* LX; Goffart, *The narrators of Barbarian history*, p. 272.

Osred's brother, a mere two years after his ascension in 718. Osric's ten-year reign ended in 729 and was followed by the apparently peaceful transfer of authority to Ceolwulf, Coenred's brother. Ceolwulf was the dedicatee of Bede's history and under his rule Northumbria regained some measure of stability. Within the first decade of the eighth century, therefore, the leadership of most of the kingdoms in northern Britain, and the putative high-kingship in Ireland, underwent significant change.

With the death of Bredei in 706, Necthon's first business in the Pictish kingship was to renegotiate old alliances – internally and externally – and make new ones. With many of the powerful political leaders of northern Britain gone, Necthon's tenure began during a period of general uncertainty. This was also an advantageous time, when an assertive monarch or cleric could make widespread political changes and petition new alliances. The leadership changes among the polities of northern Britain appear to have resulted in a period of internal consolidation. These polities sought to minimize internal dispute and consolidate the authority of their chosen leaders. In Pictland, Necthon's apparent honeymoon period in the kingship came to an abrupt end three years into his tenure. Internal dispute was nothing new to the Pictish kingship and their authority over Pictish provinces required careful maintenance. The transfer of the kingship was always going to provide an opportunity for the disaffected to challenge the rights of the new incumbent. Between 709 and 713 Necthon faced prodigious internal and external threats to his kingship. How this king faced these challenges would underpin his exercise of authority during his reign.

AU 709 – A battle over the Orkneymen, in which Artablair's son fell.[28]

The Irish chronicles make their first reference to Pictish affairs, since the obituary notice of Bredei filius Derelei, in 709. Preceding a notification of pestilence in Ireland, the annals supply a terse reference to a conflict relating to Orkney in which Artablair's son fell. This entry has received little attention, in part because it raises more questions than it is possible to answer. Fraser, however, has suggested that this entry signifies a direct challenge to Necthon, following his theory that the king was losing influence over his brother's territorial achievements.[29] It is of interest that Artablair appears to be a Brythonic rather than a Gaelic name. The context may indicate that he was the *regulus* of Orkney, quashing an internal rebellion in which one of his sons was killed. This, however, may not have registered as important to an Irish cleric, who would be more inclined to record events that had wider political ramifications. It is likely, therefore, that the entry relates to the Fortriu dynasty's interest in Orkney that may have required reinforcement at the onset of Necthon's reign.

28 *AU* 709.4 [*Bellum for Orcaidh in quo filius Artablair iacuit*]. 29 Fraser, *From Caledonia to Pictland*, p. 272.

The interest shown in Orkney by Bredei filius Bili, and later suggestions in the *Historia Brittonum* that Orkney was the territorial origin of the Picts, suggests that this region held strategic and perhaps ideological importance for the Pictish kings of Fortriu.[30] Orkney's inhabitants would have been, of a necessity, expert seafarers. Oversight of the Orkneys, by the Fortriu dynasty, may have meant a skilled naval fleet at their disposal as well as horses (attested from the excavation at Pool) and other trade goods. Bredei filius Bili's subjugation of the Orkneys in 682 would have left the king with some key hostages with which to ensure the compliance of the Orkney leadership. According to the Life of St Columba, Bridei filius Mailcon granted the saint's cleric, Cormac Ua Liatháin, safe travel to Orkney because he held the hostages of the *regulus* of Orkney.[31] It suggests that Orkney was important to the Fortriu dynasty and the chronicle entry of 709 may point to an internal coup potentially sparked by lingering disaffection and an opportunistic testing of the newly installed Necthon. As there were no further chronicle records relating to battles or disturbances in Orkney during the reign of Necthon, it is probable that this incident had no lasting effect on the balance of power. Necthon retained control over the Orkney leadership. This is confirmed by the ecclesiastical foundations dedicated to St Peter that appear to have been established in Orkney after Necthon's reforms; and the presence of Pictish symbol stones confirm Orkney's identification within a Pictish cultural continuum. Moreover, the instability in Orkney was followed in the next year by a southern conflict, possibly in the Clackmannanshire and Stirlingshire territories of the Cenél Comgaill. Both regions potentially being at the peripheries of Necthon's authority, it is notable that they both had production sites for stylistically similar penannular brooches dating roughly to this period.

AU 710 – A conflict among the Cenél Comgaill in which two sons of Nectain m. Doirgarto were killed[32]

This record has caused some confusion due to the patronymic of Dargart, which suggests that another politically powerful Nechtan, and rival to Necthon filius Derelei, was operating in northern Britain.[33] Clancy, however, views this entry as proving Necthon's (and his brother Bredei's) father as Dairgart mac Finguine of the Cenél Comgaill. In addition, Clancy found this chronicle entry suggestive of internecine conflict in which Necthon and/or his sons attempted to assert power.[34] Following this line of reasoning, Fraser suggested that the death of

30 *Nennius. British history and the Welsh annals*, V.12, pp 10, 20, 51, 61; *The Historia Brittonum; the Vatican recension*, p. 67. 31 *VC* II.42. 32 *AU* 710.4 [*Immbairecc apud genus Comghaill ubi .ii. filii Nectain m. Doirgarto iugulati sunt*]. 33 A.A.M. Duncan, 'Bede, Iona and the Picts' (1981), pp 35–6, n. 31; B.T. Hudson, *Kings of Celtic Scotland*, pp 24–5. 34 Clancy, 'Philosopher-king', pp 130–3, 138–9.

Necthon's sons resulted in the Pictish king losing the support of his Cenél Comgaill relatives, ensuring future relations were antagonistic.[35] Fraser has subsequently explored the idea that this conflict was indicative of a general breakdown in an alliance between the Strathclyde Britons, Cenél Comgaill and the Picts, possibly over territory in Clackmannanshire and Stirlingshire, but overall signifying Necthon's weakening rule.[36] There are, undoubtedly, a number of ways to read this entry; all inferential. The Cenél Comgaill gave their name to the Cowal region in Argyll where they appear to have been based and where this internecine conflict may have taken place. According to Clancy, however, Dargart's line did not belong to the Cenél Comgaill branch who ruled Cowal, but a subsidiary branch that saw new territory as a means to expand their line's political authority.[37] The other contender for the battle site may have been in the territory more recently possessed by a branch of the Cenél Comgaill which could have included parts of Clackmannanshire and Stirlingshire. In the Life of St Serf, Culross is described as *i Comgell(g)aib*, a toponym which Clancy suggests derives from the Cenél Comgaill and their lands are identified as being in Strathearn '*hi Sraith Hirend*'.[38] Culross remained a detached part of Strathearn, Perthshire, until the administrative boundary reforms of 1891 placed it in Fife.[39] This territory was probably coterminous with St Serf's properties lying between the Ochils and the Forth, encompassing parts of an older British territory of Manaw.[40] Clancy has argued that the use of the patronymic Dargart, in Bredei's donation of Culross to St Serf, reflects the king donating properties that he held by his paternal rights in the Cenél Comgaill rather than because they were Pictish territories.[41] This suggests that the Fortriu dynasty had no real claim to the territory and, instead, the gift acknowledges the Picts' indebtedness to their paternal kin for acting as a buffer between the Pictish *regnum* and Northumbrian predations. Nevertheless, this line of reasoning implies that Bredei held a superior position within the Cenél Comgaill to enable him to authorize the alienation of property.

There is a semantic issue in regard to this chronicle entry. As Dumville has pointed out, differing interpretations depend upon the translation of *apud* as 'by' or 'among', raising questions as to whether this was an internal conflict or against external aggressors.[42] This has, however, received little support, as factionalism among the Cenél Comgaill is certainly implied in the record; but in what capacity Necthon's sons were caught up in the conflict is open to doubt, as is their age. If underage, they may have been in fosterage among their Cenél Comgaill kin and learning military skills, or they might have been surety

35 Fraser, 'Ministry mission and myth', pp 202–3. 36 Fraser, 'Strangers on the Clyde', p. 104; *From Caledonia to Pictland*, p. 272. 37 Clancy, 'Philosopher-king', pp 137–8. 38 Macquarrie, '*Vita Sancti Servani*', p. 124; Clancy, 'Philosopher-king', p. 138. 39 Taylor, *The place-names of Fife*, 1, pp 224–5. 40 Clancy, 'Philosopher-king', pp 138–9. 41 Ibid., 139. 42 Dumville, '*Cethri Prímchenéla Dáil Riata*', p. 189.

hostages for continued military alliance with the Picts. If they had achieved maturity then their positions within the Cenél Comgaill may have entailed administrative oversight on behalf of their father, or as high-status leaders of the cenél. Equally, Necthon's sons could have been quashing rebellion among the cenél at their father's direction; or attempting a coup for control of the cenél and their lands. What does not seem to be in doubt is that Necthon's loss was a psychological blow that required compensation. His sons were unlikely to have been direct in line to the Pictish kingship after their father, given what can be determined from the Pictish succession system, but they held prestigious positions in the Pictish royal kindred.[43] Returning to the chronicle entry, the use of the patronymic Dargart for Necthon does suggest that the conflict was an issue internal to the Cenél Comgaill. Dissent possibly arose during the consolidation of the cenél's authority over territories in Clackmannanshire and Stirlingshire, which may have led to friction over their alliance with the Pictish kingship and the Picts' programme of territorial and ideological consolidation. What may be considered is that, instead of this conflict being indicative of Necthon's failing authority, the killing of his sons gave Necthon moral and legal capital over his paternal kin. Whether the deaths of Necthon's sons were caused by the Cenél Comgaill or their failure to prevent it, the kin ties made them responsible and, potentially, legally liable. This event may have enabled Necthon to establish an ascendant position, enforcing the fealty of his paternal kin to Pictish suzerainty at the risk of losing their territorial claim to estates in Clackmannanshire and Stirlingshire. It is also possible that, as a consequence, Necthon's brother Congal, whose obituary is recorded in 712, was placed in authority over the kin-group.[44] There does not appear to be any chronicle reference to immediate reprisals on the Cenél Comgaill for their possible complicity in the deaths of Necthon's sons.

The establishment of the Cenél Comgaill in territories within Clackmannanshire and Stirlingshire was politically advantageous to the cenél and the Pictish leadership. The cenél not only removed themselves from the internal conflicts among the western Dál Riata but, with new territories under the auspices of their own saint, they were able to expand their political prestige. In the medieval period St Serf's parish of Culross was in the diocese of Dunblane and formed a detached part of the earldom of Strathearn, Perthshire.[45] The territory appears to have been within the old British region of Manaw and, as Clancy points out, 'has no precise equivalent in any later diocesan or secular arrangement'; although he suggests that there may be similarities to the territories within the diocese of Dunblane.[46] The early ecclesiastic site of Abernethy was among the churches in the bishop of Dunblane/Strathearn's

43 See Evans, 'Royal succession and kingship', p. 25. 44 *AU* 712.4. 45 S. Taylor, *The place-names of Fife*, 1, p. 223. 46 Clancy, 'Philosopher-king', p. 139.

diocese; Culross is around thirty kilometres southwest of this Pictish church. The strategic hillfort of Clatchard Craig, a short distance east of Abernethy is also on the south bank of the River Tay and offers 'three good lines of communication from the coast through the Ochils back into the centre of Fife and on to the south'.[47] Penannular brooches were produced at this hillfort around the late seventh to early eighth century, closely followed by a period of rebuilding that transformed the hillfort into a high-status residence.[48] A Pictish symbol stone was found a short distance southwest of this fort.[49] In addition, the hillfort is strategically situated to maintain oversight of vessels sailing up the firth towards Abernethy or to high-status centres along the River Tay. The presence of Clatchard Craig in the Ochils, which formed the north-western boundary of the Comgaill territory, may suggest that the hillfort was intended to provide a measure of Pictish oversight and protection to the region.[50] The short production period of penannular brooches, followed by the 'refit' of the fort for sustained high-status occupation, points to concentrated political activity in this region, which appears to reflect a centralizing agenda. It is significant that no further mention is made of the Cenél Comgaill in the annals, and the next entry describes 'Picts' defending Mag Mannon (the Plain of Manaw). It is possible that Necthon successfully asserted Pictish interest in the region, underscored by what appears to be a Pictish presence at Clatchard Craig. The king may have cemented relations with his kin through gifts, such as penannular brooches, reflecting their participation in the political leadership. Nevertheless, a renewed Pictish presence at Clatchard Craig hillfort, given its proximity to Comgaill territories, suggests that the potential for a military presence would not be lost on Necthon's Gaelic kin. Certainly, the Cenél Comgaill appear to lose their political 'visibility' in the records at this period. Necthon's reaction to the killing of his sons is not recorded, nor is his presence noted at the conflict, or the battle of 711. Overall, Necthon's involvement in the conflict appears to have been in the pursuit of settlement rather than vengeance. A peaceful settlement was preferable as a blood-feud was costly and would have undermined Necthon's authority throughout his reign. Allies, tied by blood and conscience, were useful to retain. Moreover, allies in territories within Clackmannanshire and Stirlingshire were pivotal in order to protect access into southern Pictland from potential attack by Northumbria and the Strathclyde Britons.

AU 711 – A slaughter of the Picts by the Saxons in the district of Manaw, where Finnguine son of Deile Roith met an untimely end.[51]

47 Close-Brooks, 'Excavations at Clatchard Craig, Fife', p. 118. 48 Ibid., p. 145. 49 Allen and Anderson, *The early Christian monuments of Scotland*, ii, pp 343–4. 50 See Taylor, *The place-names of Fife*, i, p. 224. 51 *AU* 711.3 [*Strages Pictorum in Campo Manonn apud Saxones ubi Finnguine filius Deile Roith inmatura morte iacuit*].

The Northumbrians soon tested the adequacy of this protective zone in the year following the Cenél Comgaill conflict. Skene wove a heroic saga around this chronicle record, suggesting that the conflict had been instigated by the 'youthful leader Finguine', a Pict living in the district of Manaw.[52] The importance of the region as a buffer is clear, and it was in the interests of the Picts to retain it as a stable frontier.[53] The Cenél Comgaill, being among the groups settled to the north of the district of Manaw, had to respond to any threat to their territory in their own interests and, possibly secondary, to that of the Pictish king.[54] The Anglo-Saxon Chronicle adds further information on this conflict, naming the protagonist as the Ealdorman Beorhtfrith, and the site of the battle as between the Avon and the Carron.[55] From this description, Anderson placed the battle site around Falkirk, Stirlingshire, a strategic point on the Antonine wall that guards access to the main land route from the south through to Stirling and beyond.[56] The site of this conflict also makes it likely that Cenél Comgaill factions were mobilized in defence. If Fraser is correct in his suggestion of an alliance between the Cenél Comgaill and the Britons of Strathclyde then the defeat of the Britons at the hands of the Dál Riata earlier in the same year may have left the cenél severely stretched.[57] It has recently been proposed, however, that Finnguine mac Deile Roith was a member of the leading kindred of Atholl – perhaps its king.[58] The province of Atholl appears to have retained a degree of independence from the Fortriu dynasts, possibly assisted by Atholl's connections with Iona, which appears to have established an important church at Logierait.[59] Atholl's alliance with the Picts waxed and waned and at this point Finnguine appears to have sided with the Picts against a common enemy whose encroachment would also have threatened Atholl. The rather lachrymose record of Finnguine's death is indicative of affectionate partisanship. This partisanship may reflect a close connection between Finnguine, as putative king of Atholl, and the clerics of Iona. Nevertheless, the Irish entry clearly identifies the defenders of the district of Manaw as Picts, which suggests that Finnguine as well as any Cenél Comgaill forces were under Pictish political direction. These groups were fighting to protect their own territories from potential incursion but they may also have been compelled to take up arms, possibly due to alliances coerced through hostages held by the Fortriu dynasty.

Beorhtfrith was a royal commander of Osred's forces whose interest in attacking the region probably stemmed from paternal claims to the area.[60] It is

52 Skene, *Celtic Scotland*, 1, p. 270; Anderson, *Early sources of Scottish history*, 1, p. 213, n. 213. 53 D.P. Kirby, 'Bede and the Pictish Church' (1973), p. 7; Fraser, 'Ministry mission and myth', p. 203. 54 Clancy, 'Philosopher-king', pp 139–40, n. 163. 55 *ASC, Peterborough MS*, 710; also *HE* v.24. See P. Hunter Blair, 'The Bernicians and their northern frontier' (1959). 56 M.O. Anderson, 'Picts: the name and the people' (1987), p. 8. 57 *AU* 711.5; Fraser, 'Strangers on the Clyde', p. 104. See also Fraser, *From Caledonia to Pictland*, p. 273. 58 Fraser, *From Caledonia to Pictland*, p. 272. 59 Taylor, 'Seventh-century Iona abbots in Scottish place-names', p. 58. 60 Fraser, *From Caledonia to Pictland*, p. 272.

likely that Beorhtfrith's father was Brectrid (Beorht) son of Bernith, who was killed in a similar campaign in Pictish territory in 698, and the 711 offensive may have been retribution for this death.[61] The Anglo-Saxon Chronicle notes the death of Ealdorman Beorht in 699 but he was also in Ecgfrid's raiding party that attacked Ireland in the year prior to the Battle of Nechtansmere.[62] In the Life of St Wilfrid, Beorhtfrith is described as second only in rank to the king, who at this time was fourteen years of age and unlikely to have made logistical military decisions without advice.[63] Rather than revenge, it appears more likely that Beorhtfrith was either capitalizing on unrest in the region or making a pre-emptive strike due to the increasing consolidation of Pictish control in the region. It is unlikely that Beorhtfrith was acting alone, or realistically believed that Northumbria was in a position to retain any territorial gains in this region. Instead, it appears to have been a quick and powerful military action against the Picts with the aim to delineate the boundary between the two polities and establish some level of treaty. This was an ideal policy for a kingdom with a minority rule under a caretaker administration. No further evidence of Northumbrian predation on Pictland is recorded in the chronicles during Necthon's reign, while Bede confirms that a treaty of peace existed between the polities by 731.[64] The Picts' loss appears heavy, yet despite his apparent success Beorhtfrith appears to have been willing to negotiate for peace with Necthon. In order to sue for peace Necthon would have dealt with Beorhtfrith but also with the high-status clerics and nuns (probably including Abbot Ceolfrid) behind the throne of the juvenile king Osred. Bede links the treaty of peace to the polities being united in Catholic peace; and the promise of shared communion in Roman Catholic practice could have been a direct political outcome of the battle. Establishing a fixed border between Northumbria and Pictland suited both sides but the death of Finguinne in this battle appears to have resulted in an acrimonious dispute between Necthon's dynasty and Finguinne's putative kin in Atholl

AU 713.4 – Cinaed son of Derile and Mathgernan's son were killed.
713.7 – Tolarg son of Drostan is held captive by his brother [*fratrem*], King Nechtan.[65]

These records appear to relate to consecutive events. Moreover, as a number of scholars have noted and the chronicle entries imply, familial ties bound both Cinaed and Tolarg to Necthon.[66] Indeed, Clancy has concluded that Cinaed was a full brother to Necthon and Tolarg was a uterine brother whose father may

61 *AU* 698.2. **62** *ASC*, *Peterborough MS*, 684, 699. **63** *VW* LX. **64** *HE* V.23. **65** *AU* 713.4 [*Ciniod m. Derili et filius Maithgernain iugulati sunt*]; 713.7 [*Tolargg filius Drostain ligature apud fratrem suum Nectan regem*]. **66** Anderson, *Early sources of Scottish history*, p. 214, n. 213; Anderson, *Kings and kingship*, p. 176. See also Kirby, 'Bede and the Pictish Church', p. 24, n. 92.

have been a provincial king of Atholl. The annal entry may therefore recount an attempt by Tolarg to assert rights to the Pictish kingship over Necthon.[67] This explanation was also favoured by Fraser, who linked the death of Cinaed with an apparent attempt by Tolarg to usurp Necthon's sovereignty. Additionally, he suggested that the Iona clergy, led by Dúnchad, *princeps* of Iona, were complicit in the attempted coup.[68] This follows Fraser's suggestion that during the apparent hiatus in the *kathedra Iae* in 713 Necthon had installed his own candidate as *principatus* of a Pictish church, thereby threatening Iona's authority and causing them to switch allegiance to Tolarg.[69] Subsequently, Fraser has queried whether this chronicle record alludes to a plot against Necthon where Cinaed and Tolarg were co-conspirators.[70]

Tolarg makes another appearance in the annals in 739, in which year he is described as the king of Atholl.[71] His identification, however, as brother to Necthon rests on the 713 chronicle record that Clancy among others has endorsed.[72] At issue is the translation of *fratrem*, which can mean 'cousin' as well as the more usual 'brother'.[73] Nevertheless, there was evidently a consanguine connection between Necthon and Tolarg that suggests the latter may have had the necessary qualifications to contend for the Pictish kingship. There is also a possibility that Atholl retained a level of independence from the Fortriu dynasts in this period, as is suggested by its paucity of Pictish symbol stones, the title of *rex Athfoitle* in the annal entry of 739, and the ambiguous nature of the name of this province.[74] Atholl's geographic position, on a main access route from Strathearn into Moray, ensured that the province retained a prominent political position in northern affairs. Moreover, should Fraser's suggestion that Iona had established a *principatus* in Atholl be correct then there was an existing political affiliation between the *familia Columbae* and the province.[75] Certainly, the place-name evidence confirms both secular and ecclesiastical Gaelic activity in Atholl and Taylor has argued that there was a Columban monastic site near Logierait, Perthshire, by the 680s.[76] Commemorations to Bishop Coetti who died in 712 are at Logierait and in its vicinity, although there is no evidence to confirm if these foundations were established by Coetti or post-mortem dedications.[77] After Coetti's death there was a lacuna of seven months before Dorbbéne was appointed primate. This delay was possibly the result of clerical dissent among Iona clerics and instability in the north of Britain, which must have been exacer-

67 Clancy, 'Philosopher-king', pp 134–5. 68 Fraser, 'Ministry mission and myth', pp 197, 203. Dedications to this cleric are focused in east Fife: Taylor, 'Seventh-century Iona abbots in Scottish place-names', p. 60. 69 Fraser, 'Ministry mission and myth', pp 197–8; D. Dumville, 'On editing and translating medieval Irish chronicles' (1985), p. 73. 70 Fraser, *From Caledonia to Pictland*, p. 274. 71 *AU* 739.7. 72 Clancy, 'Philosopher-king', pp 133–5. 73 Anderson, *Early sources of Scottish history*, 1, p. 214, n. 3. 74 *CPNS*, pp 228–9; Fraser, *From Caledonia to Pictland*, pp 101–2. 75 Fraser, *From Caledonia to Pictland*, pp 260–2. 76 Taylor, 'Seventh-century Iona abbots in Scottish place-names', p. 42. 77 Ibid., pp 42, 59; Fraser, *From Caledonia to Pictland*, p. 257; *AU* 712.1.

bated by Dorbbéne's death after only five months in the *kathedram* of Iona.[78] Any senior cleric at Logierait would have been recalled to Iona in order to elect the next incumbent to the vacancy. Iona may also have received a political check during this period with the ascendency of the Cenél Loairn over Iona's traditional allies the Cenél nGabrain potentially leaving their seat in Atholl isolated. If the sequence of annal entries relates to consecutive events then it appears that Tolarg's captivity occurred after Dorbbéne's death, leaving no senior churchman at Logierait to petition for peaceful resolution.

There is no proof that an Iona bishop resided at Logierait, or held any unusual oversight over the Pictish church – although the relationship between Bredei filius Derelei and Adomnán may have connected clerics at this church with the Fortriu dynasty. Should Atholl have retained a degree of independence from the Fortriu dynasts' *regnum*, then it was unlikely that an Iona bishop from this position held any real effective power in Pictland. The possible exception may have been the logistical institution of the *Cáin Adomnáin* and associated correspondence between Bredei and Adomnán. Potentially, the relative autonomy of Atholl could have provided a conduit for diplomatic negotiations between Pictland and Iona's Dál Riatan supporters, particularly in the period of Cenél nGabráin supremacy. In this period, however, the Cenél Loairn assumed primacy and a direct link through the Great Glen to the northern Picts bypassed Atholl territorially and politically.

Iona lost one of its senior leaders in 712 when Bishop Coetti died. In the same period, the Cenél Loairn pursued an aggressive campaign in Argyll and Necthon's brother, Congal mac Doirgarto, may have been a casualty as he protected Cenél Comgaill interests. Coetti could also have seen the Picts begin to dispute the Columban paschal calculations, threatening Iona's liturgical authority. At the beginning of 713, with the putative *kathedram* in Atholl still vacant, Atholl's political affiliation may have been tested, with disputes among its ruling dynasty as to their direction. A traditional alliance with Pictland was made more difficult as Necthon eschewed any primatial claims that may have been made by Iona. The killing of Cinaed and the son of Maithgernan appears to be linked directly to the later captivity of Tolarg. Cinaed, on behalf of his brother Necthon, may have been caught up in disputes over Atholl's political allegiance. A dissident faction of Atholl, or a youthful Tolarg, could have taken matters into their own hands to ensure a preferred outcome. Seeking retribution or political stability, Necthon's capture of Tolarg may have received the consent of the short-lived primate Dorbbéne and the king of Atholl; who may have been the Gartnat filius Deile Roith whose death is recorded at 716.[79] This is a speculative reading of the entries. Nevertheless, Necthon's captivity of Tolarg resembles the taking of a hostage surety as a compensatory measure to prevent

78 *AU* 713.5; Fraser, *From Caledonia to Pictland*, p. 261. 79 Fraser, *From Caledonia to Pictland*, p. 272; *AU* 716.2.

ongoing bloodshed and allow a compact between Pictland and Atholl.[80] Taking Tolarg hostage was an effective means for Necthon to ensure a treaty with Atholl, particularly as Tolarg had a dynastic right to the kingship of Atholl. Moreover, the possession of these high-status hostages endorsed Necthon's own authority as king, which may be why he was afforded the title of king in this entry. Such a high-status hostage could coerce Atholl's political and military compliance. In this way, Tolarg's captivity offered Necthon the opportunity to influence this future king's partisanship. While Necthon's captivity of Tolarg may appear to be a reprisal for his brother's death, it was legally and politically justified and more effective than a large-scale military retaliation.

The records of conflict during Necthon's early career are open to various readings. There can be no doubt that Necthon's authority was sorely tested by the events they recount. Alliances made by his brother Bredei would have come under pressure as events in the north prompted a reappraisal of older connections and treaties. During this period the Cenél Loairn gained control over the Dál Riata, Atholl's partisanship came into question and the *familia Columbae* lost their ascendant position in northern liturgical affairs.[81] Necthon's reaction to these events can be interpreted as highly effective, disposed towards treaty and with recourse to legally justified retaliation combined with the pursuit for *concordia*. According to the records, Necthon's only direct action in these events was the capture of Tolarg. The evidence suggests that Necthon did not lead his *comitatus* into the battles, but his political oversight was manifest in the establishment of treaties and alliances from their outcomes. At the end of this period he gained a safe southern border – possibly with a closer oversight of the region from the reoccupied Clatchard Craig – and a hostage surety to guarantee Atholl's compliance. Furthermore, in order to consolidate his own authority over outlying provinces Necthon made a distinct break with the *familia Columbae*. By doing so he gained control over the theological direction of his kingdom and the instatement of bishops. In pursuing legitimate church reform he took an incontrovertible patriarchal position that had far-reaching consequences for the political unity of his kingdom. Necthon's decision to solicit Abbot Ceolfrid for advice on religious reform was part of a strategic plan to consolidate his personal authority and his kingdom's posterity.

ABBOT CEOLFRID'S LETTER TO NECTHON

In most cases historians have viewed Necthon's overtures to Abbot Ceolfrid as deliberately destroying the ascendant patronage of Iona in order to gain the patronage of Northumbria.[82] On the other hand, it has also been proposed that

80 Kelly, *Early Irish law*, pp 97–8. 81 Henderson, *The Picts*, pp 60–1. See also Aitchison, *The Picts and the Scots at war*, p. 35.

Necthon's initial query was suggested, if not drafted, by a pro-Romanist faction within the *familia Columbae*.[83] According to Fraser, the *Romani* cleric directly involved was Abbot Dúnchad of Iona.[84] These suggestions turn on the presumption that clerics of the *familia Columbae* dominated the higher ecclesiastical positions within Pictland. The evidence is slim but well-rehearsed. Adomnán, without naming the foundations, claims that Pictland and the Dál Riata were spared from plague due to the presence of Columban monasteries within their borders and the continuing honour with which Columba was held.[85] It is notable however that Adomnán expresses a degree of ambivalence towards the Picts, complaining of their failure to recognize Columba's intervention. Some thirty years later, Bede writes in the past tense that Iona had exercised authority over all of the monasteries of the Picts.[86] Bede also provides the binary vision of southern and northern Pictish conversion.[87] As this probably mirrored a past political division it may not reflect a contemporary ecclesiastical or political division.[88] The widespread and profuse nature of dedications to Adomnán throughout Pictland appears to support Fraser's argument that the ascendancy of the *familia Columbae* was as recent as the reign of Bredei filius Derelei.[89] The Christianization of Pictland was not strictly dichotomous. So it is of interest why this was the prevailing myth of the period. References to Adomnán in Ceolfrid's letter, and the documented relationship between Bredei filius Derelei and Adomnán, certainly suggest that the *familia Columbae* had held a prominent position in Pictland. It may be that their claim for greater authority combined with their increasing liturgical isolation in regard to paschal calculation was behind Necthon's decision to reform church practices.

The familia Columbae *in Pictland*

Under Adomnán's abbacy, and due to his diplomatic and familial connections, Iona's influence over the kings of Ireland, Dál Riata, Northumbria and Pictland was unprecedented.[90] The nature of Adomnán's relationship with King Bredei filius Derelei offered mutual spiritual and political, as well as fiscal, rewards. The evidence for this was Bredei's guarantee to promulgate Adomnán's legislative reform, the *Cáin Adomnáin*, over his own people. In theory, while the king instituted this law, the *familia Columbae* selected the judges and claimed the right to

82 Skene, *Celtic Scotland*, I, pp 276–7; Anderson, *Kings and kingship*, pp 11, 176; Cruickshank, 'The Battle of Dunnichen and the Aberlemno battle-scene', p. 74; Henderson, *The Picts*, pp 60, 83; A. Macquarrie, 'Early Christian religious houses in Scotland' (1992), p. 114; Smyth, *Warlords and holy men*, pp 75, 138, 178; Veitch, 'The Columban Church in northern Britain', p. 639. 83 Kirby, 'Bede and the Pictish Church', p. 19; Duncan, 'Bede, Iona and the Picts', pp 22–3, 27; and Veitch, 'The Columban Church in northern Britain', pp 638–9. 84 Fraser, *From Caledonia to Pictland*, p. 276. 85 *VC*. II.46. 86 *HE* III.3. 87 *HE* III.4. 88 Fraser, *From Caledonia to Pictland*, p. 275; Clancy, 'The real St Ninian', pp 1–28. 89 Fraser, 'Ministry mission and myth', pp 193–9, 204, 219; Taylor, 'Seventh-century Iona abbots in Scottish place-names', pp 56–8. 90 Herbert, *Iona, Kells and Derry*, pp 47–8, 55.

supervise the enactment of the law in every kingdom and church that had guaranteed its promulgation.[91] It may be inferred that by retaining the right to appoint judges for the enactment of the *cáin* Iona was able to extend its influence throughout the territories of its guarantors.[92] In the case of Pictland, Iona's supervision of the *cáin* would require a sufficient clerical presence in the Pictish kingdom to ensure that the legislation was upheld. The fiscal returns from enforcing the *cáin* filtered directly back to Iona and the Pictish king. As a consequence, the authority accorded to Iona's judges would have increased the general prestige of the *familia Columbae* in Pictland. Corollary to the success of Adomnán's legislation was an increase in Iona's personnel to cope with the administrative responsibilities and to capitalize on their increasing prestige. Although Iona was a monastic rather than a pastoral centre it did ordain its own bishops to minister in other ecclesiastical establishments, such as Bishop Aidan who was sent to Lindisfarne to minister to the existing Northumbrian Christians and extend conversion.[93] Cormac Bourke has suggested that very soon after Iona's founding it had a bishop, Fergna Ia, whose death is noted in 623.[94] According to Fraser, however, a 'division of the headship of Iona' was stimulated by Iona's increased involvement in Pictland during the reign of Bredei filius Derelei.[95] Commemorations to Bishop Coetti of Iona in Atholl may similarly suggest that Iona exercised temporal parochial control over other kingdoms. Parochial control allowed the collection of church dues and spiritual rights over their parishioners that could translate into influence over a territory's political direction.

The Life of St Columba does not name any Columban foundations in Pictland, but it does mention the presence of Iona's daughter houses and one such establishment may have been similar to the monastery at Portmahomack.[96] It is doubtful whether Portmahomack was established by the *familia Columbae*, but the burials found at the site confirm a male monastic presence from *c.*AD565.[97] The position of this monastery on Tarbat Ness was not isolated. It has a natural harbour and, more importantly, is a day's easy travel to the Fortriu dynasty's putative fort in Inverness. A short distance from Inverness, on the Black Isle, Rosemarkie may have been established in the same period as Portmahomack. Without archaeological proof of its foundation date, the evidence for an early ecclesiastical presence at Rosemarkie has rested on the prodigious range of Christian sculpture on the site and textual references. Andrew of Wyntoun, in the early fifteenth century, suggested that Rosemarkie had been established around AD600, to match the putative arrival of St Boniface.[98] In the late seventh century, the bishop of Rosemarkie, Curetán,

91 *CA* §37. 92 Herbert, *Iona, Kells and Derry*, p. 51. 93 Clancy and Márkus, *Iona: the earliest poetry of a Celtic monastery*, p. 24. 94 C. Bourke, 'Fergna Epscop' (2000), p. 68. *AU* 623.1. 95 Fraser, *From Caledonia to Pictland*, pp 260–1. 96 *VC* II.46. 97 Carver, *Portmahomack*, p. 76.

appears to have been an affiliate of Bredei filius Derelei. Indeed, the bishops of Rosemarkie appear ideally placed to act as spiritual advisors to the Fortriu dynasty and as a consequence Rosemarkie would have prospered. Curetán's parochial responsibilities included oversight of his diocese's ecclesiastical settlements; which may have included the monastery of Portmahomack as the parish of Tarbat was part of the bishopric of Ross.[99] Bishop Curetán's name is on the guarantor list of the *Cáin Adomnáin*, which links him to Adomnán but does not signify membership of the *familia Columbae*. Overall, there is limited evidence of an extensive Columban presence in Pictland by the eighth century; although dedications to Adomnán suggest that the prestige of this abbot in Pictland may have outshone that of Columba. There is no evidence that Iona held a 'monopoly' on Christianity in Pictland but it may have extended its presence over Pictland during Adomnán's tenure, assisted by the enactment of the *Cáin Adomnáin.*[1]

As Necthon's reforms directly targeted the liturgical practices of Iona it indicates that Iona had, at some point, influenced Pictish religious practices. Fraser argues that changing political circumstances resulted in Necthon losing the support of Iona, inspiring the king's subsequent attempts to remove the putative *familia Columbae* ascendancy in his church and kingdom.[2] There is certainly no evidence that the relationship between Adomnán and Bredei filius Derelei either extended to granting Iona spiritual authority over Pictland or compelled Necthon to continue an alliance. Factionalism regarding the paschal calculation was already prevalent among the *familia* of Iona despite Adomnán's reputed attempts to reform practices among the wider *familia Columbae*. The piecemeal evidence gives the appearance of entrenched hostility by the Iona *familia* towards adopting the Dionysiac method of calculating Easter (*pascha catholica*). Their liturgical position made it difficult for Necthon to receive counsel on the matter from Iona clerics and their own failure to reach concord left the king to seek advice elsewhere.

Divergent practices and correction

According to Bede's introduction and Ceolfrid's letter, Necthon was already in possession of nineteen-year Easter cycles and was aware, if not following, the orthodox calculations.[3] The request to Abbot Ceolfrid, Bede claims, was initiated by Necthon's own studies and with the approval of his counsellors.[4] Indeed, Necthon appears to have had copies of the nineteen-year cycles of Dionysius

98 Andrew of Wyntoun: *The Orygynale Cronykil of Scotland*, ed. and trans. D. Laing (1872), bk V, ch. XIII, p. 58 [*The tyme off this fundatyown / We efftyre the Incarnatyowne / To be reknyd sex hundyr yhere, / Quhether mare or les, bit thare-by nere*]. 99 *OPS*, 2, pt II, pp 433–4. 1 Cf. Henderson, *The Picts*, p. 79; Taylor, 'Seventh-century Iona abbots in Scottish place-names', pp 56–8. 2 Fraser, 'Ministry mission and myth', pp 204, 210–13. 3 *HE* V.21. 4 Ibid., pp 532–3.

Exiguus, the disputed eighty-four-year cycles favoured by Iona, as well as the maligned nineteen-year cycles of Victorius.[5] With such a wide selection of cycles, and lack of consensus from his clerics regarding their authority, Necthon sought an irrefutable argument in order to institute the correct method of calculation.[6] The main disputants, according to Bede, were the *familia Columbae* and their supporters who clung to an eighty-four-year paschal cycle, with its criterion of fourteen to twenty *lunae*. As Bede emphasizes at the end of the chapter, it was this cycle alone that was 'obliterated' by Necthon.[7] Curiously, however, Ceolfrid not only provides a refutation of the eighty-four-year paschal cycle but he continues with a warning for those using the criterion of sixteen to twenty two *lunae*, from Victorius' cycle, that they also deviated from correct observances.[8] Then, with recourse to rhetorical humour, he uses a Homeric reference that by turning from the fourteen to twenty *lunae* criterion, of the eighty-four-year cycle, in order to follow a sixteen to twenty two *lunae* criterion was to avoid shipwreck on *Scylla* only to fall into the whirlpool of *Charybdis* and be drowned.[9] As Clancy and Markús have noted, this mythological reference was used traditionally to highlight 'two possibilities of doctrinal error'.[10] Ceolfrid was not just arguing against the eighty-four-year cycle adopted on Iona but also the dubious nineteen-year cycles of Victorius, with their criterion of sixteen to twenty two *lunae*.

Victorius' problematic tables were the primary reason for the refusal of Irish clerics to give up their tried and tested eighty-four-year cycles.[11] Victorius' tables were riddled with computistical inconsistencies. A sincere and pleading note can be detected in Columbanus' repeated requests to the papacy, and to the synod at Châlon in 603, asking them to declare a clear ruling on the deficient cycles of Victorius. Not only were the cycles increasing error in the Gaulish churches but, according to Columbanus, they had been received with ridicule by the mathematicians of his own country.[12] As an acolyte of the monastery of Bangor under Comgall, Columbanus was fully cognisant of his countrymen's doubts and at least one member of Bangor's community, Maelrubha of Applecross, resided in Pictland during Necthon's tenure. By Necthon's reign, Bangor and other northern Irish ecclesiastical foundations appear to have already converted to nineteen-year cycles. In Columbanus' period, however, no ruling was forthcoming from the papacy and Victorius' tables continued to cause disunity. Moreover, when the Irish cleric Ségéne sought papal confirmation, after Victorius' cycles provided an erroneous date for Easter in 641, he was accused of

5 Ibid., pp 546–7. 6 Ibid., pp 532–3. 7 Ibid., pp 552–3. 8 K. Harrison, 'A letter from Rome to the Irish clergy' (1984), p. 222. 9 *HE* V.21, pp 540–1. 10 Clancy and Márkus, *Iona: the earliest poetry of a Celtic monastery*, p. 59. 11 D. Ó Cróinín, 'The Irish provenance of Bede's computus' (1983), p. 231; C.W. Jones, 'The Victorian and Dionysiac Paschal tables in the west' (1994), p. 420. 12 *Sancti Columbani opera*, *epist.* I, lines 12–14, p. 4, and lines 2–5, p. 6; also *epist.* II, p. 16 and *epist.* III, p. 24.

Pelagianism and quartodecimanism; accusations that persist in Ceolfrid's letter to Necthon.[13] Indeed, Bede's *De Temporum Ratione* continued to counter Victorius' cycles: naming and shaming Victorius for his inept calculation.[14]

Another aspect of Ceolfrid's argument, which reveals a more subtle situation on paschal matters were at issue than mere refutation of the *familia Columbae*, was his emphasis on the celebration of the Resurrection over the Passion. Ceolfrid conflates the historical chronology of the Crucifixion and Resurrection to a single night, expressed as Christ's passing 'from the world to his Father'.[15] Furthermore, he avoids any reference to the Last Supper, despite its doctrinal importance with Christ's assertion of the new covenant. Cummian of Clonfert supported the nineteen-year cycles and, in a letter sent to Ségéne of Iona and Béccán in 634, relates that some Irish clerics regarded the Passion as well as the Last Supper as equal in importance to the Resurrection.[16] In translating *Pascha* as the feast of the Resurrection, both Ceolfrid and many northern Irish clerics, including the *familia Columbae*, were in concord.[17] Cummian, however, appears to translate *Pascha* as referring to the Last Supper and the Passion itself.[18] This is a significant difference in interpretation. By concentrating on the exodus of the Israelites as prefiguring Christ's resurrection, to the exclusion of other apt references, Ceolfrid further emphasizes a division between Northumbrian practice and that outlined by Cummian who, nevertheless, approved the nineteen-year-cycles. The rarity of figural representations of the crucified Christ on Pictish sculptured cross-slabs may have been due to the Picts' adoption of a doctrine that emphasizes the Resurrection over the Passion. While this is an argument from the surviving evidence, Pictish religious sculptural design does differ from the motifs prevalent on Irish and some Anglo-Saxon crosses. Early Pictish sculptural crosses were usually ringed in iconographic representation of the 'cosmological cross' and filled by interlace and key-patterns to reinforce the image of Christ as both tree of life and eternal.[19] The closest dating evidence for Class II cross-slabs comes from the recent excavation at Portmahomack, which has dated a destruction layer covering broken fragments of cross-slabs to between AD780 and 830.[20] This is not proof of the production of these elaborate cross-slabs during Necthon's reign, but the apparent paucity of the crucified Christ image on crosses from Pictland contrasts with the extensive appearance of this iconography on Irish crosses. This makes it likely that Pictish

13 See D. Ó Cróinín, '"New heresy for old": Pelagianism in Ireland' (1985), p. 506. 14 Ó Cróinín, 'The Irish provenance of Bede's computus'; *Bedae: Opera de temporibus*, ed. C.W. Jones (1943), pp 255–7, 270–3. F. Wallis, *Bede: the reckoning of time* (1999), pp 113–15, 132–5. 15 *HE* V.21, pp 544–5. 16 M. Walsh and D. Ó Cróinín, *Cummian's letter De Controversia Paschali* (1988), pp 25–7, 66–9, 84–9. 17 *HE* V.21, pp 544–5; Walsh and Ó Cróinín, *Cummian's letter De Controversia Paschali*, p. 27. 18 Walsh and Ó Cróinín, *Cummian's letter De Controversia Paschali*, pp 26–7. 19 M.W. Herren and S.A. Brown, *Christ in Celtic Christianity* (2002), pp 199–209. 20 Carver, *Portmahomack*, p. 116.

cross-slabs conform to a liturgical understanding of the cross and the Resurrection distinct from the theological basis for Irish sculptural crosses with crucifixions in this period. As churches proliferated within the Insular kingdoms, doctrinal orthodoxy became more important as clerical authority became increasingly corporatized and hierarchical.

The political aspects of paschal dating

Division between Insular clerics over calculating Easter may be overstated, yet it was clearly a matter integral to correct religious practice and as such to the authority and legitimacy of the practitioners. Easter celebrations, after all, affirmed and reminded the faithful of a core uniting principle of their religion, divine salvation. Therefore, there was some anxiety on the part of clerics to prove they were following a legitimate method of calculation, despite limited directives from Rome.[21] The Synod of Whitby in 664 polarized the dispute between the eighty-four-year paschal cycle and what was emerging as an orthodox calculation using the tables of Dionysius Exiguus.[22] The Roman party argued that orthodox unity with Rome and the Catholic Church could only be achieved by following a nineteen-year paschal table that used the criterion of fifteen to twenty-one *lunae*.[23] The Synod of Whitby mirrored centuries of general confusion and entrenched traditions as to the correct calculation of Easter. Despite the assertions of Wilfrid's biographer, Rome appears to have taken the position that following a differing method of calculation was unfortunate rather than cause for anathema.[24] The issue, however, did not go away and failure to achieve a consensus in this matter threatened political unity. Unity in church practices, after all, promoted national unity and peace. As Columbanus argued, religious unity equates with peace and is achieved through the authority of the king and queen.[25] This stance was also taken by Isidore, who viewed religious consensus as a means to promote community peace.[26]

Necthon's request to Ceolfrid implies a growing disunity within ecclesiastical institutions in Pictland that required direct intervention by the king in order to harmonize liturgical celebrations. The social consequences of divergent Easter dating had an impact on the calculation of the king's and his nobles annual circuit of their clients – specified as between Christmas and Easter – as well as regular assemblies that may have occurred in the period around Pentecost.[27] The divergent dates for Lenten observance, which caused apparent disharmony between King Oswy and his queen, were cited as a catalyst for the Synod of Whitby. Similarly, exogamous marriage being common among the Pictish kings, as it was for other Insular kings, could have brought divergent Christian cultural

21 W.M. Stevens, 'Bede's scientific achievement' (1995), p. 43. 22 *HE* III.25. 23 Wilfrid's biographer appears confused, referring to the disputed criterion as between fourteen and twenty-two *lunae*, *VW* X. 24 *VW* X. 25 *Sancti Columbani Opera*, epist. V, lines 2–5, pp 56–7. 26 R.L. Stocking, 'Martianus, Aventius and Isidore' (1997). 27 *Críth Gablach*, §26, p. 15.

practice to a head, particularly the dating of paschal observances. Still within living memory by the early eighth century, the Synod of Whitby illustrates the political potential for a king in resolving a highly charged religious issue. Oswy's decision to side against the eighty-four-year cycles and their adherents allowed him to diffuse a tense political stalemate with his son Ahlfrith, then ruler of Deira, and gained him papal approval for his claims of *imperium*.[28] By siding with the Roman party, Oswy enacted the role of the Christian theocratic monarch, corrector of his people's orthodoxy through aligning with the superior but distant authority of Rome. Bede dismisses the supporters of the eighty-four-year cycles as a mere handful of people from a remote region daring to pit their competing theology against the orthodox unity of Rome.[29] With most of his fellow Anglo-Saxon kings following the orthodox paschal dating, it must have become increasingly clear to Oswy that it would be easier to bring his own people into line than upset any balance he retained over his, effectively vassal, kings. Achieving papal approval for his reforms not only endorsed Oswy's position as *imperator* but also the right to select the new archbishop of the English people.[30]

Necthon, as the chronicles indicate, was keen to keep factionalism within his kingdom to a minimum. Peace, as *De duodecim abusiuis saeculi* confirms, results in prosperity and scriptural typology encouraged kings to identify with the image of *rex pacificus*.[31] In order to fulfil this role, Necthon needed to curb internal dissension and violence. The peripheries were particularly vulnerable as were alliances formed during his brother's reign, many of them based on a personal relationship that ended upon Bredei's death. Necthon's politics were distinctly different from those of his brother as he dealt with swiftly changing geo-political circumstances created by a change in the leaders of northern Britain. While suggesting that Necthon's motivation was due to political insecurity, Foster argues that overall control of a church that was gaining extensive jurisdiction was a deliberate means of consolidating and extending royal and aristocratic authority.[32] Necthon's use of doctrinal orthodoxy to unite his kingdom was certainly a deliberate strategy, as Pictish ecclesiastic foundations needed to be in liturgical unanimity for his own authority to be effective. At this stage, there was no unified church in Pictland although it is likely that the king's preferred clerics established the dominant ecclesiastical doctrine. The prima facie evidence does suggest that the *familia Columbae* had influenced some aspects of liturgical and political life in Pictland as a consequence of the relationship between Adomnán and Bredei filius Derelei. Whether Adomnán had persuaded Bredei to the *pascha catholica* is impossible to verify; certainly Iona refused to authorize Dionysiac tables. Discord with the Cenél Comgaill as well as changing relations with Atholl challenged Necthon's aims for consolidation.

28 R. Abels, 'The Council of Whitby' (1983). 29 *HE* III.25. 30 Abels, 'The Council of Whitby', p. 13. 31 Pseudo-Cyprian: *De duodecim*, ix rex iniquus, pp 51–3; Kershaw, *Peaceful kings*, pp 38–9. 32 S.M. Foster, *Picts, Gaels and Scots* (1996, rev. 2004), p. 88.

By removing the dissident and competing authority of clerics from the *familia Columbae* and those endorsing differing paschal cycles Necthon, with the example of the Synod of Whitby, increased his royal authority. The overriding principle was unity. Unity of doctrine promoted a united kingdom and following the 'right' orthodoxy also endorsed Necthon's 'right' to exert his authority. It therefore behoved the king that he received the most accurate advice on the divisive issue of paschal dating.

Abbot Ceolfrid's letter outlines a programme of orthodox observances that disparaged not only the practices of the *familia Columbae* but other contrary observances present in Insular practice. It is suggestive that Adomnán was the only church leader referred to in this letter, initially in appreciative and honorific tones.[33] Ceolfrid was aware of Necthon and his dynasty's connection to Adomnán and his letter presents a rather one-sided dialogue between himself and Adomnán in which Ceolfrid appears to successfully challenge the elder abbot of Iona on his paschal stance. Adomnán, according to Ceolfrid, subsequently convinced large numbers of Irish to the 'Catholic observance of Easter'. This constituted a very public reminder to the *familia Columbae* clerics in Pictland that their esteemed abbot had previously approved the reform. Ceolfrid further observes that Adomnán was unable to correct the monks on Iona to the *pascha catholica*, or the Petrine tonsure, as he had insufficient authority over his clerics.[34] This is a damning indictment on Adomnán's authority and Iona's apparent recalcitrance. In essence, if they refused to acknowledge the wisdom of their rightful head, on what authority can they claim liturgical legitimacy.

Given that the clergy within Pictland had reached no concord on paschal dating, it appears that Necthon, in making his appeal to Ceolfrid, was attempting to use the authority of a non-partisan senior cleric.[35] As Kenneth Veitch notes, Abbot Ceolfrid does not attempt to assert Northumbrian primatial status over the Pictish churches as Bishop Wilfrid had once claimed.[36] Nevertheless, Ceolfrid was a leading ecclesiastical figure in Northumbria and had close connections with Oswy's dynasty. These connections could have included an esteemed position as counsellor to Osred within a regency administration. Ceolfrid also had intimate connections with Bishop Wilfrid who had ordained him at Ripon in 669, and through whom Ceolfrid must have gained a full, if one-sided, report of the Whitby synod.[37] Computistical sources of Irish provenance were available to Aldhelm, abbot of Malmesbury, around the same period that Wearmouth was founded and it is probable that Ceolfrid studied the Dionysiac paschal cycles under Wilfrid.[38] Moreover, Wearmouth and Jarrow were institutions of learning with extensive libraries and scholastic links with other

33 *HE* V.21, pp 550–1. 34 Ibid. 35 M. Miller, 'The disputed historical horizon of the Pictish king-lists' (1979), p. 15. 36 Veitch, 'The Columban Church in northern Britain', p. 637; *HE* V.19. 37 *The anonymous history of Abbot Ceolfrith*, §3, p. 214; Abels, 'The Council of Whitby', p. 9. 38 Ó Cróinín, 'The Irish provenance of Bede's computus', pp 242, 246; D. Mc

Anglo-Saxon and Continental ecclesiastical foundations. At the time of Necthon's paschal deliberations Ceolfrid was one of the longest serving abbots of a prestigious monastery neighbouring Pictland. The reinforcement of diplomatic relations between Pictland and Northumbria was a further inducement for Necthon to solicit Ceolfrid for advice. It is unlikely that Necthon's request for clarification of doctrinal issues was the first time Ceolfrid and other Northumbrians had dealings with a Pictish king. Having offered a safe-haven to Northumbrian aethelings fleeing rival dynasts, Pictland had historical and consanguine ties to Northumbria.[39] Inherent in Bede's descriptive summary of Necthon's reception of Ceolfrid's letter is the expectation of a continuing relationship where Northumbria provided Necthon with stonemasons. Furthermore, evidence for the maintenance of these relations is found in Bede's final chapter in which he declares that a treaty exists between the two kingdoms.[40] Existing ties between the kingdoms' various ecclesiastical foundations continued, irrespective of their allegiance to their founding fathers' theological stance. Ceolfrid's scholarship appears well known to Necthon's own clergy and the abbot was witness to the political benefits that Oswy had achieved from the Synod of Whitby. In soliciting Ceolfrid for advice, Necthon received the outcome he wanted: a ruling that accorded with his own studies and one that allowed him to legitimately authorize liturgical reform and remove the initiative from dissenting clerics. The issue of paschal dating also had political ramifications that may serve to date the letter and the institution of the *pascha catholica* in Pictland.

Dating Ceolfrid's letter

Bede provides no date for Ceolfrid's letter, simply beginning the chapter with an ambiguous *eo tempore* (at that time); perhaps reflecting the theological transcendence of the subject. As the previous chapter spans a period of twelve years this is hardly informative and Plummer, with some hesitancy, suggested 710 as an appropriate date, with which Henderson concurred.[41] Ceolfrid retired from the abbatial office at the beginning of June 716 in order to travel to Rome and the Columban clergy on Iona adopt the *pascha catholica* in the same year.[42] This provides a possible date range for the letter from the beginning of Necthon's reign in 706 to early 716. As Duncan points out, however, the various paschal tables only diverged in 712 and 716 of that period, and he suggests that the discrepancy of 712 had instigated Necthon's request.[43] David Kirby proposed 715 as the date for the letter, on the basis that Iona conformed in 716 to the nineteen-year cycles as, he surmised, a direct result of Pictish conformity in the

Carthy, 'The lunar and paschal tables of *De Ratione Paschali*' (1996), pp 310–11. **39** Miller, 'Eanfrith's Pictish son'. **40** *HE* V.23. **41** *Venerabilis Baedae: Historiam ecclesiasticam*, ii, p. 331; Henderson, *The Picts*, pp 82–3. **42** Bede: *Lives of the abbots of Wearmouth and Jarrow*, ch. 16, p. 204; *AU* 716.4. **43** Duncan, 'Bede, Iona and the Picts', pp 26–7, 35.

previous year.[44] While agreeing with Duncan's proposition, Fraser proposes the simultaneous institution of paschal reforms in Iona and Pictland in 716.[45] Wyntoun dated the foundation of Rosemarkie by Necthon to 716, which may preserve a memory of paschal reform; his source for this date, however, is not known.[46] The 712 divergence appears the most likely impetus for the reform of paschal cycles, whether advance notification of the conflicting calculations stimulated debate or if this occurred after celebrations in 712 is uncertain. A similar circumstance had occurred when calculation tables provided different paschal dates for 641. Anticipation of this problem provoked a great deal of concern in Ireland, with letters written to the papacy in 640 requesting clarification.[47] Similarly, the Synod of Whitby was convened due to the impending divergence of paschal cycles in 665.[48] It suggests that there was advance notification of the divergent paschal dates, for either 712 or 716, which required the reconciliation of the correct calculations prior to the event. By 716 Easter celebrations in Pictland did follow the orthodox date, but when the Dionysiac calculations were instituted remains debated.

Paschal dating was a live issue among Insular clerics and advance notification of divergences in calculation was more likely than reactive responses after the event. It is likely that a faster resolution of this issue occurred than the proposed three- to five-year lag between the initial divergence and Necthon's adoption of orthodox cycles. The records of conflict relating to Necthon's reign from 710 to 712 suggest that Necthon urgently required a means to retain a coherent identity for his kingdom so that he could maintain his authority and control his borders. The use of divergent cycles was an inauspicious symbol and potentially a cause of further division among political groups in his kingdom. The imminent divergence in the dates for Easter celebrations would have motivated debate among Pictland's clerics and potentially divided the loyalties of parishioners, including those who may have been under the religious care of clerics from the *familia Columbae*. In focusing on the divisions within the *familia Columbae* over their paschal stance, Necthon may have been able to limit or at least diffuse their political influence. It may be significant that after Bishop Coetti's death on 24 October 712 it took over nine months to replace him, during which time Iona clerics appear to have failed to reach an accord.[49] In addition, should Necthon have responded to Northumbrian aggression after the Picts' defeat in 711 by promising to align his kingdom with communal orthodox unity, it would have eased negotiations towards truce and had a concomitant effect on his relations with Atholl and the primacy of the *familia Columbae*. It was certainly a strategic political decision to initiate paschal reform. Ceolfrid's address to the king,

44 Kirby, 'Bede and the Pictish Church', pp 9, 13, 19. 45 Fraser, 'Ministry mission and myth', pp 203, 208. 46 Andrew of Wyntoun: *The Orygynale Cronykil of Scotland*, II, bk 5, XIII, p. 58. 47 Ó Cróinín, '"New heresy for old": Pelagianism in Ireland', pp 505–16. 48 J. Moreton, 'Doubts about the calendar' (1998), p. 54. 49 Fraser, *From Caledonia to Pictland*, p. 261.

moreover, suggests that it was a tactical move combining a religious conscience and scholarship with a pro-state agenda.

THE PHILOSOPHER KING

The sources indicate that Necthon filius Derelei did not continue his brother Bredei's association with the *familia Columbae*. Necthon was not, however, working alone against a united and powerful *familia*. Internal dispute over paschal dating and the loss of Adomnán's leadership had dismantled their unity and much of their political influence. Necthon, according to Bede, made his own assiduous study of church writings; which suggested to Clancy that Necthon may have been destined for clerical office before attaining the mantle of kingship.[50] Ceolfrid alludes to Necthon as a king who marries the fear of god with wisdom. In seeking out the truth, Necthon could also call upon the advice of his counsellors and the bishop of Rosemarkie. During Bredei's reign the bishop of Rosemarkie, Curetán, had been a major player on the ecclesiastical and political field as signatory of the *Cáin Adomnáin*. Curetán had powerful connections with other leading clerics from close and distant polities as was likely for Rosemarkie's subsequent bishops. Necthon was an obedient son of the church and his tactical response to conflict reveals a desire to establish a peaceful realm in the manner of an ideal Christian ruler. His reign corresponds to a period in which clerical intellectuals (many from the *familia Columbae*) were rewriting the role of kingship as theocratic and paternal, on which he was able to capitalize. In soliciting advice from Abbot Ceolfrid on paschal dating and the correct method of tonsure Necthon was behaving as a 'just' Christian ruler.[51] This role also conforms to Old Testament imagery, alluded to in Bede's description of Edwin's reign, of the peace established for Israel under the wisdom of Solomon's rule.[52]

Ceolfrid's letter to Necthon, structured according to Classical rhetorical principles ideal for the purpose of public oratory, displays a familiarity with the relationship between Pictish kings and Adomnán.[53] At the same time, however, Ceolfrid intimates that Adomnán had a distinct lack of orthodoxy and authority over his own clerics.[54] In the opening address, Ceolfrid praises Necthon that 'whenever rulers themselves take trouble to learn and teach and watch over the truth, it is a heaven-sent gift to God's holy Church'.[55] He completes this encomium with a reference from Plato's *Republic*, 'that the world would be in a happy state if kings were philosophers and philosophers were kings'. Bede records a similar tribute in a letter sent to King Oswy from Pope Vitalian; praising the king 'that race is indeed blessed which has been found worthy to

50 Clancy, 'Philosopher-king', p. 137. **51** *HE* V.21. **52** Kershaw, *Peaceful kings*, p. 33. **53** See M. Lapidge, 'Gildas's education and the Latin culture' (1984), pp 41–3. **54** *HE* V.21, pp 550–1. **55** *HE* V.21, pp 534–5.

have so wise a king'.[56] Plato's reference to philosopher-kings also appears in Boethius' *Philosophiae Consolatio* where it is used to argue that the love of justice was the correct motivation for pursuing high office.[57] Ceolfrid's is not a direct quote, but rather a rhetorical memory of the *res.*[58] Nevertheless, Ceolfrid's address to Necthon is more than mere flattery. It reiterates one of the major *speculum principum* themes of texts such as the ninth abuse of *De duodecim abusiuis saeculi*, the king's responsibility to correct his people. Ceolfrid congratulates Necthon for both teaching and watching over the truth and by soliciting advice on orthodox practice Necthon took direct responsibility for the religious direction of his people. This was not an unusual response, as the early Christian fathers perceived no division between church and state instead the division was between the orthodox Catholic ruler and the non-orthodox ruler.[59] The opening address finishes on an emphatic statement that, as a powerful 'man of this world', Necthon should induce his subjects to observe the instructions for correct Catholic practice by his example together with his authority.[60] In his summary, Bede suggests that the reforms proposed by Necthon received collective approval, although Ceolfrid frames his exhortation to the king as autocratic action. The letter signs off with an encouragement that Necthon institute the orthodox observances because God had placed him in the office of king and his actions would gain him a place in heaven among God's elect.[61] This was a public letter that was carefully constructed to enhance Necthon's Christian credentials, his authority and wisdom, while demonstrating to the Pictish audience the orthodox failings of the Iona *familia* and Victorius' paschal cycles. Naturally, Ceolfrid was supportive of a king who engaged in the spiritual direction of his subjects but his letter also sets out to validate Necthon's rights over religious foundations in his kingdom. Ceolfrid would not have missed the political implications in sanctioning autocratic religious directives.

Despite retaining a moral ascendency throughout the letter, Ceolfrid does not claim prerogatives over liturgical life within Pictland. His complimentary greetings to Necthon suggest that the diligent efforts of clerics to define the behaviour of a Christian king flowered in this king's reign. Instead of demanding virtuous behaviour, Ceolfrid urges a greater exercise of authority by the king as one who could 'judge correctly about the governance of this world'.[62] Necthon was clearly adhering to the prescribed virtues of the 'just' king by pursuing the alignment of his people to orthodox observances and soliciting the advice of a senior cleric. For, as the ninth abuse of *De duodecim abusiuis saeculi* reminded a ruler, 'the throne is raised in the king's justice, and the governance of peoples is secured in the king's truth'.[63] Moreover, should Clancy be correct in his sugges-

56 *HE* III.29. **57** Anicii Manlii Severini Boethii: *Philosophiae Consolatio*, ed. L. Bieler, 94 (1957), I.IV, p. 10. **58** M.J. Carruthers, *The book of memory* (1990), p. 191. **59** R.A. Markus, 'The Latin fathers' (1988), pp 94–6. **60** *HE* V.21, pp 534–5. **61** *HE* V.21, pp 550–1. **62** *HE* V.21, pp 534–5.

tion that Necthon had received clerical training prior to his accession to the kingship then Ceolfrid's classical reference would have been familiar and evoked a memory of the context within Boethius that described the necessity for just government.[64] In turn, this quote could recall a range of contemporary political ideas on the constitution of Christian government. There is no reason to disbelieve Bede's portrait of Necthon's 'assiduous study of Church writings' as Insular Christian kings in this period were being actively encouraged to attain knowledge. Moreover, in studying western Christian writings on the constitution of government, such as Gregory the Great's extensive writings on the subject, Necthon was equipped with a range of ruling principles that promoted national consolidation and an increase in the effective authority of kingship.[65]

Separating Necthon's political ambitions from his religious convictions is unproductive. What can be elicited, particularly from Ceolfrid's letter, is that Necthon had a desire to conform to a wider Catholic communion. Success, whether spiritual or temporal, was seen as a mark of God's favour and the promotion of Catholic adherence in his subjects was the prime role of a Christian king. By enjoining his people to follow orthodox Catholic practice, Necthon exemplified contemporary Christian expectations that the king provided protection to his subjects in the herein and hereafter. The king was also ensuring that his people celebrated their liturgical rituals in Catholic communion with Rome and their immediate neighbours. Conformity in collective ritual also endorsed a collective identity among the Pictish communities. Combining liturgical alignment to Rome with a proposed new church of stone, built in the Roman manner and consecrated to St Peter, was a powerful message of Catholic participation. Moreover, although it is never clearly stated, Ceolfrid's allusion to Necthon's wise rulership and desire for a new ecclesiastic foundation suggests that Ceolfrid, if not Necthon himself, was consciously identifying with the example of King Solomon.

CONCLUSION

According to the chronicles, the first half of Necthon's reign severely tested the king's military and diplomatic authority. Internal unrest and conflict at the fringes of the Pictish kingdom highlights the tenuous nature of political and territorial consolidation. Necthon's reaction to these perils reveals a ruler with keen diplomatic skills wresting political advantage from personal tragedy. Necthon's political actions are open to a positive interpretation that mitigates the general trend in the historiography to view him as a weak and reactionary ruler.

63 Pseudo-Cyprian: *De duodecim*, ix rex iniquus, lines 8–9, p. 51. 64 Clancy, 'Philosopher-king', pp 126–7. 65 R.A. Markus, 'Gregory the Great on kings' (1991).

It should be borne in mind that the heartland of Pictland remained uncontested during Necthon's reign, with assembly sites, such as the one proposed for Rhynie, mediating the consolidation of Pictish territories. Necthon did experience challenges to his rule and his leadership qualities can be judged by his response to these threats and his retention of the kingship. Necthon began his reign in a period when the balance of political power in northern Britain and Ireland underwent significant change. The triumph of Selbach of the Cenél Loairn helped to realign political authority away from Iona, which had already lost influence with the death of Adomnán. In the north-east of Britain, Necthon negotiated a safe southern border and reinstated his control over Orkney. The death of Necthon's sons among his paternal kin, the Cenél Comgaill, was potentially damaging to his authority but it also allowed him to extract compensation possibly in the form of political suppression and obedience. Atholl's intrigues were similarly diffused and Necthon held Tolarg hostage against further assaults on his dynasty. Likewise, religious reform curbed the ambitions of the *familia Columbae* in Pictland. Indeed, Iona's refusal to adopt the *pascha catholica* appears to have left them further marginalized with discord among their ranks. In Pictland, conflicting religious practice among clerics were rationalized according to the superior understanding of orthodox practice espoused by Ceolfrid. There is certainly no evidence that Pictland was a peripheral latecomer to Christianity or that Necthon was unaware of the potential for political consolidation through religious change.

By allying himself with Roman Catholic orthodoxy, Necthon viewed his kingdom as a significant entity. Necthon emerges, from these early challenges to his reign, politically strengthened with profitable diplomatic ties to Northumbria and a defined border. Necthon's visible reforms united his churches under a shared ideology and forged a new identity in direct communion with Rome. As an exemplar of the ideal Christian king, a model developed and propagated by clerical intellectuals including Adomnán, Necthon was able to evoke an image of the 'just' king to achieve a greater exercise of authority. As a result, Necthon served as an exemplar to his people, claiming responsibility for the temporal and spiritual well-being of his subjects, the state of his soul reflecting the state of his kingdom. Necthon's leadership was effective, an assiduous scholar capable of instituting religious reform with collective approval. Indeed, the means by which Necthon consolidated his control over the kingdom underscores his diplomatic and strategic talents as a theocratic king.

5

Necthon the just king

Necthon's assertion of orthodox Catholic reform resulted in significant social and political transformations within his kingdom. Bede describes Necthon as a model of Christian kingship, whose actions conform to a range of contemporary political ideas on the exercise of secular authority. By conscious adoption of this model, Necthon was able to test the limits of his constitutional authority in order to unify Pictish identity and ensure his dynastic legitimacy. In convoking his kingdom's clergy and nobles to authorize the adoption of the *pascha catholica*, Necthon ensured the coalescence of his own Christian theocratic monarchy. Moreover, in aligning Pictish ecclesiastical houses to orthodox observance, organizational reforms could be implemented in order to create a more united and powerful church structure. Challenges to Necthon's kingship and territorial authority early in his reign indicate that his geo-political control over the provinces was in flux. In order to achieve full political oversight of a united Pictish kingdom, Necthon used ecclesiastical expansion to impress his authority over the territories and Pictish polity. The final half of Necthon's reign is characterized by his institution of liturgical reform. Adopting the *pascha catholica* was the beginning of a wider political strategy of unification. The political ramifications of his actions may be read in his expulsion of clerics, the silence of the records and the apparent proliferation of ecclesiastical foundations. The king's choice to retire from temporal office similarly illustrates an underlying religious conviction that dominates his political manoeuvring. His retirement, however, presaged a dynastic conflict that fractured the peace of his kingdom. That this conflict did not threaten the inherent consolidation of his kingdom argues against the political fragility of this emergent Pictish state. The closing years of Necthon's reign appear to shift between apparent serenity and internecine conflict, which may suggest the dissipation of his authority. Nevertheless, Necthon's posterity should be considered in light of the state of his kingdom under his successor's reign, which saw an expansion from a consolidated base. In effect, King Necthon's achievements in unifying his kingdom left a functioning Pictish nation on the path to becoming a fledgling state.

ECCLESIASTICAL REFORM

Upon receipt of Abbot Ceolfrid's letter, Bede informs his audience, Necthon was so grateful for the advice that he fell to his knees and publicly proclaimed his adherence to the measures on behalf of himself and his people. This was not an impetuous response, as Bede provides a vignette of Necthon discussing the letter in some detail with his 'more learned men', before making his devout promise to his assembled nobles. Indeed, the visual emphasis Bede places on Necthon's first rising among his leaders before falling to his knees in thanks is suggestive of a public performance, instilling the moment with due solemnity before reinforcing his authority with a proclamation of kingdom-wide adherence to his strictures. Bede may be accused of hyperbole, but some level of reform was instituted in ecclesiastical institutions with a concomitant impact on governmental organization. The instigation of ecclesiastical reform in Pictland under Necthon's direction appears to be supported by the Irish chronicle entry of 717, relating to his expulsion of Iona clergy.[1] Scholars have argued for a direct link between Pictish paschal reform and Iona's expulsion, as a consequence of Iona's failure to submit to orthodox correction. Most perplexing to this simple reading of Columban clerics being swept aside by religious reform is the chronicle record in the previous year that announces Iona's conformity to what had become the *pascha catholica*.[2] This entry argues against a straightforward causal relationship between the paschal debate and the expulsion of Iona clerics. Instead, an explanation for the expulsion may be found through contextualizing the recorded events against broader issues of political autonomy and the erosion of Iona's relationship with the Pictish kingship. It appears that Necthon's active interest in the theological direction of his people, and the correction of clerics operating within his kingdom, did impact on Iona's political interests. In this way, Necthon's reforms reveal the implementation of long-term strategies that centralized his authority over a territorially defined political constituency.

Most analyses of Necthon's ecclesiastical reforms turn on the presumption that clerics of the *familia Columbae* dominated ecclesiastical positions within Pictland. The idea has recently been refined to suggest that the ascendancy of the *familia Columbae* only occurred during the reign of Bredei filius Derelei under the guidance of Adomnán; who thereby ensured the primacy of the *familia Columbae* in Pictland.[3] It was the loss of clerical support from Iona, Fraser suggests, that caused Necthon to solicit advice from Abbot Ceolfrid in order to remove an Iona-led ascendancy from his church and kingdom.[4] Necthon's reforms were certainly calculated strategies, yet there is limited evidence for an existing ecclesiastical organization over which Iona could exert

1 *AU* 717.4; *AT* 717.3. 2 *AU* 716.4. 3 Fraser, 'Ministry mission and myth', pp 193–9, 204, 219. 4 Ibid., 204, 210–13.

control. The evidence, instead, suggests that a range of ecclesiastical foundations were present in Pictland, providing limited overall political coherence or, potentially, direct fealty to the Pictish kingship. While the prima facie evidence does suggest the *familia Columbae* achieved authority over some aspects of ecclesiastical life in Pictland, this was, arguably, directly through the close relationship between Adomnán and Bredei filius Derelei; and possibly as a result of the imposition of the *Cáin Adomnáin*. Should the *familia Columbae* have held a bishopric located within Atholl they would have been marginalized, as northern and southern Pictland were consolidated under the control of the Fortriu dynasts. Indeed, the paucity of Pictish Class I symbol stones within Atholl may point to this province's autonomy from a Pictish cultural continuum. With the death of Adomnán, the personal relationship between abbot and king ended, resulting in a similarly deleterious impact on Iona's authority within Pictland. Necthon began to cultivate rival establishments: such as Wearmouth and Jarrow, which brought him into contact with Ceolfrid; and possibly with Bangor and Lismore through his contacts with the Cenél Loairn and Maelrubha of Applecross. Older foundations, like Rosemarkie, were endowed with additional saintly associations and new foundations were consecrated. In reforming the date of paschal celebrations, Necthon established himself as arbiter and corrector of the spiritual life of his people.[5] The support of a Pictish *primepscop* ensured Necthon's reforms were actualized and control over the senior clerics in his kingdom was the foundation from which the king could alter the entire political direction and destiny of his kingdom.

Bede concludes the chapter, in which he has included Ceolfrid's letter, by describing how King Necthon 'enforced his word by royal authority'; namely that the *pascha catholica* was to be instituted and all clerics in his kingdom were to receive the Petrine tonsure.[6] Control of the paschal reckoning also meant control over the timing of all activities centred on this primary feast of the Christian calendar.[7] Necthon's reforms aligned churches under a unified authority that was 'the source of authenticating discourse' and which fortified the king as possessor of 'truth'.[8] Unity was clearly Necthon's aim and Fraser has argued that, by this decree of conformity to Roman practice, Necthon gained the power to elect his church leaders and reduce the authority of dissenters, the *familia Columbae*.[9] Certainly, Bede's summary supposes that Necthon had sufficient authority to enforce adherence, yet there remains limited evidence that Necthon exercised rights over clerical elections. Instead of autocratic measures that may have had limited life beyond initial coercion, Necthon could use the authority of his bishops and senior clerics to entrench his own political

5 For example, Pseudo-Cyprian: *De duodecim*, ix rex iniquus, lines 3–4, p. 51. 6 *HE* V.21, pp 552–3. 7 E. Edson, 'World maps and Easter tables' (1996), p. 26. 8 T. Asad, 'Anthropological conceptions of religion' (1983), p. 244. 9 Fraser, 'Ministry mission and myth', p. 212.

oversight. To do so, he used the church's own hierarchical structure to impose unity.

Comparisons with contemporary clerical hierarchies indicate that the bishop of the oldest foundation was the first to sign ecclesiastical acts and convene convocations of regional bishops.[10] This was the expectation of the church of Armagh, which legitimized its claim to primacy through Patrick having been the first bishop to proselytize Christianity in Ireland.[11] Nevertheless, its assertions also rested on the patronage of the Uí Néill kings. Indeed, the bishop of the king's familial territory may have asserted primacy over other bishops in the kingdom; in the same way Wilfrid claimed his diocese was coterminous with King Oswy's kingdom.[12] This may be the implication of Curetán standing as guarantor to the *Cáin Adomnáin* in Pictland mirroring Bredei filius Derelei's guarantees on behalf of his people.[13] By doing so, Curetán may have established a precedent. Bishop Curetán's diocesan church and abbey at Rosemarkie was among the oldest foundations north of the Mounth. In the Martyrology of Gorman he is named both bishop and abbot of *Ruiss Meinn*.[14] It appears, however, that alongside the venerableness of its bishopric it was the bishop's relationship with the king that maintained its superiority. Indeed, this association of the dynasty with a chief bishop is evident in a later period. The annals record the death of Túathal son of Artgus, *primepscop* of Fortriu, abbot of Dunkeld in 865.[15] The king of Fortriu was thus paired with a *primepscop* of Fortriu and it is tempting to see an earlier instance of this chief bishop in the Brec of Fortriu who died in 725.[16] Similarly, it is possible to view Túathal's abbacy of Dunkeld as indicative of the geographic shift in the centre of political activity from the north into southern Pictland by the ninth century. This would suggest that the concept of Fortriu came to embody rulership and authority rather than a territory. This would be useful, particularly within the prevailing system of peripatetic kingship, where the chief bishop accompanied the king on his circuit of the kingdom and otherwise resided in close proximity to the caput of Fortriu. The, albeit slim, evidence suggests that during Necthon's tenure the chief bishop was also abbot of Rosemarkie, from which it may be inferred that the caput of Fortriu was nearby. While Archbishop Theodore may have declared that seniority of consecration alone determines precedence among bishops, his argument may not have withstood the authority of the king, as patriarch, to favour and promote his own candidate.[17]

As *primus inter pares*, the chief bishop was able, and expected, to call synods

10 Reynolds, 'Clerics in the early Middle Ages: hierarchies and functions', p. 17. 11 *The Patrician texts in the Book of Armagh*, 'E. Liber Angeli', §(13), pp 186–7 [*Nonne utique contentus sum esse apostolicus doctor et dux principalis omnibus Hiberionacum gentibus* …]. 12 *HE* V.19. 13 Ní Dhonnchadha, 'The guarantor list of the Cáin Adomnáin', p. 191. 14 *Félire Húi Gormáin: The Martyrology of Gorman*, ed. and trans. W. Stokes (1895), pp 56–7. 15 *AU* 865.6. 16 *AU* 725.7. 17 *HE* IV.5.

and host ordinations. The traditional ordination of bishops and presbyters occurred during Pentecost, which was part of the moveable cycle celebrated fifty days after Easter. This had more than a liturgical impact as the ceremonies were held at the church of the chief bishop and lack of consensus regarding the date of celebration would have polarized allegiances.[18] By enforcing the *pascha catholica*, Necthon's chief bishop was in an ideal position to select and confirm new bishops and clerics who adhered to the reforms. These senior clerics, in turn, would reinforce their fealty to the reforms within their own territories, ensuring unity with their fellow bishops and Necthon's ecclesiastical corrections. Endowments to existing ecclesiastical establishments and the consecration of new ones by the king furthered the obligation of these institutions. This ensured that Necthon had a greater input in the selection of church prelates, the prelates being spiritual as well as civil agents. As previously noted, towards the end of the seventh century the active participation of bishops and senior clerics in society increased, both as spiritual authorities and through their participation in legal procedures. Similarly, ecclesiastical establishments accrued greater land holdings as fear of the afterlife and prestige in the temporal world led to property donations. The agglomeration of church lands encouraged long-term strategies for the management of church estates that further enhanced their profitability and economic power. A profitable estate also increased the local authority of bishops and abbots and, as spiritual directors of their local rulers, the prelates could ensure unity of spiritual and political purpose. Furthermore, the chronicles record clerics with Pictish names who are active during the seventh and early eighth century and, as with comparative examples in Ireland and among the Anglo-Saxon kingdoms, it is likely that these clerics were members of the ruling dynasties. By working with ecclesiastical hierarchies and promoting the consolidation of their authority, Necthon could achieve a greater degree of personal authority over his people and promote their identification with a distinct national identity and a political process that promoted centralizing authority.

The manifestation of reform

Necthon encouraged a visible consensus by giving his allegiance to Roman orthodox practices. In particular, the adoption of the Petrine tonsure created an observable mark of orthodox adherence. In his letter, Ceolfrid openly confronts Adomnán about the form of his tonsure. Having earlier indicated that diverse methods of tonsure were not 'hurtful to those whose faith in God is untainted', he refers to the *familia Columbae* and Adomnán's tonsure as that adopted by Simon Magus.[19] Ceolfrid was not accusing Adomnán of the practice of simony, but may have been alluding to an apocryphal tale of the Magus' attempt to

18 R.E. Reynolds, 'The ordination of clerics in the Middle Ages' (1999), pp 4–5. 19 *HE* V.21, 548.

subvert Peter's establishment of Christianity in Rome.[20] The inference is clear; the doubtful theology of the *familia Columbae* was a hindrance to Necthon's reforms. The imposition of the Petrine tonsure made a clear distinction between those who adhered to Necthon's decrees and those who dissented. The tonsure style was another cause for internal debate among Iona clerics, who did not agree to the adoption of the Petrine tonsure until 718.[21] Necthon's ruling on the Petrine tonsure resulted in clerical unity being an observable fact, and failure to adhere to the stricture was a political declaration of non-affiliation. Conformity to the Petrine tonsure would have been difficult to deny, particularly if it became a condition of holding an office. After all, before Theodore of Tarsus took up the archbishopric he had to wait four months for his Eastern style tonsure to grow out in order to adopt the prescribed Petrine one.[22] Necthon appears to have been fully cognisant of the political and ecclesiastical ramifications in instituting the Petrine tonsure. This was a period in which hair styling indicated political affiliation or ethnic identity and a change in tonsure style may be seen as a distinct declaration of new political membership.[23] In effect, the tonsure distinguished a cleric from the lay community; separating him from secular society and binding him into a greater spiritual community and authority.[24] By effectively politicizing the style of clerical tonsure, Necthon made it simple for lay communities to know the liturgical affiliations of their local clerics and the spiritual implications of being led by a 'non-conforming' priest.

Another example of the visible adoption of orthodoxy was Necthon's desire for architects to build a church in the Roman manner, which was to be dedicated to St Peter.[25] A notable precedent for this new form of architecture was the church at Wearmouth. In 674, Benedict Biscop had imported stonemasons from France to build Wearmouth in the Roman style and Biscop dedicated it to St Peter.[26] According to his *Vita*, Wilfrid's first new foundation at Ripon was dedicated to St Peter, and like Moses' earthly tabernacle it was consecrated to God. The kings attending this ceremony are described in the *Vita* as 'like Solomon the wise' for their confirmation of this dedication and their promise of further lands.[27] The erection of a stone church was a distinct departure from the usual, Irish-influenced, ecclesiastical architecture constructed in wood.[28] Necthon made a clear statement of reform by building a stone church, marginalizing the old Insular tradition to appropriate the 'superior' construction of Rome.[29] Building in stone required a considerable economic investment, but the

20 A. Ferreiro, *Simon Magus in patristic, medieval and early modern traditions* (2005), pp 212–19. **21** *AT* 718.6. **22** *HE* IV.1. **23** E. James, 'Bede and the tonsure question' (1984), p. 93. **24** Ibid., pp 93–4. **25** *HE* V.21, pp 532–3. **26** Bede: *Lives of the abbots of Wearmouth and Jarrow*, ch. 5, p. 191. **27** *VW* XVII. **28** Henderson, *The Picts*, p. 77; *HE* III.25; A. Hamlin, 'The archaeology of the Irish Church in the eighth century' (1985), p. 283. **29** I. Smith, 'The archaeology of the early Christian church in Scotland', p. 32; Foster, *Picts, Gaels and Scots*, p. 90. Skene, *Celtic Scotland*, 2, p. 233.

ideological implications made the endeavour worthwhile. Bede makes it clear that a church in stone imitated the 'Roman fashion', and allowed Necthon to exhibit his architectural participation in communion with Rome. The reuse of ancient Roman buildings to build stone churches has been observed in early English sites, such as Canterbury, and legionary forts north of the Antonine Wall may have been similarly salvaged for church construction. The presence of megaliths and symbol stones within the landscape had accrued permanence and legitimacy that would have been logically transferred to a religious building of stone.[30]

Necthon, like Solomon building the temple promised to and by God, incorporated a new technology in support of a new religious direction. This new architectural style imposed a new order and form on the physical as well as social landscape and symbolically endowed Necthon, as the patron, with transformative authority.[31] The transformative analogy also occurs in the late Life of St Boniface when Necthon is baptized by the saint and donates the land of his baptism for the first of many churches; a new baptism accompanied by a new consecration indicating complete change rather than a simple renewal.[32] Necthon's promise to dedicate the stone church to St Peter may have copied Benedict Biscop but, more importantly, it reflected the founding church in Rome. The ideology is unambiguous in that Peter was the rock upon which Jesus proclaimed that his church was to be built and, as first apostle of Rome, he was head of the church. A stone church dedicated to St Peter has an inherent congruity that is supported by patristic literature that viewed the members of the church as living stones.[33] Necthon was directing his orthodoxy not to Northumbria but to Rome, so that churches within Pictland were not subject to primatial overlordship from Canterbury, York or to Irish clerical *federati*. Answering to the remote authority of Rome and St Peter was advantageous to the Picts in securing ecclesiastical and political autonomy and equal status with their neighbours. Most scholars are convinced that Necthon's request to Ceolfrid for a stone church was realized, but J.H.S. Burleigh suggested that in addition to a stone and mortar structure it symbolized the introduction of a form of organized episcopacy.[34] Like Oswiu at Whitby, Necthon could also take credit for reforming and consolidating Christian practice to win Rome's approval and a place in heaven. In closing, Bede states that the reformed Pictish nation placed itself directly under St Peter's protection.[35]

Necthon's ecclesiastical reforms introduced other changes in ritual practice in line with orthodox Easter observance and regular commemoration. These religious changes may have been similar to those claimed for Wilfrid who, Bede

30 Bradley, 'Time regained', pp 1–17. 31 Helms, *Craft and the kingly ideal*, p. 78. 32 MacDonald, *Curadán, Boniface and the early church of Rosemarkie*, p. 16. 33 B.V. Repsher, *The rite of church dedication* (1998), pp 28, 33. 34 Burleigh, *A church history of Scotland*, p. 31; Anderson, *Kings and kingship*, p. 176. 35 *HE* V.21, pp 552–3.

asserts, introduced the Catholic way of life to the Anglo-Saxons through reforms to the monastic rule, liturgical music and associated rituals.[36] All reforms were intended to align churches in Pictland into direct communion with Rome and by doing so ensure a closer degree of conformity among clergy in Pictland. Reforms such as the adoption of orthodox liturgical music gave a potent assurance of vocal and spiritual harmony with Rome.[37] More explicitly, councils held at Toledo during Isidore's tenure promoted the idea that liturgical conformity preserved the stability of a kingdom and united its provinces.[38] Adherence to synodical decrees made at regular convocations would have meant greater control over clerics, such as permission to travel or leave their institution. These restrictions concentrated the human resources available in monasteries and churches and established a stronger internal hierarchy within the churches where competition for promotion encouraged a degree of social mobility and political adherence. Royal protection and establishment of monasteries and their 'sacred zones' likewise enhanced the authority of the king.[39] With an appreciation for the potency of learning, Necthon would have benefited from the fact that a harmonious clergy in his kingdom and a close alliance with Wearmouth and Jarrow, Bangor and other institutions opened the way for extensive sharing of texts between clerics. Within this environment of concord, it is likely that new dioceses were established and existing bishops' territories of authority were extended and consolidated.[40]

There were real political outcomes for a king instituting church reform. Bede endows Necthon with the authority to order the convocation of clergy and nobles within his kingdom in order to discuss the reforms. Bolstered by the arguments supplied by Ceolfrid, the king exercised his authority with the appearance of collective agreement to institute corrections to church practice. The consolidation of churches following orthodox practices ensured the extension of the king's authority through his bishops. New Peter dedications arguably emerge in Orkney and elsewhere around this period, indicative of an active reforming move by the bishops who consecrated the churches to the head Apostle.[41] As advisors, diplomats, counsellors and confessors, bishops were effective civil actors who extended their influence over governance through their close associations with the king and his nobles. Moreover, their possession of extensive estates combined with their spiritual authority provided a platform from which to mediate the will of the king. Conversely, bishops could hold the king's moral credibility and legitimacy hostage.

36 *HE* IV.2. 37 E. Fletcher, *Benedict Biscop* (1981), p. 11. 38 Stocking, 'Martianus, Aventius and Isidore', pp 175, 178, n. 47. 39 M. de Jong, 'Monastic prisoners or opting out?' (2001), p. 293. 40 G. Donaldson, 'Scottish bishops' sees before the reign of David I' (1952–3), p. 108; Cowan, 'The post-Columban church', p. 255; I.B. Cowan, 'Early ecclesiastical foundations' (1975), p. 19. 41 Macquarrie, 'Early Christian religious houses in Scotland', p. 114; Foster, *Picts, Gaels and Scots*, pp 89, 91; Kirby, 'Bede and the Pictish Church', p. 18; J.M. MacKinlay, *Ancient church dedications in Scotland: scriptural dedications* (1910), pp 218–34.

EXPULSION OF THE FAMILIA COLUMBAE

Necthon's ecclesiastical reforms had a wider political outcome than just the adoption of the *pascha catholica* and the Petrine tonsure. Some reforms took longer to implement than the distribution of accurate Easter tables, which were allegedly issued immediately after Necthon's declaration of conformity. Orthodox paschal observance was a potent symbol of his nation's participation in Catholic unity and obedience to Rome. Iona's refusal to adopt the *pascha catholica*, attested to by Ceolfrid, resulted in the isolation of the *familiae Iae* and opened the way for legitimate criticism of their practices and authority.[42] Ceolfrid's is the only source to describe Adomnán's conversion to the nineteen-year paschal cycles. There is no evidence in Adomnán's own writing as to how he viewed the paschal disputes. Although sceptical of Adomnán's conversion, Clancy and Márkus concede that Adomnán may have 'laid the groundwork' for Iona's later reform'.[43] Adomnán's concession to the *pascha catholica*, as described by Ceolfrid and Bede, occurred during his diplomatic mission to Northumbria in 687 and allegedly resulted in a conversion mission to Ireland.[44] While Bede claims that Adomnán's intervention in the debate won over large numbers of churches in Ireland to orthodox observance, churches within the south of Ireland and many in the north had already adopted orthodox Easter tables.[45] Adomnán's evangelical mission, should it have occurred, was unsuccessful as Iona held onto their old *computus* until 716.[46]

The date of Iona's final acceptance of the *pascha catholica* in 716 was the first year since 712 that the disputed paschal tables produced a divergent date. It was, therefore the first time Iona's reform could be observed and Bede suggests a *consessus* on the topic occurred earlier that year due to the persuasions of Bishop Ecgberht.[47] Nevertheless, after abstaining from reform for so long it is curious that Iona finally accepted the *pascha catholica* after the Picts had adopted the cycles. There have been numerous suggestions by historians as to why this was the case. Burleigh suggested that Iona was influenced by King Necthon to pursue reform, whereas Kirby speculated that Iona wanted to forestall Necthon's expulsion of their brethren in the following year.[48] Another suggestion favoured by Duncan centres on the exogenous influence of Bishop Ecgberht in first reforming Pictland then advancing to Iona, flushed with success and armed with Necthon's authority, to demand Iona's reform.[49] According to Fraser, Ecgberht was just one of a number of faithful bishops called to Iona in 715 to attend a *consessus* on the paschal question with, he suggests, a concurrent

42 *HE* V.15. 43 Clancy and Márkus, *Iona: the earliest poetry of a Celtic monastery*, p. 15. 44 *AU* 687.5; *HE* V.15. 45 Hughes, *Early Christian Ireland: introduction to the sources*, p. 76; D. Ó Cróinín, *Early medieval Ireland* (1995), p. 152; Herbert, *Iona, Kells and Derry*, p. 49. 46 *AU* 716.4. 47 *HE* V.22. 48 Burleigh, *A church history of Scotland*, p. 31; Kirby, 'Bede and the Pictish Church', p. 19. 49 Duncan, 'Bede, Iona and the Picts', p. 35.

meeting held by Necthon from which both parties agreed the reform.[50] However, while members of the *familiae Iae* appear to have held debates about paschal dating their internal hierarchy was inchoate due to the quick succession of abbots and bishops of limited longevity.[51] The obituary notices of Iona senior clerics also indicate that some administrative powers were devolved onto bishops away from the headship of the abbot of Iona; possibly resulting in Adomnán's reputed inability to reform his own monastery.[52] This was also a period of political instability for the monastery, with an ascendant Cenél Loairn quashing their favoured Dál Riatan dynasty, the Cenél nGabrain.[53] At the same time, the interests of the wider *familia Columbae* were directed towards Ireland after the killing of an Uí Néill king in 715.[54] Albeit of the Southern Uí Néill, this death represents just one of numerous battles that were rewriting the political map in Ireland.[55] Obviously of more critical immediacy, the chronicle record of Iona's reform to the *pascha catholica* was upstaged by the killing of King Osred of Northumbria, son of the Irish educated King Aldfrid.[56] Iona's favoured position, having been reliant on siding with dominant dynasties and the charismatic leadership of Adomnán had waned. In addition, Necthon's reforms do appear to have materially affected Iona's presence in Pictland and offered a direct challenge to their own ecclesiastical observances.

The historiography has generally emphasized the singular transcendence of the *familia Columbae* in Pictland and a direct causal relationship between Iona's acceptance of the *pascha catholica* and their expulsion by Necthon in the following year has been difficult to reconcile.[57] The presence of commemorations to Columba and the continued veneration of this saint into the modern era in Scotland is understood to indicate that Necthon's reforms and expulsion of Columban clerics were of limited effect.[58] As Barrow and more recently Clancy have usefully pointed out, however, the ninth-century merger of the Scots and Picts revived Columban Irish ecclesiastical influence, which (re)introduced the widespread veneration of Columba.[59] The record of the expulsion is singular, with an authoritative Necthon expelling the *familiae Iae* across the *Dorsum Brittaniae*.[60] Instead of a mass clerical removal, however, this expulsion was

50 Fraser, 'Ministry mission and myth', p. 208; *HE* V.22. 51 Anderson, *Early sources of Scottish History*, p. 215, n. 214. 52 *HE* V.21. 53 *AU* 714.2. 54 *AU* 715.2. 55 See T.M. Charles-Edwards, *The chronicle of Ireland* (2006), 1, p. 188, n. 1. 56 *AU* 716.1. 57 Anderson, *Early sources of Scottish history*, p. 217, n. 213; Anderson, *Kings and kingship*, pp 11, 176; Anderson, 'Picts: the name and the people', p. 84; *Venerabilis Baedae: Historiam ecclesiasticam*, 2, p. 331; Skene, *Celtic Scotland*, 1, p. 284; Skene, *Chronicles of the Picts, chronicles of the Scots*, p. clviii. Subsequently, Kirby, 'Bede and the Pictish Church', p. 19; Smyth, *Warlords and holy men*, pp 75, 138–9; Sharpe, *Adomnán of Iona*, pp 76–7; Foster, *Picts, Gaels and Scots*, p. 89; Fraser, 'Ministry mission and myth', pp 213, 216; Veitch, 'The Columban Church in northern Britain', p. 642; Herbert, 'The legacy of Columba', p. 4; Márkus, 'Iona: monks, pastors and missionaries', p. 138. 58 Veitch, 'The Columban Church in northern Britain'. 59 Barrow, *Kingship and unity*, p. 71; Clancy, 'Deer and the early church in north-eastern Scotland', p. 364, n. 3. 60 *AU* 717.4.

limited to members of the Iona *familia* rather than the wider Columban clerical community.[61] Following on from a brief footnote by Duncan, Fraser insisted that that term *familia Iae* signifies that the expulsion only affected Iona clerics.[62] He suggested that the election of Fáelchú to the *kathedra* of Columba in 716 was an attempt to reassert their primacy in northern Britain, but their expulsion was of limited effect and caused little change to the Columban clergy operating within Pictland.[63] The chronicle record describing this transfer of the *kathedra* is unusual as the previous incumbent, Dúnchad, does not die until a year later so that it would appear the election was a political attempt to unite the *familia Columbae*.[64] Likewise, the *kathedra* implies a bishop's seat, but whether the *kathedra* of Columba is usually combined with the abbacy of Iona and headship over the *familia Columbae* or a more localized bishopric that encompassed foundations in Pictland is uncertain. An earlier holder of the *kathedra*, of *Iae* rather than of Columba, Bishop Coetti who was signatory to the *lex innocentum* possibly had a foundation at Logierait (*Locin Mo Chedd*) in Atholl.[65] Commemorations to this bishop are confined to Atholl, echoing an area of authority that may have been recent and short-lived.[66] Coetti died in 712 and was succeeded briefly by Dorbbéne and, possibly after a three-year lacunae, Fáelchú was next recognized in the *kathedra* of Columba.[67] The evidence suggests that after the death of Abbot Dúnchad in 717 Fáelchú added the abbatial office to his duties as bishop.[68] Taking into consideration that Iona underwent a period of swift successions in the offices of bishop and abbot, and internal disputes that saw the eventual adoption of the *pascha catholica*, it was not until 717 that Iona achieved stability and was able to reassess its position. Fraser has suggested that reforms in Pictland may have interfered with the 'episcopal succession' and rendered the oversight of Iona on Pictish affairs redundant.[69] Nevertheless, it would have been difficult to abandon the prestige of any daughter houses they may have established in Pictland and the *tributum* that accompanied them.[70] That Fáelchú initiated a tour of Columban houses in Pictland after attaining the abbacy, only for his emissaries to be ejected by Necthon, is also a possibility.[71]

Returning to the chronicle entry, however, the geographic element of the expulsion across the *Dorsum Brittaniae*, or Druim Alban, indicates a localized event. The province of Atholl stands along this topographic border. Should Logierait in Atholl indeed have been a major foundation of the bishop of Iona, then the chronicle entry may relate to the removal of Iona clerics from this

61 Skene, *Celtic Scotland*, 2, p. 61, n. 47. See *AU* 714.8, 719.9. 62 Duncan, 'Bede, Iona and the Picts', p. 35, n. 31. 63 Fraser, 'Ministry mission and myth', p. 214. 64 Charles-Edwards, *The chronicle of Ireland*, 1, p. 190, n. 6. 65 Taylor, 'Place-names and the early church', p. 102; Fraser, *From Caledonia to Pictland*, p. 257. 66 Taylor, 'Seventh-century Iona abbots in Scottish place-names', p. 42. 67 *AU* 712.1, 713.5, 716.5. 68 *AU* 724.1. 69 Fraser, *From Caledonia to Pictland*, p. 261. 70 Henderson, *The Picts*, p. 78; L.M. Bitel, *Isle of the saints* (1990), pp 127–8. 71 J. Grigg, 'Expulsion of the family Iona' (2005).

putative bishopric.[72] Bede, however, makes no mention of the expulsion. This is a curious omission given Bede's critical stance on Iona and it suggests that the event had a limited political outcome. Indeed, Veitch argued that it was merely a small group of Iona clerics who were expelled from Atholl which, he proposed, was Necthon's familial territory.[73] The suggestion that Atholl was the point of expulsion has the potential to explain some of the perplexing anomalies of this record; nevertheless, a very wide bow needs to be drawn. Should Atholl have remained an autonomous kingdom in the face of Pictish consolidation then the expulsion would be manifestly political. It may be recalled that Necthon took the future king of Atholl hostage in 713 by which he may have gained political oversight of the province. Indeed, an important hostage to limit competing claims from Atholl's leading dynasty would have been a political imperative. It is possible that the Gartnat filius Deile Roith who died in 716 was a king of Atholl.[74] If this were the case then Atholl's treaty with Necthon required a renegotiation or formal confirmation by the succeeding ruler of Atholl. Mediation between kings and nobles, and organizing the release of hostages, was a critical role for bishops and abbots and Adomnán had been particularly skilled in this area. A Columban presence at Logierait suggests that the *familia Columbae* were closely associated with the ruling dynasty of Atholl. It would be likely, in this scenario, that the newly installed Abbot Fáelchú of Iona sent a party on a diplomatic mission to Necthon in order to negotiate terms for the release of Tolarg. It is highly unlikely that Necthon gave up such valuable political capital particularly on the back of reforms that were marginalizing the influence of the *familia Columbae* in his kingdom. Exercising his full authority, as king and overlord of Atholl by right of his hostages, Necthon would have had no choice politically other than to refuse negotiation and expel the *familiae Iae* delegation.

Whatever the catalyst that caused Necthon to expel the clerics, it is testament to his authority that he was able to do so. The expulsion provides a stern warning to his people and neighbouring polities that the king had sufficient power to order an eviction from Atholl. Indeed, the interest of the annalists in Necthon's actions indicates that this king was being carefully observed and his actions had wider political consequences than internal liturgical reform. These reforms were, of course, of great interest to any Insular cleric, nevertheless an aetiological relationship between the expulsion of the *familiae Iae* and their late acceptance of the *pascha catholica* appears unlikely. Having won a small victory over the *familiae Iae*, Necthon applied his state-building strategies to an *ecclesiastica Pictorum*.

72 Fraser, *From Caledonia to Pictland*, p. 257. 73 Veitch, 'The Columban Church in northern Britain', p. 642. 74 *AU* 716.2.

ECCLESIASTICA PICTORUM

The chronicles are silent on Pictish matters until 724 when Necthon resigned his kingship to take up a clerical office. Likewise, Bede provides no further information on Necthon and the king's reforming ventures can only be adduced from problematic evidence such as hagiography, dedications and toponymics. Nevertheless, analysis of obscure or discrete clusters of saint commemorations can be of use in augmenting the slim documentary and archaeological evidence in order to build a fragmentary picture of a dynamic period in ecclesiastical growth.[75] From the seventh to the early eighth century there is an increase in chronicle references to clerics who were active within Pictland; and the excavation of the monastery at Portmahomack, likewise, suggests an organized and large-scale industrial development of the site after the mid-seventh century.[76] These are signs of a maturing ecclesiastical presence, fully integrated within the social system, extending its own networks and consolidating economic advantages. The considerable economic investment in Pictish ecclesiastical foundations during this period highlights their socio-political integration. This period of active growth in ecclesiastical establishments within Pictland coincided with a *floruit* in Irish clerical texts and Northumbrian illumination, seen in the Lindisfarne gospels. A growing sophistication in the internal church hierarchies encouraged the development of a complex network of internal and external relationships that were stimulated by the patronage of kings. The late hagiographical account of Bishop Curetán/Boniface associates him with Necthon who is thereby memorialized for his expansion of the Pictish church and organizational reform.

Necthon's bishops

The cleric most closely associated with Necthon in hagiographical records was Curetán, bishop and abbot of Rosemarkie and signatory to the *Cáin Adomnáin*.[77] His feast day is 16 March and there are a discrete range of commemorations to the saint along the north bank of Loch Ness and in Ross and Cromarty.[78] Scholarship accords this cleric with the near single-handed reform of Pictish churches to orthodoxy, bolstered by the influence of a 'romanizing' Adomnán.[79] The late *Vita* of Curetán's Romanized alter ego, St Boniface, credits Necthon with endowing the saint land in Restenneth for a church dedicated to St Peter

75 Clancy, 'Deer and the early church in north-eastern Scotland', p. 366. 76 Carver, *Portmahomack*, p. 64. 77 Ní Dhonnchadha, 'The guarantor list of the Cáin Adomnáin', p. 191. 78 *CPNS*, p. 315; MacDonald, *Curadán, Boniface and the early church of Rosemarkie*, pp 38–9. 79 Veitch, 'The Columban Church in northern Britain', pp 636–8; Skene, *Celtic Scotland*, 1, p. 278, 2, pp 229–31; Kirby, 'Bede and the Pictish Church', pp 17–18; Smyth, *Warlords and holy men*, p. 138; Fraser, 'Ministry mission and myth', pp 212–13, 215; Miller, 'The disputed historical horizon', p. 14.

(possibly *Egglespether*).[80] This *Vita* portrays the saint as a pope who renounced his office for the mission field. His baptism of Necthon at Restenneth, in the territory of Angus, acts as a claim of tenure to the region pointing to the king consolidating his control over this territory by the establishment of an ecclesiastical foundation. Dedications to Boniface in Scotland are rare and he appears to be more closely associated with introducing commemorations to St Peter, as at Restenneth.[81] Aidan MacDonald has suggested that the introduction and dissemination of the *cultus* of St Peter can be directly associated with Boniface/Curetán, and it is compelling that Rosemarkie is dedicated to both Boniface and St Peter.[82] The traditional association of Necthon with Rosemarkie and Boniface can be traced to one of Scotland's earliest historians. Indeed, Andrew of Wyntoun attributed Necthon with the founding of Rosemarkie in 716 – 'wyndyr Saynt Bonyface lyvand thare' – but he also states that it had been established in 600; suggesting that Necthon was rededicating the church, probably to St Peter, rather than founding a new one.[83] This fits typologically with Necthon's baptism by the putative ex-Pope Boniface, in the *Vita*, into full communion with Rome. The *Vita* describes Boniface arriving in Pictland with six other bishops and a large retinue of mostly secular churchmen. Skene took this tradition to represent the establishment of seven dioceses, created by Boniface and his attendant six bishops, in his postulated seven Pictish provinces.[84] Both Donaldson and Cowan similarly link Necthon's reforms to the emergence and formal establishment of territorial episcopal dioceses.[85] Comparison with Anglo-Saxon episcopal organization, however, suggests that some level of parochial organization was already established by the eighth century, with senior clerics claiming *tributum* for pastoral services within their territories.[86] With limited evidence for episcopal dioceses in Pictland there were, nevertheless, existing ecclesiastical establishments servicing their communities with pastoral services. These were the monks and ministers of the altar, referred to by Bede, who were ordered to adopt the Petrine tonsure and *pascha catholica*.[87] As more churches were established, particularly under Necthon, it would have become increasingly necessary to formalize their territorial responsibilities and limits.

One of Boniface's companions, St Serf (Servanus), has a similar legend to

80 *Breviarium Aberdonense*, ed. W. Blew and D. Laing (1854), Mar. 16; Skene, *Chronicles of the Picts, chronicles of the Scots*, pp 421–3; MacDonald, *Curadán, Boniface and the early church of Rosemarkie*. 81 MacKinlay, *Ancient church dedications in Scotland: scriptural dedications*, pp 220–2. 82 MacDonald, *Curadán, Boniface and the early church of Rosemarkie*, pp 18–19; Skene, *Celtic Scotland*, 2, p. 230. 83 Andrew of Wyntoun: *The Orygynale Cronykil of Scotland*, bk V, ch. XIII, p. 58; MacDonald, *Curadán, Boniface and the early church of Rosemarkie*, p. 41. 84 Skene, *Chronicles of the Picts, chronicles of the Scots*, pp clviii–clix. 85 Donaldson, 'Scottish bishops' sees', p. 108; Cowan, 'Early ecclesiastical foundations', p. 19. 86 S. Bassett, 'Church and diocese in the West Midlands' (1992); A. Thacker, 'Monks, preaching and pastoral care in early Anglo-Saxon England' (1992). 87 *HE* V.21, pp 552–3.

that of St Boniface, both having resigned from the papacy to pursue life as missionaries.[88] According to his hagiographer, St Serf appeared in southern Pictland in the time of Bredei filius Dereli and Adomnán. This has suggested to some scholars that Serf's *Vita* provides evidence for the adoption of Roman orthodox reforms during the time of Bredei, under the guidance of Adomnán.[89] These saints' alleged prior incumbencies in the papal office are a significant *topos* that legitimized the adoption of Roman orthodoxy to recognizably historical kings. Moreover, St Serf also appears as a companion to St Boniface in the later life, emphasizing his subordination in Boniface's great mission.[90] While Adomnán was reputedly the agent for Serf's first foundation, the *Vita* stipulates that the abbot also gave up all future claims to another property, at Lochleven, Kinross-shire, when he is alleged to have formally donated it to Serf.[91] This latter foundation may be later than Necthon's reign, but the *Vita* appears to both legitimize Serf's parochial possessions and remove all prior Columban proprietorship.

The *Vitae*, while late, may suggest a cultural memory of the sons of Derelei being engaged in the endowment and creation of churches, particularly in the south outside of their traditional northern political centre. Alexander Grant suggested that there had also been a mission to Orkney following Necthon's reforms, instigated by Bishop Curetán who, he asserted, held episcopal authority over northern Pictland.[92] Jocelyn Rendell's contention that the church of St Boniface on Papa Westray, Orkney, was dedicated to the Anglo-Saxon missionary Boniface/Winfrid is unconvincing in light of the nearby Loch of St Tredwell who appears in the *Vita* as a companion of Boniface/Curetán.[93] There is no obituary notice for Curetán in the Irish annals, but it appears more likely that his successor was the agent assisting the dissemination of the St Peter *cultus* and indeed the Romanizing of Curetán: possibly Brec of Fortriu. The expansion of the St Peter *cultus* under Necthon was an effective message of consolidation under regnal authority. It is interesting to note that, half a century later, Offa of Mercia was granted a papal privilege to take all ecclesiastical communities dedicated to St Peter under his care.[94] Another historically attested bishop during Necthon's reign was *Fergustus Episcopus Scotiae Pictus*, who was present at a council in Rome in 721.[95] Commemorations to a St Fergus, who may be the

88 Skene, *Chronicles of the Picts, chronicles of the Scots*, pp 412–20; W.M. Metcalfe, *Pinkerton's Lives of the Scottish saints* (1889), pp 283–93; Macquarrie, 'Vita Sancti Servani'. 89 Kirby, 'Bede and the Pictish Church', p. 17; Miller, 'The disputed historical horizon of the Pictish king-lists', pp 14–15; Veitch, 'The Columban Church in northern Britain', pp 635–7. 90 MacDonald, *Curadán, Boniface and the early church of Rosemarkie*, p. 15. 91 Macquarrie, '*Vita Sancti Servani*', pp 140, 149. 92 Grant, 'The province of Ross and the kingdom of Alba', p. 95. 93 J. Rendell, 'St Boniface and the mission to the Northern Isles' (2002), pp 31–7; MacDonald, *Curadán, Boniface and the early church of Rosemarkie*, p. 18. 94 C. Cubitt, 'Universal and local saints in Anglo-Saxon England' (2002), p. 449. 95 *Councils and ecclesiastical documents*, ed. A.W. Haddan and W. Stubbs (1878), 2, p. 7; Clancy, 'Deer and the early

same Fergus who travelled to Rome, are primarily in the north-east of Scotland and at Wick and Halkirk in Caithness.[96] These commemorations, within Pictish territory, suggest that this bishop was held in importance by Picts as well as the *Scotiae*. Whether the latter were from Ireland or from Dál Riata is uncertain. Clancy suggested that the bishop could have been in Rome to gain a ruling on the correct tonsure.[97] Whatever Fergus' purpose in journeying to Rome, it indicates a clerical perspective that placed central importance on Rome and the papacy as ultimate authority. In Rome, Fergus was in an excellent position to attest to Necthon's Catholic orthodoxy and may have taken the king's petitions for relics or recognition to the papal court. Clancy also made an excellent case for a number of other bishops contemporary with Fergus, and Necthon's reign, having a similar north-eastern spread of dedications: Uoloch, Talorcan, Gartnait and Drostan.[98] While Drostan and Fergus are commemorated in the north-east, they both have commemorations at Halkirk, Caithness, as well as in the south in Angus and Fife.[99] The discrete spread of commemorations to these clerics into the north and south appears purposeful. It is possible that these commemorations reveal the direction of territorial activity by clerics of the saints' *familiae* out from their patrons' primary foundations. This may suggest that, from church foundations in the heartland of northern Pictish territories, new foundations were established in areas of interest to the expansionary Fortriu dynasts. The geographic direction of these commemorations may suggest the active approval, if not assistance, of the Pictish kings. The exception, the *cultus* of St Serf, appears to have come under the patronage of the Fortriu dynasty and was confined to the south. The expansion of these saints' cults into southern Pictland and into Orkney and Caithness may, therefore, have been politically motivated as part of Necthon's centralizing strategy.

Saints' cults and territorial expansion

Dynastic marriages, treaties, hostage and fosterage were all effective political tools to establish centralizing kingship. Indeed, it is likely that Necthon was related to most of the leading dynasties within his kingdom and to neighbouring rulers. The rulers of Atholl would certainly have had consanguine connections to the Fortriu dynasty and, as a consequence, may have had a potential claim to the Pictish kingship. These relationships, however, could promote competition as easily as accord, given the nature of early medieval kingship succession. In order to maintain suzerainty over the far reaches of his kingdom, Necthon's best choice, as Isidore had established, was to become the agent for religious unity.[1] The development of saints' cults, through the patronage of the king, was also a way to renew and consolidate church practices and gain a wider political

church in north-eastern Scotland', p. 379. **96** *CPNS*, pp 322–3. **97** Clancy, 'Deer and the early church in north-eastern Scotland', p. 381. **98** Ibid., pp 377–85. **99** Ibid., p. 375; Watson, *CPNS*, pp 317–18. **1** Stocking, 'Martianus, Aventius and Isidore'.

oversight. The postulated expansion of the St Peter *cultus* under Necthon was an effective message of consolidation under regnal authority. This was augmented by the increasing territorial activity of bishops and senior clerics in Pictland during Necthon's reign. Pictland was not alone in the expansion of saints' cults. As Schulenburg has shown, the late seventh to early eighth centuries mark a significant 'golden-age' in the creation of male and female saints' cults across north-western Europe.[2] Necthon's interest in ecclesiastical reform is documented and his long reign during a period of Insular ecclesiastical expansion makes it likely that Pictland likewise saw the proliferation of foundations and associated saints' cults. Moreover, it appears probable that Necthon deliberately employed saints' cults, and the *pascha catholica* reforms, as a means of expanding his oversight over southern Pictland and consolidating his authority over Caithness and Orkney. As Fouracre has observed, the veneration of a saint's cult transcends the preserve of any one ethnic group and was more importantly 'a principal element in the ... construction of a non-ethnic ... identity'.[3] The creation of a saint's cult in the early medieval period was often a result of local communal veneration, but Kemp also found that kings played a direct role in their establishment.[4] Necthon's nearby bishopric at Rosemarkie was likely to have had a role in promoting and extending the cult of St Peter throughout Pictland. Indeed, Rosemarkie appears to have been the centre for Necthon's Romanizing reforms. It also became a legendary repository for a number of saints, suggesting that it was attempting to bolster its primatial position. In the same period, Armagh strengthened its claims to superiority by housing the relics of St Patrick and a number of other saints as well as a linen cloth bearing the blood of Christ.[5] Rosemarkie may have competed for seniority with older southern Pictish foundations, such as Abernethy. The need for Rosemarkie to legitimize its venerableness may underlie the 'Romanizing' of Bishop Curetán, transforming him into St Boniface, and the accrual of traditions that associate the saints MoLuóc of Lismore and Maelrubha of Applecross with Rosemarkie.

Maelrubha was active during Necthon's reign, having established his primary foundation at Applecross, Ross and Cromarty, around 673 his death is recorded in 722.[6] Significantly earlier, MoLuóc founded a major ecclesiastical site on the island of Lismore within the Dál Riatan territory of the Cenél Loairn and his obituary notice is at 592.[7] The Martyrology of Oengus enters his feast day as 25 June, and describes him as 'pure, brilliant, the sun of Lismore of Alba'.[8] Late

2 Schulenburg, 'Female sanctity', p. 104. 3 P. Fouracre, 'The origins of the Carolingian attempt to regulate the cult of saints' (1999), p. 150. 4 E. Waldram Kemp, *Canonization and authority in the Western Church* (1948), pp 21, 32–5. 5 *The Patrician texts in the Book of Armagh*, 'E. Liber Angeli', §19, pp 186–9 [*quod in ea secreta consitutione exstat sacratissimus sanguis Iesu Christi redemptoris humani generis in sacro lintiamine simul cum sanctorum reliquiis in aeclessia australi, ubi requiescunt corpora sanctorum perigrinorum de longue cum Patricio transmarinorum caeterorumque iustorum!*]. 6 *AU* 722.1, 673.5. 7 *AU* 592.1; *AT* 591. 8 *Félire Óengusso:*

traditions, however, describe MoLuóc as a confederate and travelling companion of St Boniface and assign them both burials at Rosemarkie.[9] According to the Martyrology of Aberdeen, MoLuóc was full of the spirit of prophecy and his 'glorious relics' lay at Rosemarkie.[10] A fragmentary reference to the saint, as Lugaid, survives in Bernard of Clairvaux's Life of St Malachy of Armagh, where he is remembered as 'the founder ... of a hundred monasteries'.[11] Despite this encomium, it is highly unlikely that the saint personally established this number of ecclesiastic sites during his lifetime. Nevertheless, the surviving Scottish commemorations are numerous in the Hebrides, including a surviving chapel at Eoropie Ness on Lewis, and in north-eastern Scotland.[12] Taken together with the surviving spread of commemorative evidence, these late traditions suggest that this saint's *cultus* was deliberately imported into Pictland. Furthermore, the emphasis on MoLuóc's relics residing at Rosemarkie may suggest that the *cultus* began with the donation, or acquisition, of relics from Lismore. A chapel commemorating the saint at Ballaggan, Loch Ness, Inverness-shire, falls half way between Lismore and Rosemarkie along the direct route from Loch Linnhe, through the lochs Lochy and Ness, which may preserve a ritual progression of his relics from the saint's primary foundation.[13] The chapel at Kilmonivaig, Inverness-shire, preserves a commemoration to MoLuóc's successor, St Neamhan (d. 611), which indicates a prior interest by Lismore clerics in establishing their presence along this route.[14]

The importation of a MoLuóc *cultus* into north-eastern Pictland points to the appropriation of the saint's spiritual capital to reinforce Rosemarkie's primacy. Nevertheless, the date in which the MoLuóc *cultus* arrived in Scotland is a subject of debate. The lack of secure dating for early church dedications in Scotland is insurmountable. In the case of MoLuóc, the earliest textual evidence for a dedication in north-east Scotland is an 1165 to 1171 charter in which the earl of Mar granted the church of Moluag in Tarland to the priory of St Andrews.[15] Similarly, the *cultus* may have emerged over a long period of veneration, or was renewed after an associated miracle. While any conclusions remain inferential, the distribution of St MoLuóc's north-eastern *cultus* has stimulated a number of theories. Isabel Henderson suggested a direct link with Curetán and the *familia* of MoLuóc, whereas MacDonald proposed a transplant of the cult by a sept of the Cenél Loairn moving into north-eastern Scotland during the Viking period.[16] Woolf, however, contends that the *cultus* of MoLuóc was

Martyrology of Oengus, p. 142. **9** P. Dransart, 'Saints, stones and shrines' (2003), p. 240. **10** *Brevarium Aberdonense*, Iunius fo. vii. **11** *St Bernard of Clairvaux's Life of St Malachy of Armagh*, ed. H.J. Lawlor (1920), §12 (7), p. 27. **12** *CPNS*, pp 292–3. **13** *CPNS*, p. 293; MacKinlay, *Ancient church dedications: non-scriptural dedications*, p. 161; NMRS: NN18SE 1. **14** MacKinlay, *Ancient church dedications: non-scriptural dedications*, p. 161. **15** I.B. Cowan, *The parishes of medieval Scotland* (1967), p. 195. **16** Henderson, *The art and function of Rosemarkie's Pictish monuments*; MacDonald, *Curadán, Boniface and the early church of Rosemarkie*, pp 45–6.

encouraged by King Máel Coluim mac Donnchada, and centred on the monastic centre of Mortlach, Banffshire, whose titular saint was MoLuóc.[17] According to later tradition, the monastery of Mortlach was the site of a battle between King Máel Coluim's forces and Norwegian Vikings. Facing near defeat, the king petitioned St MoLuóc for succour and his subsequent victory was attributed to the saint's intervention. As a result, the king raised Mortlach to a bishopric – paying for extensive refurbishment.[18] Subsequently, the see was translated to Aberdeen by 1139. Woolf, however, argued that the see at Mortlach may have replaced the see at Rosemarkie and encouraged the renewed veneration of St MoLuóc with the political aim of pacifying the Moray rulers, who had ancient claims to the Scottish kingship and links to the Cenél Loairn.[19] The Cenél Loairn appear to be pivotal to the appearance of a St MoLuóc's *cultus* in the north-east of Scotland, as the saint's primary foundation at Lismore was within their territory. The rise of this cenél under the leadership of Selbach, during Necthon's reign, may offer an earlier date for contact between the two polities that may have stimulated the diffusion of MoLuóc's *cultus* into Pictish territory. This may reconcile the saint's traditional association with Rosemarkie, St Boniface, and the geographic distribution of commemorations (fig. 3). Similarly, the distribution of the *cultus* corresponds to Necthon's strategy of territorial consolidation through ecclesiastical expansion.

MoLuóc was a contemporary of Columba and possibly had superior connections and ecclesiastical pedigree to Iona's founder, with his connections to Bangor.[20] It is of interest that St Maelrubha was also educated at Bangor and his foundation at Applecross was a dependency of Bangor.[21] This connection will be explored further. Returning to MoLuóc, traditions associate this saint with Rosemarkie and he is commemorated nearby at Strathpeffer, Ross and Cromarty, and at Ardclach (or Ferness), Nairn, and at sites in Banffshire and Aberdeenshire.[22] There are commemorations to the saint at Chapelpark, Inverness-shire, and Cromdale, Morayshire, on the banks of the River Spey, the latter in the vicinity of the putative site of the Battle of Nechtansmere. The saint is also commemorated at Mortlach and to the south-east, now linked by the A941, is the putative assembly site of Rhynie, whose church is dedicated to the saint in the form of St Luag.[23] Nearby, Clatt and Clova (now a single parish) and Kildrummy, in Aberdeenshire, are associated with the saint. A short distance to the south, among the Grampians (the Mounth), St MoLuóc is commemorated at Migvie and Tarland (Tarland and Migvie were united into a single parish), Aberdeenshire.[24] There is only one commemoration to the saint south of the

17 A. Woolf, 'The cult of Moluag' (2007), pp 299–334; Clancy, 'Deer and the early church in north-eastern Scotland', p. 388. 18 L. Shaw, *The history of the province of Moray* (1882), 1, pp 136–40. 19 Woolf, 'The cult of Moluag', pp 309–10. 20 Fraser, *From Caledonia to Pictland*, pp 105–6. 21 Charles-Edwards, *The chronicle of Ireland*, 1, p. 158, n. 6. 22 *CPNS*, p. 293; NMRS: NH94NE 3.00. 23 Dransart, 'Saints, stones and shrines', pp 236–8. 24 *CPNS*, pp

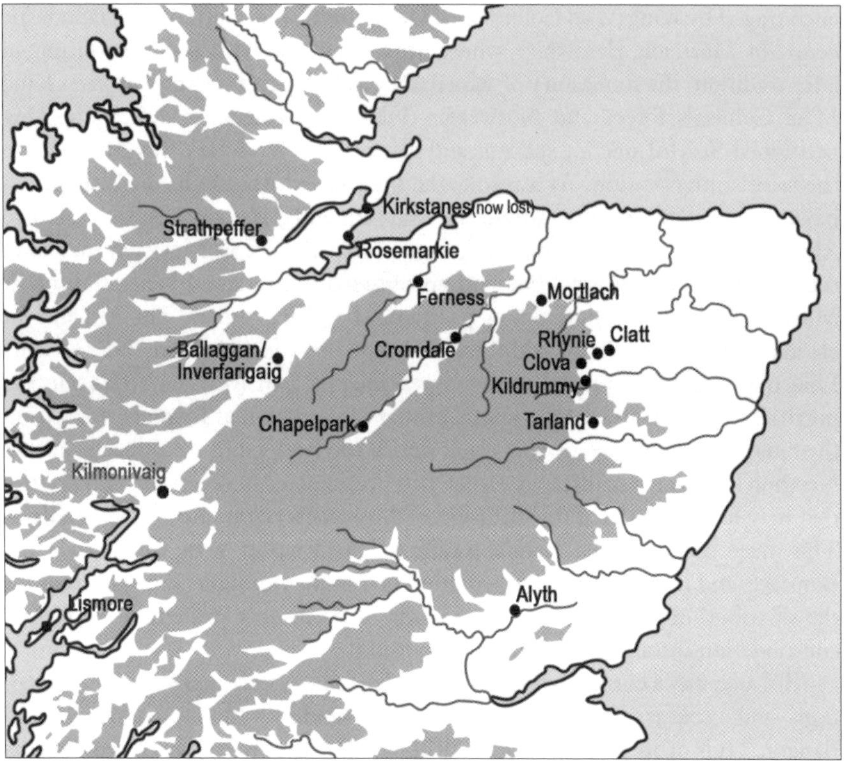

3 North-eastern distribution of St MoLuóc commemorations.

Mounth, in southern Pictish territory, and this is at Alyth in Perthshire. This southerly commemoration is some distance from the main spread of the *cultus*, and appears significant.

The tight north-eastern cluster of commemorations is intriguing, particularly as they fall within the vicinity of Rhynie, which witnessed a significant investment in Pictish symbol stones. Sculptural remains are a primary indicator of an early medieval presence. Other than at Rhynie, Class I Pictish symbol stones are also found at Mortlach, Clatt, Tarland and Strathpeffer. Class II cross-slabs are found at Rosemarkie, Mortlach and Alyth, and the simple hewn crosses at Clova appear to be early. Holy wells similarly point to potentially early sites and wells attributed to MoLuóc are found at Mortlach, Cromdale and Clova. Traditional fairs may also preserve an early titular saint with Tarland celebrating 'Lung's fair', 'St Molloch's fair' at Clatt, 'Molouach's' at Alyth and St MoLuag's fair at Milton of Balveny, Banffshire.[25] In addition, Barrow has suggested that there is

292–3. **25** Black, 'Scottish fairs and fair-names', pp 3–4, 42; *CPNS*, p. 293.

more than a coincidental pairing of St Bride and MoLuóc dedications in a number adjacent parishes or chapels reflecting early centres of worship.[26] As discussed, Rhynie may constitute an important assembly site in use during the reigns of the sons of Derelei. Moreover, the place-names of the Mains and Milton of Lesmore (Lesmoir) and Lesmore Castle at the foot of the Tap O'Noth, by Rhynie, calls to mind MoLuóc's primary foundation on the island of Lismore. The castle at Lesmore, dating from the thirteenth to seventeenth centuries, is situated at a strategic point on the Essie/Rhynie pass.[27] The place-name, however, preserves the early P-Celtic **lis–* element meaning court or important aristocratic and administrative residence (British **lis–* developed into Welsh *llys*, meaning court or hall).[28] This may suggest that this 'British' place-name, which is rare in the north-east of Scotland, referred to a significantly early prestige residence. Moreover, its similarity to MoLuóc's primary foundation at Lismore, coupled with a dedication to this saint in the nearby church of Rhynie, may suggest that this was the foci for the cluster of MoLuóc dedications in this area. Rhynie was a geographically strategic site on a 'major routeway through the hills north and south' as well as east and west.[29] The saint's feast day, 25 June, was a favourable date to convoke an annual assembly. There are a number of glens through the Grampians connecting the north-east through the Correen Hills to the south into Angus and Perthshire. In the eighteenth century a drove road began in Huntly, travelled south through Rhynie to Kildrummy and then a number of routes were available (including through Tarland) through Glen Clova or Glen Isla to Alyth.[30]

The commemorations appear to reflect a physical momentum from the north through the Grampians ending just within the southern territory at Alyth. The parish of Alyth is ideally positioned to provide access into south-eastern territories without crossing into Atholl. Indeed, a church at this site could have provided a diplomatic venue for negotiations between Atholl and the Fortriu kings. Immediately to the south, divided by the water of Isla, is the parish of Meigle, which has numerous early medieval crosses of beautiful workmanship, suggesting a wealthy and venerable foundation. The church at Meigle, Perthshire, is dedicated to St Peter and is possibly contemporary with King Necthon's commemorative initiatives.[31] According to later records, the forest (or moorland) of Alyth belonged by ancient right to the Scottish kings. An earlier, prestige presence is verified by the remains of a substantial ramparted fort on

26 G.W.S. Barrow, 'Badneoch and Strathspey' (1989), p. 6. 27 Simpson, 'Lesmoir Castle and the church of Essie'. 28 MacDonald, 'Caiseal, Cathair, Dùn, Lios and Ràth in Scotland', p. 51; S. Taylor, 'Place-names of Lesmahagow' (2009), p. 72. 29 RCAHMS, *In the shadow of Bennachie*, pp 119–21. 30 A.R.B. Haldane, *The drove roads of Scotland* (1968), pp 115–32. 31 MacKinlay, *Ancient church dedications in Scotland: scriptural dedications*, p. 221; Allen and Anderson, *The early Christian monuments of Scotland*, 2, pp 296–305. Alyth and Meigle both belonged to the medieval diocese of Dunkeld: *NSA*, 10, 1110.

Barry Hill, which overlooks the parish where there was an annual fair held on St MoLuóc's day.[32] This most southerly dedication to MoLuóc could represent the first attempt by Necthon to consolidate his control over southern territory through the agency of religion. A foothold in Alyth opened access to other southern territories and an ecclesiastical endowment by the king would result in a regular visitation where he could exact tribute and possibly hunting privileges (these medieval rights were preserved by the crown until the fifteenth century).[33] The importation of the MoLuóc *cultus* may represent a commemorative experiment in territorial consolidation, which was repeated to a greater effect by the expansion of the *cultus* of St Peter, such as at Meigle.

The primary foundation of MoLuóc at Lismore was in the territory of the Cenél Loairn, who could have had some involvement with the diffusion of the saint's *cultus*. The Cenél Loairn became pre-eminent in Dál Riata coincident with Necthon's reign. The political career of their king, Selbach, bears a striking similarity to that of Necthon's – both kings retiring into religion only to be drawn back into politics by civil unrest. Significantly, there is no record of conflict between these two kings who held sway over the north of Britain for over twenty years. As the two major powers in the north, Necthon and Selbach would certainly have reached some form of agreement that limited any overt friction between the two kingdoms during their reigns. As an *entente cordiale*, Selbach may have offered relics of MoLuóc to Necthon. Should this be the case then Selbach's gift of relics was an ideal means to cement a personal, affectionate bond between the kings.[34] Usually the dynamics of gifting would have placed Necthon under obligation, but in the case of saints' relics the political implications may have been different. The gift could be considered one of cosmological brokerage – offering both leaders privileged participation in the supra-natural to endorse their actions. It remains unproven as to whether a translation of relics *per se* did occur. Evidence for the use of corporeal relics in early Insular churches is unhelpfully patchy. Irish saint's lives suggest that contact relics were more widely incorporated into petitionary practices than corporeal relics. Adomnán, for instance, records a ritual procession on Iona of St Columba's shirt to pray for rain.[35] It remains uncertain, however, whether his own relics, recorded as returning from Ireland in 730, were corporeal or contact relics.[36] Early Irish legal proceedings could incorporate the use of relics, possibly contact relics, to validate contracts.[37] Although, it may also be considered that these oaths could be sworn over the saint's cist which housed his remains and was likely to be a place of veneration. The corporeal relics of a church's founding saint did provide it with irrefutable sanctity, as St Patrick's remains asserted the prece-

32 *OSA*, 6, pp 397–406; *NSA*, 10, pp 1110–28; NMRS: NO25SE 23.00, Barry Hill. 33 RCAHMS, *North-east Perth: an archaeological landscape* (1990), p. 6. 34 Geary, *Living with the dead in the Middle Ages*, p. 210. 35 *VC* II.44. 36 *AU* 730.3. 37 Stacey, *Dark speech*, p. 47; Kelly, *Early Irish law*, pp 198–9.

dence of the church of Armagh. Later church consecration rites often required a relic of the titular saint, although there is no evidence of when this became regulated for Insular churches. Anglo-Saxon evidence is also problematic. Bede relates a story of St Oswald's cult being implanted in Sussex with no translation of relics, but a vision of intercession.[38] Nevertheless, Benedict Biscop, founder of Wearmouth, returned from one of his trips to Rome with 'an abundant supply of relics of the blessed apostles and Christian martyrs that were such a boon for many churches in the land'.[39] This may suggest that these relics were used for the consecration of new churches or granting liturgical rights, such as baptism, to a church. Miracles could also be expected with attendant revenue from those seeking a more material focus for their veneration. In the late sixth century there were papal directives against the partial or full removal of holy bones, but these directives appear to have been largely ignored. Certainly, Bede records the partial removal of the bones of Aidan from Lindisfarne.[40] Whether St MoLuóc's corporeal or contact relics were translated to Rosemarkie, the geographic spread of the *cultus* is suggestive of a formal translation.

The late tradition of MoLuóc's association with St Boniface and Rosemarkie could suggest that his *cultus* was established in Pictland during the period of ecclesiastical reforms that were instigated during Necthon's reign. Should Necthon have wished to make a distinct break with the traditions of Columba, this saint offered a favourable pedigree. Indeed, he was reputed in later hagiography to have studied under Columba's colleague, St Comgall of Bangor.[41] Comgall's *familia* included the preeminent missionary Columbanus, and Bangor may have been at the forefront of paschal reforms well before Necthon contemplated his own conversion to the *pascha catholica*.[42] Veneration of MoLuóc would have strengthened clerical ties with Bangor, encouraging alliances, trade and the sharing of scholarship. It is possible that dedications to MoLuóc displaced foundations previously associated with the *familia* of Columba. As Fouracre had observed, 'control over cults was achieved by leading patronage away from saints associated with their opponents'.[43] It could be significant that St Comgall of Bangor was of the Dál nAraidi, the Irish Cruthin (Picts), and MoLuóc was reputedly from the same kin.[44] Similarly, the founder of Applecross, Maelrubha (d. 722), was closely associated with Bangor and traditionally was said to have passed away after (or on) a visit to Rosemarkie; he is commemorated at Urquhart on the Black Isle.[45] Maelrubha does not appear to have had any affiliation with the *familia Columbae* and there are a number of

38 *HE* IV.14. 39 Bede: *Lives of the abbots of Wearmouth and Jarrow*, ch. 6, p. 192. 40 *HE* III.26; A. Thacker, 'Membra disjecta' (1995), pp 108–9. 41 *St Bernard of Clairvaux's Life of St Malachy of Armagh*, §12 (7), p. 28. 42 D. Ó Cróinín, 'Mo-Sinnu Moccu Min and the computus of Bangor' (1982), pp 294–5. 43 Fouracre, 'The origins of the Carolingian attempt to regulate the cult of Saints', p. 150. 44 *St Bernard of Clairvaux's Life of St Malachy*, p. 28, n. 3. 45 W. Reeves, 'Saint Maelrubha: his history and churches' (1857–60), p. 290.

theories as to how he found his way to Applecross. Smyth argued that Maelrubha was reviving the defunct mission of St Donan of Eigg, while Macquarrie has suggested that the family of Gartnait (recorded as returning to Skye in 670 after exile in Ireland) requested a bishop from Bangor and received Maelrubha.[46] Drawing these threads together, Fraser questioned whether the spread of commemorations to MoLuóc and Maelrubha is indicative of an alliance between Fortriu, the Cenél Loairn and the family of Gartnait of Skye.[47] Early connections between Maelrubha of Applecross and Rosemarkie are likely given the geographic proximity. Furthermore, the presence of Pictish symbol stones in Skye and Raasay, combined with the MoLuóc commemorations, places the family of Gartnait within a Pictish cultural continuum.[48] This suggests that Maelrubha was familiar with Necthon in a diplomatic capacity if not more closely affiliated with the king's ecclesiastical reforms as a cleric trained at Bangor.

The primacy of Rosemarkie was fortified by the 'Romanization' of its Bishop Curetán and it was given further embellishment with a tale of St MoLuóc's visit and approbation. Royal initiative may be behind the spread of commemorations to MoLuóc. Similarly, commemorations to saints contemporary with Necthon's reign, such as Drostan and Fergus, appear to spread from a north-eastern base into southern territories as well as into Caithness and Orkney, possibly under royal approval if not direction. Overall, however, the *cultus* of St Peter was the most widely effective in drawing together the geo-political extremes of northern and southern Pictland. The choice of St Peter was ideal; he was a supra-regional, non-partisan saint who held ultimate authority over the church and reminded the faithful of their participation in the wider Catholic world. Likewise, Rosemarkie's range of saints, under the supreme headship of St Peter, offered stiff competition to any foundation that may have claimed an earlier consecration. Rather than importing saints to dilute any 'native' church, or to encourage exogenous expansionism, Necthon's main aim was the unification of church practices. Importing a well-recognized spiritual saintly authority, such as MoLuóc or Peter, was more effective than raising a local one: particularly as it endorsed the primacy of Necthon's favoured bishopric and fostered diplomatic ties. By the eighth century many of the clerics operating in Pictland had received some degree of Irish scholastic training, but this did not make them part of a Gaelic expansion.[49] Instead, the political links and relationships that were developed by high-ranking churchmen from Irish, British, Anglo-Saxon and Pictish foundations transcended geo-political boundaries and these connections made them highly useful to the Fortriu dynasts

Rosemarkie's bishop, as a chief agent of the king, could ensure widespread obedience among the clergy through regular synods that endorsed the king's

46 *AU* 670.4; Smyth, *Warlords and holy men*, pp 107–11; A. Macquarrie, *The saints of Scotland* (1997), pp 167–71.

political agenda. This would establish the political *status quo* that was disseminated at regular political assemblies, such as at Rhynie. The increase in ecclesiastical foundations encouraged a concomitant parochial expansion over communities within their territories. Necthon did not have to rely solely on his regional rulers' approval as his senior clerics extended their interests across the territories and exercised their spiritual authority over the people. By using the spiritual authority of his bishops and senior clergy, Necthon's own authority was effectively consolidated. The spread of new foundations under the auspices of the king increased his territorial authority. In visiting these foundations and endowing them with gifts, Necthon made a claim over the territories through his physical presence and that of his court. The itinerary of the royal circuit was arranged to manifest the king's presence at new ecclesiastical foundations within territories that needed a reminder of the king's dominance.[50] These foundations were a strategic means by which the king could ensure the territorialization of his authority. Under Necthon, Pictland was united by orthodox religious practice in direct communion with Rome, an expanding orthodox church, and a clear political identity promoted by national assemblies. In concert with his bishops and senior clerics, Necthon used ecclesiastical dedications and foundations to impose his presence over the Pictish territories. This was a versatile political strategy, which may have been married with a religious conviction that prompted Necthon's eventual retirement into *clericatus*. This retirement was not a sign of a weak king but was representative of his identification with the correct behaviour of a Christian ruler. Unfortunately, his retirement appears to have instigated a period of internecine strife.

CLERICATUS

Ceolfrid's final benediction to Necthon was that 'the grace of the eternal king keep you in safety to reign for many years and so bring peace to us all'.[51] The silence of the chronicles from 717 until 724 on matters relating to the Picts suggests that Necthon did indeed have peaceful relations with his neighbours. This peaceful period undoubtedly allowed Necthon to expand his oversight over the southern and northern reaches of his kingdom by the increase in ecclesiastical establishments and continuance of treaties. The epitome of a 'just king', in 724 Necthon entered the clerical office and, after engineering peace and

47 Fraser, *From Caledonia to Pictland*, p. 252. 48 *CPNS*, p. 292. MoLuóc commemorations are found at NMRS: Skye NO47SW 2; Raasay NG53NW 1 (the chapel was a dependency of Lismore); as well as Lewis at Europie NB56NW 3 and Harris at Pappay NF88NE 2. 49 See Clancy, 'Deer and the early church in north-eastern Scotland', p. 392. 50 Bernhardt, *Itinerant kingship*, pp 50–1. 51 *HE* V.21. 52 *AT* 724.2 [*Clericatus Neactain reigis Pictorum. Drust postea regnat*]. Pseudo-Cyprian: *De duodecim*, ix rex iniquus, line 10, p. 53 [*sibimet ipsi spes futurae beatitudinis*].

abundance, he sought 'for himself hope in future blessedness'.[52] There have been differing views on Necthon's retirement into religious life. Some have argued that it was due to a genuine Christian devotion,[53] whereas others have asserted that he was merely a pawn to political pressure, with his chosen successor, Drest, forcing the old king into involuntary retirement.[54] Combining the twin views of Necthon's religious zeal and political pressure, Alfred Smyth saw Necthon forced to abdicate after 'hovering uncertainly between kingship and monastic retirement'.[55]

The arguments espousing Necthon's forced retirement appear to be based on Continental examples of kings removed from office and subsequently cloistered. This was the situation for the Visigothic king Wamba who was forcibly tonsured, and there are similar Merovingian cases that illustrate the tonsuring of kings as an effective means to ban them from maintaining office.[56] According to Clare Stancliffe, this is not representative of the political ramifications for Insular kings entering *clericatus*. Rather, it appears that many of the examples of Insular kings 'opting out' are indicative of a penitential desire in the individual king, answering an entrenched Christian demand for personal redemption.[57] It is notable that taking clerical vows did not prevent the king from regaining his position, as is apparent from Necthon's political involvement in the destiny of his kingdom four years after his retirement.[58] For this reason, Yorke has suggested that it was politically astute for kings to retreat to a monastery in times of crisis and that temporary retirement may have been under penitential conditions.[59] With the usual competition between factions it appears unlikely that a king went into voluntary retirement and expected to reclaim their position after serving penance or sitting out a political crisis. It is also doubtful whether *clericatus* can be interpreted as taking monastic vows or ordination, as the 'clerical office' provides only an ambiguous outline of the type of religious commitment that Necthon may have taken.[60] Despite his veneration of St Peter, Necthon did not undergo a pilgrimage to Rome; which may indicate that the king was not quite willing to abandon all interest in the welfare of his kingdom or, indeed, the world. Nevertheless, the records do suggest that Necthon considered his retirement as permanent, for his successor is named in the same entry.

Necthon's eventual retirement came after an eighteen-year rule and it was only after his retirement that, what appears to be internecine, conflict occurred.

53 Most recently, see Clancy, 'Philosopher-king', pp 126, 143, 145; Anderson, *Early sources of Scottish history*, p. 221, n. 224; Duncan, 'Bede, Iona and the Picts', pp 35–6, n. 31; Skene, *Celtic Scotland*, 2, p. 233. **54** *Venerabilis Baedae: Historiam ecclesiasticam*, 2, p. 331; Fraser, 'Ministry mission and myth', p. 216 (revised in: *From Caledonia to Pictland*, p. 286); Kirby, 'Bede and the Pictish Church', p. 8; Veitch, 'The Columban Church in northern Britain', p. 645, n. 610; Anderson, *Kings and kingship*, p. 177. **55** Smyth, *Warlords and holy men*, pp 73, 75. **56** James, 'Bede and the tonsure question', pp 89–93. **57** C. Stancliffe, 'Kings who opted out' (1983), p. 176. **58** Ibid., p. 163; *AT* 728.5. **59** Yorke, *The conversion of Britain*, pp 165–6. **60** Cf. *HE* III.18; Dumville, 'On editing and translating medieval Irish chronicles', pp 74–5.

The sites of these conflicts have only been tentatively identified, but they nevertheless suggest that the battles were concentrated within a tight geographic area and were between apparently related claimants. The records do not indicate that the battles devastated large armies or descended into general civil conflict, which suggests that there was minimal disruption to administrative and social structures. It is of interest that Selbach of the Cenél Loairn also enters *clericatus*, one year earlier than Necthon, in 723 but by 727 is fighting against a competing faction to regain the kingship for his son.[61] Similarly, in 728 Necthon is actively participating in a contest for the kingship of the Picts. In both these cases, Selbach and Necthon retire from rule after a significant period in office and appear to have chosen their successors. The king of Brega, Fínsnechta of the Uí Néill, provides an earlier example of this temporary retirement. Having entered *clericatus* in 688, just one year later he is reinstated in the kingship.[62] While Necthon's retirement into religion may argue a diffidence to rule, the king also appears to have been an astute politician who used religion as a vehicle for the consolidation of his authority. This does not discount Necthon's personal religious convictions, as he appears to have received a level of religious training. It is probable that he had access to the latest political ideas on governance, law and religious reform that were being discussed (and to some degree implemented) in the courts of Ireland, England and in western Europe. Like the Northumbrian king Aldfrid, Necthon could have shared a similar intellectual and theological training that exposed him to authors such as Augustine and Isidore, a range of patristic authors and the popular writings of Gregory the Great. The links drawn by Gregory between temporal and ecclesiastical rulership, and the burden of temporal concerns, may have stimulated a Christian ruler to consider retirement into religious devotion.[63] Rather than being a weak king who was forced into early abdication, Necthon appears to have been a man ready to relinquish the reins of power in order to devote his remaining years to the serious preparation of his soul for the afterlife. Arguably, Necthon's retirement placed the king in a positive position to select his successor, one who would ensure the continuity of the Fortriu dynasty and its political agenda. It was, therefore, unfortunate that Necthon's successor Drest was not universally accepted. Instead of a peaceful retirement, Necthon was forced back into secular politics to secure his nation's future from an apparently bitter rivalry and the division that ensued from a divisive succession system.

61 *AU* 723.4, 727.3. 62 *AU* 688.3, 689.2. 63 S. Gregorii Magni, *Registrum epistularum: Libri I–VII*, ed. D. Norberg, 140 (1982), liber 1, epist. V, p. 5.

INTERREGNAL CONTEST

Necthon's retirement had unfortunate ramifications. This is apparent only one year after his retreat with the records noting the binding of King Drest's son.[64] This was followed in the next year by the notification that Necthon was 'bound' by King Drest, suggesting a retaliation that resulted soon after in Drest removed from office and Elpín taking his place as king.[65] The records certainly suggest that Drest did not have a full consensus for his rule and, as Fraser suggests, he may have seized Necthon with the hope of providing his rule with increased legitimacy.[66] On the other hand, it has been suggested that the binding of Drest's son was the opening gambit for Necthon's supporters to place him back on the throne.[67] In general, arguments have revolved around a genealogical debate as to which protagonist had the closest legitimate claim. The binding of Drest's son was a severe blow to Drest's authority to rule, holding him in subjugation to whichever party held his son hostage. Drest responded by using Necthon as a hostage. This suggests that Necthon retained considerable political authority and, as Anderson asserted, retained the strongest constitutional right to rule.[68] Necthon's reputation was politically potent and Clancy suggested that Necthon was not a mere political pawn in the proceedings with his emergence from seclusion prompted by 'dismay at the way things had gone'.[69] Necthon had reigned for a considerable period – a period in which the Picts achieved and maintained peaceful relations with their neighbours. It is likely that with peace came prosperity. Necthon was therefore held in considerable esteem and retained a degree of support from his leading magnates who saw the dangers of civil unrest to their own prosperity.

The brevity of the chronicle records, which outline the contest between the rival claimants, allows for a range of speculations. The record of 726, which styles Elpín as king, suggests that there were rival contenders for the Pictish succession, with no clear constitutional arrangements to broker a peaceful settlement. The aim of any contender to the kingship was to ensure that he had control over all the provinces consolidated under the previous ruler. This would be a difficult task without the full consensus of the regional rulers. Moreover, the consanguine bonds created over generations of alliances resulted in a rival dynasty having an equally legitimate claim. It may be, as Fraser suggests, that Elpín was from the leading dynasty of Atholl, and cousin to Necthon.[70] The

64 *AU* 725.3 [*Simul filius Druis constringitur*]. 65 *AU* 726.1 [*Nectan m. Derile constringitur apud Druist regem*]; *AT* 726.4 [*Druist de reghno Pictorum iectus et Elphin pro eo regnat*]; Skene, *Celtic Scotland*, 1, pp 285–6. 66 Fraser, *From Caledonia to Pictland*, p. 289. 67 Anderson, *Early sources of Scottish history*, pp 221, n. 224, 226, n. 221; Anderson, *Kings and kingship*, p. 177; D.P. Kirby, '... Per Universus Pictorum Provincias' (1976), p. 302. 68 Anderson, *Kings and kingship*, pp 177, 183; Kirby, '... Per Universus Pictorum Provincias', p. 302. 69 Clancy, 'Philosopher-king', p. 143. 70 Fraser, *From Caledonia to Pictland*, p. 290.

Pictish king lists add the intriguing information that Drest and Elpín shared a joint rule over Pictland for five years.[71] If this were the case, then Elpín moved quickly to dissipate Drest's potential authority. It may be that Elpín ruled from Atholl, where he could exploit any disaffection for Drest's rule by the leaders of the Pictish provinces with the view to wresting the kingship from Drest. Atholl was certainly involved in the battles, and its connection with Iona may be why the chronicler waxed lachrymose over Elpín's defeat, describing it as a 'woeful battle'.[72] It is notable that Atholl appears to have retained their kings as other provinces in Pictland appear to have acceded to the overlordship of the dynasty of Fortriu. Nevertheless, they may have been legitimate rivals for the Pictish *regnum*. Drest appears to have been either unlucky or lacking the ingenuity required of a king. If allowing his son to become a hostage was unfortunate, responding with the imprisonment of Necthon was a disastrous tactical error. The conflict between these rivals was fierce, with four distinct affrays in two years, as can be seen from the following chronicle entries.

*AU*728 – The Battle of Monidhcrobh between the Picts themselves, in which Aengus was victor, and many were slain on the side of King Eilpín. A woeful battle was fought between the same parties near Caissel Créidi, where Eilpín was put to flight.[73]
*AU*729.2 – The Battle of Monid Carno near Loch Laegde between the hosts of Nectan and the army of Aengus, and Nectan's exactors fell, i.e. Biceot son of Monet, and his son, Finnguine son of Drostan, Feroth son of Finnguine, and many others; and the adherents of Aengus were triumphant.[74]
*AU*729.3 – The Battle of Druim Derg Blathug in the territory of the Picts between Aengus and Drust, king of the Picts, and Drust fell.[75]

These entries are surprisingly detailed and may have formed part of a longer report abbreviated by the chronicler. The records provide no similar descriptive references to interregnal battles for any other group in this period, despite obvious similarities in the career of Selbach of the Dál Riata. There are significant differences between the accounts of the annals of Tigernach and Ulster, which are difficult to account for. In particular, after Elpín's defeat in 728 the Annals of Tigernach add that Necthon regained the kingship.[76] The Annals of

71 Anderson, *Kings and kingship*, pp 248–9, 263. 72 *AT* 728.4. 73 *AU* 728.4 [*Bellum Mónidchroibh inter Pictores inuicem, ubi Oenghus uictor fuit et multi ex parte Eilpini regis perempti sunt. Bellum lacrimabile inter eosdem gestum est iuxta Castellum Credi, ubi Elpinus efugit*]. 74 *AU* 729.2 [*Bellum Monith Carno iuxta Stagnum Loogd et inter hostem Nectain et excercitum Oengusa et exactores Nectain ceciderunt; hoc est: Biceot m. Moneit et filius eius, Finguine m. Drostain, Feroth m. Finnguine et quidam multi et familia Oengussa triumphauit*]. 75 *AU* 729.3 [*Bellum Dromo Dergg Blathuug in regionibus Pictorum inter Oengus et Drust regem Pictorum et cecidit Drust*]. *AT* 729.3 includes the detail that Drest fell on 12 August. 76 *AT* 728.4 [*Cath truagh iter Pocardachaib ac Caislen Credhi, ⁊ ro memaidh ar in Ailphin cetna, ⁊ ro benadh a chricha ⁊ a daine de uile, ⁊ ro gab*

Clonmacnoise also include the information that a certain Eolbeck son of Moydan with the rest of the nobles turned their backs on Elpín and received Necthon as king once again.[77] This detail indicates a first-hand report. It also implies that the kingship was validated by martial success and the consensus of the nobles. What does appear to be clear from the records is that Onuist (Aengus) was the instigator of events on behalf of Necthon.[78]

Onuist, as Kirby pointed out, does not appear to have been a candidate for the kingship at this stage despite his later success.[79] Should Evans' thesis on the naming of Fortriu dynasts be correct, then his brothers Bridei and Talorcan were potential contenders for the kingship while Onuist lacked the appropriate consanguine link.[80] It is notable that the annals refer to Onuist as *regis Pictorum*, whereas his successor Bridei was described as *rex Fortrenn*.[81] Nevertheless, as Bredei filius Bili had proven, succession could be legitimated through force of arms. Onuist may not have been from the correct lineage to inherit the kingship, but he was close to the Fortriu dynasty. It is likely that he held a position similar to that of Ealdorman Beorhtfrith. A skilled campaigner, Onuist may have taken the battle to Elpín, possibly at the hill of Moncrieffe near Abernethy. This area was to be the focus of political activity in the later kingdom of Alba and was strategically and ideologically important to a consolidated Pictish kingdom. The hill may have been a major assembly site for southern Pictish polities and in use in this period. The proximity of the battle to Abernethy may also imply that this foundation supported the rival king, Elpín, perhaps hoping to gain episcopal primacy under their chosen king. The battle moved on to Castellum Credi, tentatively identified by Skene with Scone, where Onuist routed the remains of Elpín's supporters.[82]

In the next year, Onuist appears to take the battle directly to the borders of Atholl, as Stagnum Loogdae has been identified with Loch Lochy, to the west of the Perthshire border.[83] Earlier in the same year, the Annals of Tigernach notes the wrecking of 150 Pictish ships off Ross Cuissine, which has been identified with Troup Head on the Banffshire coast.[84] It is tempting to view this fleet as Necthon's 'navy' sent south to the Tay in order to quash any lingering opposition. Unfortunately, there is no information as to the direction of the fleet at the time they came to grief. The description of the battle at Monid Carno in 729, however, has excited a degree of speculation.[85] Woolf has recently refuted previous assumptions that this battle marked the end of Necthon's brief return to the kingship at the hands of his postulated rival Onuist. Instead, a closer reading of the chronicle entry suggested to Woolf that *hostem* (hostis) and

Nechtain mac Der Ili ríghi na Picardach]. 77 *AClon.* 725. 78 Anderson, *Kings and kingship*, pp 135, n. 146, 178. 79 Kirby, '... Per Universus Pictorum Provincias', pp 302–3, n. 349. 80 Evans, 'Royal succession and kingship', p. 25. 81 *AU* 761.4, 763.10. 82 Skene, *Chronicles of the Picts, chronicles of the Scots*, p. 280, n. 5. 83 *CPNS*, p. 50. 84 *AT* 729.2. *CPNS*, pp 63, 507. 85 Fraser, *From Caledonia to Pictland*, pp 288–91.

exactores should be read as 'enemy' and 'oppressors', significantly changing the sense of the entry.[86] Translating *exactores* in this way, rather than as 'tax gatherers', has brought into question a number of theories on Pictland having a bureaucratic centralized government manned by royal officials.[87] Woolf's argument sits far better with the evidence than the theory of a Pictish state run by royally appointed bureaucrats. The implication of this revision is that, instead of Onuist making his own push for kingship, Onuist and his army fought against Necthon's enemies. Moreover, the named fallen, oppressors of Necthon (Biceot son of Monet, and his son, Finnguine son of Drostan, Feroth son of Finnguine), appear to have been members of the Atholl dynasty.[88] Soon after, Onuist fought with and defeated Drest – who is styled king of the Picts in the Annals of Ulster, whereas Onuist is designated king in the Annals of Tigernach – at an unidentified site, which Skene suggests was in Angus near Kinblethmont.[89]

These battles are clearly a contest for the kingship of the Picts. The confusion of the entries, as to who retained the kingship, suggests the dissemination of multiple, confused reports. Only two main contenders were responsible for the violence, suggesting a small pool of legitimate claimants to the kingship. Furthermore, the action appears to have occurred in the south and west of the country (barring the alleged shipwrecks at Troup Head, Bannfshire), which may imply that the northern regions remained faithful to the Fortriu dynasts. Similarly, these battles do not represent civil war but targeted action. Woolf's reinterpretation of the first battle of 729 would suggest that Necthon retained the kingship until his death in 732.[90] This follows Clancy's earlier suggestion that Bede's silence on this issue could be interpreted as Necthon remaining the legitimate king.[91] Onuist is first designated the king of the Picts in 736 where he is given his full name and title: *Oengus m. Fergusso rex Pictorum*.[92] This record announced Onuist's attack on Dál Riata, which signalled a reign of militant expansionism that was only possible if he had a consolidated and unified kingdom from which to launch an offensive. Without the pro-state strategies of Necthon, Pictland could not have played such a major part in political affairs during Onuist's reign. Necthon's creation of an *ecclesiastica Pictorum* effectively welded his kingdom into a nation. While we can rule out a precocious administration of tax gatherers and royal agents, Necthon's authority was nevertheless centralized through his senior clerics and regional rulers. The succession system was his major weakness. After rewriting the conditions to promote a uniting myth in favour of matrilineal succession, the competition for the kingship would have increased. Likewise, having created a

86 Woolf, 'AU 729.2 and the last years of Nechtan mac Der-Ilei', p. 132. 87 Anderson, *Kings and kingship*, p. 178; Skene, *Celtic Scotland*, 1, p. 288, n. 220; Foster, *Picts, Gaels and Scots*, p. 34; Clancy, 'Philosopher-king', p. 136. 88 Clancy, 'Philosopher-king', pp 136–7. 89 Skene, *Celtic Scotland*, 1, p. 289. 90 *AT* 732.7. 91 Clancy, 'Philosopher-king', p. 146. 92 *AU* 736.1.

peaceful and increasingly wealthy cohesive nation, Necthon's kingship was a plump prize worthy of a fight.

CONCLUSION

Necthon's reign appears to represent the idealization of a Christian monarch. He instituted religious correction, endowed new foundations and oversaw the expansion of his bishops' authority by ensuring their independence from outside primatial claims. Furthermore, his actions received collective approval. A King Solomon for his people, Necthon's religious reforms were a proactive example of a king sharing in contemporary theological and political ideas on theocratic kingship and authority. Using liturgical correction as a means to control dissent and the political direction of his kingdom was an astute strategy. In allying himself with Roman orthodoxy, Necthon considered his kingdom as a significant entity within the Catholic world, unity in liturgy leading to political unity. Control over his territories was centralized through establishing ecclesiastical foundations, granting royal privileges and his royal presence at assembly. In this way, churches and their senior clerics became key partners in ensuring the supremacy of the Fortriu dynasty and a unified communal identity. St Peter dedications, alongside those of St Boniface, in Orkney point to the institution of reforms at the territorial limits of the Pictish nation. Necthon's visible reforms enhanced and increased his authority as a 'just' ruler duty-bound to correct his people and safeguard their spiritual and temporal wellbeing.

The exercise of Necthon's power remained patriarchal rather than bureaucratic and was therefore reliant on maintaining ideological legitimacy and support. This may not have been the basis of lasting governance or statehood as this structure relied on the individual character and political skill of the king. This, of course, was the situation among most of western European kingdoms. Nevertheless, the Fortriu dynasts exercised real and effective authority to unify a Pictish nation and nourish the institutional framework of centralizing governance. Inviolable while in office, Necthon's retirement opened the way for rival claimants ready to risk everything for the rewards of kingship. At the conclusion of his reign, Necthon left a powerful nation emerging into statehood, able to marshal armies to fight beyond the borders of Pictland and make alliances among Anglo-Saxon kings.

Conclusion

The aim of this study has been to reintegrate the Picts into the historical narrative of the early medieval west. Due to the elusive nature of the sources – including Adomnán's portrait of a barbarous people whose king was in the thrall of magicians – the Picts have been assigned a regressive role in terms of political development. Instead of sharing in the centralizing ambitions of their neighbours, scholarship has often regarded Pictish regnal authority as weak and diffused. This has particularly been the case with King Necthon. Despite a long reign for an early medieval king, Necthon has been viewed as clinging vainly to power, willing to dissipate his authority to the cultural and religious dictates of neighbouring polities. This reading appears influenced by modern expectations of coercive and aggressive displays of authority, taking limited account of early medieval notions on the operation of 'just' rule. In negotiating peace to demarcate his kingdom's borders, Necthon was defining and controlling his kingdom to stimulate stability and prosperity. Likewise, liturgical reform had extensive political consequences for the operation of his authority and the consolidation of Pictish identity and unity.

Authoritative Pictish kingship was, nevertheless, underpinned by economic, military and institutional factors. Indeed, the political roots of the Pictish kingdom can be detected in sixth-century economic transitions that impacted on existing hierarchical power. This is seen in the climatic amelioration that, alongside agricultural innovations, expanded the opportunities for surplus production and created new opportunities for trade. Expansion in external trade networks had a direct impact on the upward transfer of resources that thereby encouraged the accretion of wealth in the hands of fewer rulers. As a result, existing hierarchies were able to exploit both production and trade, leading to competition that rationalized their control over the productive landscape. The operation of clientage similarly transmitted social and political power upwards, culminating in a wider territorial purview for those achieving ascendancy. This is reflected in the settlement record, where high-status sites became less fortified and less numerous while dispersed upland farms, scattered across the landscape, proliferated. Similarly, existing territorial units regulated social customs that were communally negotiated and enforced, consolidating lordship. These territorial divisions, or units of lordship, were the bedrock of local administration over which control could be consolidated internally and externally. Rulers of these units of lordship promoted the regulation of property rights and the organized division of the landscape, leading to the commodification of production and land. Surplus production also encouraged social mobility with a concomitant effect on hierarchical control and status, and with it came the expansion of specialist trades under patronage. Status through land prerogatives, specialized skills and knowledge bestowed social authority and mobility.

The most influential institutional force in Pictland was Christianity. The corporate organization of Christianity encouraged emulation among Insular rulers. Christ as the king of kings made for an excellent temporal exemplar; an exemplar that could be realized through the institutional provisions of clientage. Clientage expanded the opportunities for rulers to consolidate their authority through personal, vertical relationships. These were reciprocal negotiations, both parties being accountable for their maintenance. Clientage offered the primary means for the exercise of social and political power. In addition, clientage stimulated external social networks of control, which had a direct impact on the consolidation of the office of kingship. Personal displays of status reflect a sophisticated response to these changing social dynamics. Adornments, such as the penannular brooch, made visible, political statements of affiliation and the wearer's relationship to authority. Moreover, the semiotics of status inherent in the brooches was legible to neighbouring polities suggesting an increasing degree of inter-kingdom mobility. Assemblies exploited this, albeit, restricted mobility. Central to political identity, the assembly was the arena of functioning governance where public authority promoted public order. Occurring at local, regional to national venues, assemblies offered the ideal means to enact public power in the form of law making, justice, contracts and political change. Local and regional assemblies bound communities together through public rituals that reinforced social obligations and concepts of belonging. As is still the case in the modern era, political assemblies were dynamic centres of government where political change could be enacted and communal rights negotiated. In addition, the operation of organized governance, through the assembly, promoted increased local and regional connections. This encouraged communal identification with neighbouring territories that expedited participation in the political construct of a kingdom. Communal participation, likewise, reinforced hierarchical status and control. Kings established and fortified their authority through their public performance at assemblies, and consolidated their visible rule over their people by a regular circuit of their kingdom.

While social fora, such as assemblies, assisted the coalescence of collective identity the evidence also points to the conscious appropriation of dominant political ideologies that had nation building objectives. The agents propelling the political transition in Pictland were the consecutive Pictish kings: Bredei filius Bili, Bredei filius Derelei and his brother Necthon filius Derelei. These kings initiated a change in the practice of kingship and the perception of collective identity. The fulcrum of this transition was the Battle of Nechtansmere. Indeed, the Pictish historical horizon begins with the actions of King Bredei filius Bili as he united Pictish provinces to remove Northumbrian suzerainty from southern Pictland. Alliances were coerced from many of the Pictish provinces, but this king ultimately unified the polities and removed Northumbrian dominance at the Battle of Nechtansmere. A causal outcome of Nechtansmere was the syncretism of regional polities, who identified with the mutual aims of the battle and their mutual adversary. The collective success helped to affirm their unanimity of identity under the militarily mighty King Bredei filius Bili. Pictish kingship prospered, particularly as succession became dynastic with a new symbolic designation as kings of Fortriu. By retaining the kingship within the dynasty, fiscal opportunities from sword land and coercive dominance could be transformed into long-term strategies that achieved political dominance over regional rulers through gift-giving, hostage, fosterage, marital alliances and culturally defined artistic display. This may be seen in the production of penannular brooches and the proliferation of Pictish symbol stones, which materially manifest the social and territorial authority of the Fortriu dynasts. The distribution of Pictish symbol stones (including those on Class II sculptured crosses) appears to represent an active statement of cultural dominance and coherence. Like their neighbours, however, kin ties and hostages remained pivotal to ensuring political adherence. Likewise, the Fortriu kings continued to require architectural statements of their superiority, through the use of hillforts like Clatchard Craig. This suggests that military as well as ideological supremacy was still required. The Fortriu kings were reliant on regional rulers to cooperate with their political decisions in order to enact them over the territories. At the same time, regional rulers relied on the Fortriu kings to legitimize their positions and authority. The exercise of a ruler's power, after all, was only possible through the reciprocal complicity of their subjects and other rulers. This cooperation allowed an expansion in the executive functions of Pictish kingship, consolidated under dynastic succession and legitimized through the production of origin myths and king lists.

The perception of kingly authority was as important as its actuality and clerical engagement in the development of ideas on theocratic kingship conceptually transformed the office into one of centralizing authority. Indeed, the creation of Pictish king lists promoted the Fortriu dynasty as the single focus of legitimate authority and power in Pictland. The executive functions of kingship were re-conceptualized by clerical manifests on the exercise of Christian virtue during this period. New constitutional expectations of kingship required appropriate moral behaviour and the exercise of virtue while promoting patriarchal domination. On the other hand, the increasing political and economic authority of ecclesiastical foundations directly assisted the territorial and financial purview of the Pictish kings. For example, the dynast Bredei filius Derelei expanded his geo-political authority through legislative actions that brought fiscal rewards to the king as well as moral legitimacy to underscore his primacy. Clerics were embedded in all social and political activities, promoting western political ideas on governance and kingship. These ideas promoted the concept of nationhood and identification with a sovereign authority. All the conditions for emergent statehood became manifest under the direction of these Fortriu dynasts.

The reign of Necthon filius Derelei represents an important stage in the political effectiveness of 'the just' Christian king. This king enforced the territorial boundaries of his kingdom through military action, treaties and hostages. More importantly, he expanded his oversight over the provinces through ecclesiastical reform. Necthon's paschal reforms were more than a simple calendrical adjustment as they had far-reaching ramifications for ecclesiastical and political unity. These reforms reinforced the primacy of Necthon and his favoured clerics resulting in Pictish ecclesiastical coherence. Clerics could become the mouthpieces and activists for national unity and conformity. In addition, the king's territorial control was strengthened through the establishment of saints' cults and churches across northern and southern provinces. After the model of Solomon, the philosopher king Necthon built a new stone church dedicating it and his people into the communal embrace of St Peter. Consequently, an *ecclesiastica pictorum* emerged, with active, native clerics and the proliferation of local and supra-regional saints' cults; a commemorative exercise in territorial consolidation. A reassessment of the evidence indicates that Necthon was not a weak ruler with limited political agency. He faced down early challenges to win tactical and diplomatic advantage that stabilized his territorial boundaries. The presence of St Peter dedications and identifiable Pictish symbols in Orkney and Fife indicate the full incorporation of these, apparently, peripheral territories into Necthon's kingdom. Necthon's foreign policy was conciliatory. His ecclesiastical reforms indicate authoritative and paternal action that resulted in a coherent Pictish identity and nation. This king manipulated the existing institutional organizations and systems, such as assembly, clientage and the church, to effect the coalescence of the emergent state of Pictland.

When Abbot Ceolfrid addressed King Necthon, *regi Naitano*, it would seem that the abbot understood the king to be ruler of a distinct and cohesive nation. King Necthon was certainly a nation builder. Underlying Ceolfrid's argument for paschal dating was a clear message on the organization of Christian government and the operation of the king's authority. Unity of Catholic observance extended and strengthened profitable diplomatic ties to Northumbria and their trade routes, at a time when Northumbrian kings were no longer a serious threat to Pictish territories. Likewise, reforms allowed Pictish clerics more immediate participation in a wider western intellectual culture. The Picts were not isolated, rather they were active players in the politics of the Insular world. They traded in goods and intellectual ideas with their neighbours and with western European polities. Pictish artisans developed distinct artistic styles, implemented with a high degree of virtuosity. The collaborative energies of rulers and clerics engineered the geo-political expansion of authoritative kinship that espoused a collective identity. This resulted in the formation of a Pictish nation with aspirations of statehood that were arguably realized under King Onuist. Despite the vagaries of the succession system that encouraged damaging competition, governmental authority and its institutional underpinnings remained stable under the Fortriu dynasts. Indeed, Necthon's legacy of unification provided the base for King Onuist's expansion into England, through military means and diplomatic negotiations, and the continuance of the Fortriu dynasty under his brothers and sons. The Fortriu dynasts shaped a powerful and dynamic nation and left a lasting geo-political legacy that underpinned the formation of Alba and, eventually, the kingdom of Scotland.

Bibliography

Abels, Richard, 'The council of Whitby: a study in early Anglo-Saxon politics', *Journal of British Studies*, 23:1 (1983), 1–25.

Ailred of Rievaux's Life of St Ninian, in *Ancient Lives of Scottish saints*, trans. W.M. Metcalfe (Paisley, 1895).

Airlie, Stuart, 'Talking heads: assemblies in early medieval Germany' in P.S. Barnwell and M. Mostert (eds), *Political assemblies in the earlier Middle Ages* (Turnout, 2003), pp 29–46.

Aitchison, Nick B., 'Kingship, society and sacrality: rank, power and ideology in early medieval Ireland', *Traditio*, 49 (1994), 45–75.

Aitchison, Nick B., *Armagh and the royal centres in early medieval Ireland* (Woodbridge, 1994).

Aitchison, Nick B., *The Picts and the Scots at war* (Stroud, 2003).

Alcock, Leslie, 'A survey of Pictish settlement archaeology' in J.G.P. Friell and W.G. Watson (eds), *Pictish studies: settlement, burial and art in Dark-Age northern Britain* (Oxford, 1984), pp 7–41.

Alcock, Leslie, 'Pictish studies: present and future' in A. Small (ed.), *The Picts: a new look at old problems* (Dundee, 1987), pp 80–92.

Alcock, Leslie, 'The activities of potentates in Celtic Britain, AD500–800: a positivist approach' in S.T. Driscoll and M.R. Nieke (eds), *Power and politics in early medieval Britain and Ireland* (Edinburgh, 1988), pp 22–39.

Alcock, Leslie, 'The Rhind lectures, 1988–9: a synopsis. An heroic age: war and society in northern Britain, AD450–850', *PSAS*, 118 (1988), 327–34.

Alcock, Leslie, *Kings and warriors, craftsmen and priests: in northern Britain, AD550–850* (Edinburgh, 2003).

Alcock, Leslie, Elizabeth A. Alcock and Stephen T. Driscoll, 'Reconnaissance excavations of early historic fortifications and other royal sites in Scotland, 1974–84:3: excavations at Dundurn, Strathearn, Perthshire, 1976–7', *PSAS*, 119 (1989), 189–226.

Aldhelmi Opera, ed. Rudolf Ehwald (Berlin, 1961).

Alfonso, Isabel, 'Judicial rhetoric and political legitimation in medieval Léon-Castile' in I. Alfonso, H. Kennedy and J. Escalona (eds), *Building legitimacy: political discourses and forms of legitimation in medieval societies* (Leiden and Boston, 2004), pp 51–87.

Allen, J. Romilly, and J. Anderson, *The early Christian monuments of Scotland*, 2 vols (Balgavies, 1993).

Anderson, Alan Orr, *Early sources of Scottish history, AD500 to 1286*, 1 (Edinburgh, 1922).

Anderson, Benedict, *Imagined communities: reflections on the origin and spread of nationalism* (Thetford, 1983).

Anderson, Marjorie O., *Kings and kingship in early Scotland* (Edinburgh, 1973).

Anderson, Marjorie O., 'Picts: the name and the people' in A. Small (ed.), *The Picts: a new look at old problems* (Dundee, 1987), pp 7–14.

Andrew of Wyntoun: *The Orygynale Cronykil of Scotland*, ed. and trans. David Laing (Edinburgh, 1872).

Anicii Manlii Severini Boethii: *Philosophiae consolatio*, ed. Ludwig Bieler, *Corpus Christianorum, Series Latina*, 94 (Turnhout, 1957).

Armit, Ian, 'Epilogue: the Atlantic Scottish Iron Age' in I. Armit (ed.), *Beyond the brochs: changing perspectives on the later Iron Age in Atlantic Scotland* (Edinburgh, 1990), pp 194–210.

Armit, Ian, *Celtic Scotland* (London, 1997).

Asad, Talal, 'Anthropological conceptions of religion: reflections on Geertz', *Man*, 18:2 (1983), 237–59.

Ashmore, P.J., 'Low cairns, long cists and symbol stones'; *PSAS*, 110 (1978–80), 346–55.

Ashmore, P.J., 'Orkney burials in the 1st millenium AD' in J. Downes and A. Ritchie, *Sea change: Orkney and northern Europe in the later Iron Age, AD300–400* (Balgavies, 2003), pp 35–50.

Audacht Morainn, ed. and trans. Fergus Kelly (Dublin, 1976).

Bangor-Jones, Malcolm, 'Pennylands and Ouncelands in Sutherland and Caithness' in L.J. Macgregor and B.E. Crawford (eds), *Ouncelands and Pennylands: the proceedings of a day conference held in the centre for advanced historical studies on 23 February 1985* (St Andrews, 1987), pp 13–23.

Bannerman, John, *Studies in the history of the Dalriada* (Edinburgh, 1974).

Barney, Stephen A., W.J. Lewis, J.A. Beach and Oliver Berghof (eds), *The Etymologies of Isidore of Seville* (Cambridge, 2006).

Barnwell, P.S., 'Kings, nobles and assemblies in the Barbarian kingdoms' in P.S. Barnwell and M. Mostert (eds), *Political assemblies in the earlier Middle Ages* (Turnhout, 2003), pp 11–28.

Barnwell, P.S., 'Political assemblies: an introduction' in P.S. Barnwell and M. Mostert (eds), *Political assemblies in the earlier Middle Ages* (Turnhout, 2003), pp 1–10.

Barrett, John C., 'Fields of discourse: reconstituting a social archaeology', *Critique of Anthropology*, 7:3 (1988), 5–16.

Barrow, Geoffrey W.S., *The kingdom of the Scots: government, church and society from the eleventh to the fourteenth century* (London, 1973).

Barrow, Geoffrey W.S., *Kingship and unity: Scotland, 1000–1306* (Toronto, 1981).

Barrow, Geoffrey W.S., 'Popular courts in early medieval Scotland: some suggested place-name evidence', *Scottish Studies*, 25 (1981), 1–24.

Barrow, Geoffrey W.S., 'Badneoch and Strathspey, 1130–1312: the church', *Northern Scotland*, 9 (1989), 1–16.

Barrow, Geoffrey W.S., *Scotland and its neighbours in the Middle Ages* (London, 1992).

Barrow, Geoffrey W.S., 'The uses of place-names and Scottish history: pointers and pitfalls' in S. Taylor (ed.), *The use of place-names* (Edinburgh, 1998), pp 54–74.

Bartrum, P.C., *Early Welsh genealogical tracts* (Cardiff, 1966).

Bassett, Steven, 'Church and diocese in the West Midlands: the transition from British to Anglo-Saxon control' in J. Blair and R. Sharpe (eds), *Pastoral care before the parish* (Leicester, 1992), pp 14–40.

Bechbretha, ed. Thomas Charles-Edwards, Early Irish law series, 1 (Dublin, 1983).
Bedae: Opera de temporibus, ed. C.W. Jones (Cambridge, MA, 1943).
Bede: *Epistola ad Ecgbertum episcopum*, in C. Plummer (ed.), *Venerabilis Baedae: Historiam ecclesiasticam gentis Anglorum, historiam abbatum, epistolam ad Ecgberctum una cum historia abbatum auctore anonymo*, 2 vols, 1, pp 405–23 (London, 1896; repr. 1956).
Bede: *Lives of the abbots of Wearmouth and Jarrow*, in D.H. Farmer and J.F. Webb (ed. and trans.), *The age of Bede* (London, 1965; repr. 1998).
Bemmer, Jaqueline, 'The types of pledges in early Irish law: form, function and context' in A. Ahlqvist and P. O'Neill (eds), *Medieval Irish law: text and context* (Sydney, 2013), pp 3–24.
Bernhardt, John W., *Itinerant kingship and royal monasteries in early medieval Germany, c.936–1075* (Cambridge, 1993).
Betha Adamnáin: the Irish Life of Adamnán, ed. Máire Herbert and Pádraig Ó Riain (Cork and London, 1988).
Bhreathnach, Edel, 'Termoria: caput Scotorum?' *Ériu*, 47 (1996), 67–88.
Binchy, Daniel A., 'The date and provenance of *Uraicecht Becc*', *Ériu*, 18 (1958), 44–54.
Binchy, Daniel A., *Celtic and Anglo-Saxon kingship* (Oxford, 1970).
Binchy, Daniel A., 'An archaic legal poem', *Celtica*, 9 (1971), 152–68.
Bitel, Lisa M., *Isle of the saints: monastic settlement and Christian community in early Ireland* (Ithaca, NY, 1990).
Black, Jonathan, 'The divine office and private devotion in the Latin West' in T.J. Heffernan and E.A. Matter (eds), *The liturgy of the medieval Church* (Kalamazoo, MI, 2001), pp 47–71.
Black, Ronald I.M., 'Scottish fairs and fair-names', *Scottish Studies*, 33 (1999), 1–75.
Blair, John, *The Church in Anglo-Saxon society* (Oxford, 2005).
Blair, Peter Hunter, 'The Bernicians and their northern frontier' in Nora Chadwick (ed.), *Studies in early British history* (Cambridge, 1959), pp 137–72.
Bond, J.M., 'A growing success? Agricultural intensification and risk management in late Iron-Age Orkney' in J. Downes and A. Ritchie (eds), *Sea change: Orkney and northern Europe in the later Iron Age, AD300–800* (Balgavies, 2003), pp 105–10.
Bourke, Cormac, 'Fergna Epscop', *IR*, 51:1 (2000), 68–71.
Bradley, J., 'Moynagh Lough: an Insular workshop of the second quarter of the 8th century' in R.M. Spearman and J. Higgitt (eds), *The age of migrating ideas: early medieval art in northern Britain and Ireland* (Edinburgh, 1993), pp 74–81.
Bradley, Richard, 'Time regained: the creation of continuity', *Journal of the British Archaeological Association*, 140 (1987), 1–17.
Bray, Daniel, 'The myth of Tara' in P. O'Neill (ed.), *Nation and federation in the Celtic world* (Sydney, 2003), pp 288–97.
Breatnach, Liam, 'Canon law and secular law in early Ireland: the significance of the *Bretha Nemed*', *Peritia*, 3 (1984), 439–59.
Breatnach, Liam, 'The first third of *Bretha Nemed Toísech*', *Ériu*, 40 (1989), 1–40.
Breen, Aidan, 'The text of the Constantinopolitan Creed in the Stowe Missal', *PRIA*, 90C (1990), 107–21.

Breen, Aidan, '*De XII Abusiuis*: text and transmission' in P. Ní Chatháin and M. Richter (eds), *Ireland and Europe in the early Middle Ages: texts and transmissions* (Dublin, 2002), pp 78–94.

Breviarium Aberdonense, ed. William Blew and David Laing (Edinburgh, 1854).

Broun, Dauvit, 'The seven kingdoms in *De situ Albanie*: a record of Pictish political geography or imaginary map of ancient Alba?' in E.J. Cowan and R.A. McDonald (eds), *Alba: Celtic Scotland in the Middle Ages* (East Linton, 2000), pp 24–42.

Broun, Dauvit, 'The church of St Andrews and its foundation legend in the early twelfth century: recovering the full text of version A of the foundation legend' in S. Taylor (ed.), *Kings, clerics and chronicles in Scotland, 500–1297* (Dublin, 2000), pp 108–14.

Broun, Dauvit, 'The Picts' place in the kingship's past before John of Fordun' in E.J. Cowan and R.J. Finlay (eds), *Scottish history: the power of the past* (Edinburgh, 2002), pp 11–28.

Broun, Dauvit, 'Alba: Pictish homeland or Irish offshoot?' in P. O'Neill (ed.), *Exile and homecoming: papers from the 5th Australian Celtic conference* (Sydney, 2005), pp 234–75.

Broun, Dauvit, 'The property records in the Book of Deer as a source for early Scottish society' in K. Forsyth (ed.), *Studies on the Book of Deer* (Dublin, 2008), pp 313–60.

Brown, P. Hume, *History of Scotland: to the accession of Mary Stewart* (Cambridge, 1909).

Brunner, Karl, 'Continuity and discontinuity of Roman agricultural knowledge in the early Middle Ages' in D. Sweeney (ed.), *Agriculture in the Middle Ages: technology, practice and representation* (Philadelphia, 1995), pp 21–40.

Burleigh, J.H.S., *A church history of Scotland* (London, 1960).

Byrne, Francis J., 'Tribes and tribalism in early Ireland', *Ériu*, 22 (1971), 128–66.

Byrne, Francis J., *Irish kings and high-kings* (Dublin, 2001).

Camden, William, *Camden's Brittania* (London, 1695).

Campbell, James, *Bede's Reges and principes* (Jarrow, 1979).

Campbell, James, 'Anglo-Saxon courts' in C. Cubitt (ed.), *Court culture in the early Middle Ages: the proceedings of the first Alcuin conference* (Turnhout, 2003), pp 155–69.

Campbell, James, 'A nearly, but wrongly, forgotten historian of the Dark Ages' in J. Barrow and A. Wareham (eds), *Myth, rulership, church and charters: essays in honour of Nicholas Brooks* (Aldershot, 2008), pp 31–44.

Campbell, James, 'Archipelagic thoughts: comparing early medieval polities in Britain and Ireland' in S. Baxter, C. Karkov, J.L. Nelson and D. Pelteret (eds), *Early medieval studies in memory of Patrick Wormald* (Farnham, 2009), pp 47–63.

Canning, Joseph, *A history of medieval political thought, 300–1450* (London and New York, 1996).

Carrier, James, 'Gifts, commodities and social relations: a Maussian view of exchange', *Sociological Forum*, 6:1 (1991), 119–36.

Carruthers, Mary J., *The book of memory: a study of memory in medieval culture* (Cambridge, 1990).

Carver, Martin, 'Environment and commodity in Anglo-Saxon England' in J. Rackham (ed.), *Environment and economy in Anglo-Saxon England: a review of recent work on*

the environmental archaeology of rural and urban Anglo-Saxon settlements in England (London, 1994), pp 1–6.
Carver, Martin, 'An Iona of the East: the early medieval monastery at Portmahomack, Tarbat Ness', *MA*, 48 (2004), 1–30.
Carver, Martin, 'Sculpture in action: contexts for stone carving on the Tarbat Peninsula, Easter Ross' in S.M. Foster and M. Cross (eds), *Able minds and practised hands: Scotland's early medieval sculpture in the 21st century* (Leeds, 2005), pp 13–36.
Carver, Martin, *Portmahomack: monastery of the Picts* (Edinburgh, 2008).
Carver, Martin, and Cecily Spall, 'Excavating a parchmenerie: archaeological correlates of making parchment at the Pictish monastery at Portmahomack, Easter Ross', *PSAS*, 134 (2004), 183–200.
Catling, Christopher, 'Village of the Pictish symbol stones', *Current Archaeology*, 263 (2012), 8–9.
Cederman, Lars-Erik, *Emergent actors in world politics: how states and nations develop and dissolve* (Princeton, NJ, 1997).
Chadwick, Nora K., *Celtic Britain* (London, 1963).
Chalmers, George, *Caledonia; or, A historical and topographical account of north Britain from the most ancient to the present times* (Paisley, 1807; repr. 1887).
Charles-Edwards, Thomas M., 'Kinship, status and the origins of the Hide', *Past and Present*, 56 (Aug. 1972), 3–33.
Charles-Edwards, Thomas M., 'The distinction between land and moveable wealth in Anglo-Saxon England' in P.H. Sawyer (ed.), *Medieval settlement: continuity and change* (London, 1976), pp 180–7.
Charles-Edwards, Thomas M., 'Boundaries in Irish law' in P.H. Sawyer (ed.), *Medieval settlement: continuity and change* (London, 1976), pp 83–7.
Charles-Edwards, Thomas M., 'The church and settlement' in P. Ní Catháin and M. Richter (eds), *Irland und Europa: die Kriche im Frümittelalter* (Stuttgart, 1984), pp 167–75.
Charles-Edwards, Thomas M., 'A contract between king and people in early medieval Ireland?: *Críth Gablach* on kingship', *Peritia*, 8 (1994), 107–19.
Charles-Edwards, Thomas M., *Early Christian Ireland* (Cambridge, 2000).
Charles-Edwards, Thomas M., 'The Uí Néill, 695–743: the rise and fall of dynasties', *Peritia*, 16 (2002), 396–418.
Charles-Edwards, Thomas M., 'Gorsedd, Dadl and Llys: assemblies and courts in medieval Wales' in A. Pantos and S. Semple (eds), *Assembly places and practices in medieval Europe* (Dublin, 2004), pp 95–105.
Charles-Edwards, Thomas M., *The chronicle of Ireland* (Liverpool, 2006).
Charles-Edwards, Thomas M., 'Celtic kings: "priestly vegetables"?' in S. Baxter, C. Karkov, J.L. Nelson and D. Pelteret (eds), *Early medieval studies in memory of Patrick Wormald* (Farnham, 2009), pp 65–80.
Claessen, Henri J.M., and Jarich G. Oosten, 'Introduction' in H.J.M. Claessen and J.G. Oosten (eds), *Ideology and the formation of early states* (Leiden, 1996), pp 4–7.
Clancy, Thomas O., *The Triumph Tree: Scotland's earliest poetry, AD550–1350* (Edinburgh, 1998).
Clancy, Thomas O., 'The real St Ninian', *IR*, 52:1 (2001), 1–28.

Clancy, Thomas O., 'Philosopher-king: Nechtan Mac Der-Ilei', *SHR*, 83 October (2004), 125–49.

Clancy, Thomas O., 'Deer and the early church in north-eastern Scotland' in K. Forsyth (ed.), *Studies in the Book of Deer* (Dublin, 2008), pp 363–95.

Clancy, Thomas O., and Gilbert Márkus, *Iona: the earliest poetry of a Celtic monastery* (Edinburgh, 1994).

Close-Brooks, Joanna, 'Excavations in the Dairy Park, Dunrobin, Sutherland, 1977', *PSAS*, 110 (1981), 328–45.

Close-Brooks, Joanna, 'Pictish and other burials' in J.G.P. Friell and W.G. Watson (eds), *Pictish studies: settlement, burial and art in Dark-Age northern Britain* (Oxford, 1984), pp 87–111.

Close-Brooks, Joanna, 'Excavations at Clatchard Craig, Fife', *PSAS*, 116 (1986), 117–84.

Clover, Carol J., 'The politics of scarcity: notes on the sex ratio in early Scandinavia', *Scandinavian Studies*, 60 (1988), 147–88.

Connon, Anne, 'The *Bannshenchas* and the Uí Néill queens of Tara' in A.P. Smyth (ed.), *Seanchas: studies in early and medieval Irish archaeology, history and literature in honour of Francis J. Byrne* (Dublin, 2000), pp 98–108.

Councils and ecclesiastical documents relating to Great Britain and Ireland, ed. A.W. Haddan and W. Stubbs, 2 (Oxford, 1878).

Cowan, Ian B., *The parishes of medieval Scotland* (Edinburgh, 1967).

Cowan, Ian B., 'The post-Columban church', *Records of the Scottish Church History Society*, 18:3 (1974), 245–60.

Cowan, Ian B., 'Early ecclesiastical foundations' in P. McNeill and R. Nicholson (eds), *An historical atlas of Scotland,* c.*400*–1600 (St Andrews, 1975), pp 17–19.

Críth Gablach, ed. Daniel A. Binchy (Dublin, 1941).

Cruickshank, G.D.R., 'The Battle of Dunnichen and the Aberlemno Battle-Scene' in E.J. Cowan and R.A. McDonald (eds), *Alba: Celtic Scotland in the Middle Ages* (East Linton, 2000), pp 69–87.

Cubitt, Catherine, 'Universal and local saints in Anglo-Saxon England' in A. Thacker and R. Sharpe (eds), *Local saints and local churches in the early medieval West* (Oxford, 2002), pp 423–53.

Curle, Cecil L., *Pictish and Norse finds from the Brough of Birsay, 1934–74* (Edinburgh, 1982).

Curran, Michael, *The antiphonary of Bangor and the early Irish monastic liturgy* (Dublin, 1984).

Dalglish, Chris, 'Scotland's medieval countryside: evidence, interpretation, perception' in N. Christie and P. Stamper (eds), *Medieval rural settlement: Britain and Ireland, AD800–1600* (Oxford, 2012), pp 270–87.

Davies, Wendy, 'Land and power in early medieval Wales', *Past & Present*, 81 (1978), 3–23.

Davies, Wendy, *Patterns of power in early Wales: O'Donnell lectures delivered in the University of Oxford, 1983* (Oxford, 1990).

Davies, Wendy, and Paul Fouracre, 'Introduction' in W. Davies and P. Fouracre (eds), *Property and power in the early Middle Ages* (Cambridge, 1995), pp 1–16.

de Jong, Mayke, 'Monastic prisoners or opting out? Political coercion and honour in the Frankish kingdom' in M. de Jong, F. Theuws and C. van Rhijn (eds), *Topographies of power in the early Middle Ages* (Leiden, 2001), pp 291–328.

Dodgshon, Robert A., *Land and society in early Scotland* (Oxford, 1981).

Doherty, Charles, 'Some aspects of hagiography as a source for Irish economic history', *Peritia*, 1 (1984), 300–28.

Donaldson, Gordon, 'Scottish bishops' sees before the reign of David I', *PSAS*, 87 (1952–3), 106–17.

Dransart, Penelope, 'Saints, stones and shrines: the cults of Sts Moluag and Gerardine in Pictland' in J. Cartwright (ed.), *Celtic hagiography and saints' cults* (Cardiff, 2003), pp 232–48.

Driscoll, Stephen T., 'The early historic landscape of Strathearn: the archaeology of a Pictish kingdom', PhD, University of Glasgow, 1987.

Driscoll, Stephen T., 'Power and authority in early historic Scotland: Pictish symbol stones and other documents' in J. Gledhill, B. Bender and M. Trolle Larsen (eds), *State and society: the emergence and development of social hierarchy and political centralization* (London, 1988), pp 215–36.

Driscoll, Stephen T., 'The archaeology of state formation in Scotland' in W.S. Hanson and E.A. Slater (eds), *Scottish archaeology: new perceptions* (Aberdeen, 1991), pp 81–111.

Driscoll, Stephen T., 'Political discourse and the growth of Christian ceremonialism in Pictland: the place of the St Andrews sarcophagus' in S.M. Foster (ed.), *The St Andrews sarcophagus: a Pictish masterpiece and its international connections* (Dublin, 1998), pp 168–78.

Driscoll, Stephen T., 'The archaeological context of assembly in early medieval Scotland: Scone and its comparanda' in A. Pantos and S. Semple (eds), *Assembly places and practices in medieval Europe* (Dublin, 2004), pp 73–94.

Dumville, David N., '"Primarius Cohortis" in Adomnán's Life of Columba', *Scottish Gaelic Studies*, 13:1 (1978), 130–1.

Dumville, David N., 'Kingship, genealogies and regnal lists' in P.H. Sawyer and I.N. Wood (eds), *Early medieval kingship* (Leeds, 1977; repr. 1979), pp 72–104.

Dumville, David N., 'On editing and translating medieval Irish chronicles: the Annals of Ulster', *CMCS*, 10 (1985), 67–86.

Dumville, David N., '*Cethri Prímchenéla Dáil Riata*', *Scottish Gaelic Studies*, 20 (2000), 170–91.

Duncan, Archibald A.M., 'Bede, Iona and the Picts' in R.H.C. Davis and J.M. Wallace-Hadrill (eds), *The writing of history in the Middle Ages* (Oxford, 1981), pp 1–42.

Duncan, Archibald A.M., *The kingship of the Scots, 842–1292: succession and independence* (Edinburgh, 2002).

Dunlop, Annie I., 'Bagimond's Roll', *Miscellany of the Scottish History Society*, 6 (Edinburgh, 1939), 3–77.

Easson, A.R., 'Ouncelands and Pennylands in the west Highlands and islands of Scotland' in L.J. Macgregor and B.E. Crawford (eds), *Ouncelands and Pennylands: the proceedings of a day conference held in the centre for advanced historical studies on 23 Feb. 1985* (St Andrews, 1987), pp 1–11.

Edson, Evelyn, 'World maps and Easter tables: medieval maps in context', *Imago Mundi*, 48 (1996), 25–42.
Edwards, Nancy, 'Rethinking the Pillar of Eliseg', *Antiquaries Journal*, 89 (2009), 143–77.
English historical documents: c.*500–1042*, ed. Dorothy Whitelock (London, 1955).
Enright, Michael J., 'Royal succession and abbatial prerogative in Adomnán's *Vita Columbae*', *Peritia*, 4 (1985), 83–103.
Enright, Michael J., *Iona, Tara and Soissons: the origin of the royal anointing ritual* (Berlin and New York, 1985).
Erler, Mary C., and Maryanne Kowaleski, 'Introduction. A new economy of power relations: female agency in the Middle Ages' in M.C. Erler and M. Kowaleski (eds), *Gendering the master narrative: women and power in the Middle Ages* (Ithaca and London, 2003), pp 1–16.
Etchingham, Colmán, 'The early Irish church: some observations on pastoral care and dues', *Ériu*, 42 (1991), 99–118.
Etchingham, Colmán, *Church organisation in Ireland, AD650 to 1000* (Maynooth, 1999).
Etchingham, Colmán, and Catherine Swift, 'English and Pictish terms for brooch in an 8th-century Irish law-text', *MA*, 48 (2004), 31–49.
Evans, Nicholas, 'Royal succession and kingship among the Picts', *IR*, 59:1 (2008), 1–48.
Faith, Rosamond, *The English peasantry and the growth of lordship* (London and Washington, 1997).
Félire Húi Gormáin: The Martyrology of Gorman, ed. and trans. Whitley Stokes (London, 1895).
Félire Óengusso Céli De: The Martyrology of Oengus, the Culdee, ed. and trans. Whitley Stokes (London, 1905; repr. Dublin, 1984).
Felix's Life of Saint Guthlac, ed. and trans. Bertram Colgrave (Cambridge, 1956).
Ferreiro, Alberto, *Simon Magus in patristic, medieval and early modern traditions* (Leiden and Boston, 2005).
Fletcher, Eric, *Benedict Biscop* (Jarrow, 1981).
Forsyth, Katherine, *Language in Pictland: the case against 'Non-Indo-European Pictish'*, *Studia Hameliana*, 2 (Utrecht, 1997).
Foster, Sally M., 'Pins, combs and the chronology of the later Atlantic Iron-Age settlement' in I. Armit (ed.), *Beyond the Brochs: changing perspectives on the later Iron Age in Atlantic Scotland* (Edinburgh, 1990), pp 143–74.
Foster, Sally M., 'The state of Pictland in the age of Sutton Hoo' in M. Carver (ed.), *The age of Sutton Hoo* (Woodbridge, 1992), pp 217–34.
Foster, Sally M., 'Brochs: domestic architecture and changing social configurations in prehistoric and early historic Scotland', *PSAS*, 123 (1993), 463–4.
Foster, Sally M., 'Before Alba: Pictish and Dál Riata power centres from the fifth to late ninth centuries AD' in S.M. Foster, A. Macinnes and R. Macinnes (eds), *Scottish power centres: from the early Middle Ages to the twentieth century* (Glasgow, 1998), pp 1–31.
Foster, Sally M., 'Discovery, recovery, context and display' in S.M. Foster (ed.), *The St*

Andrews Sarcophagus: a Pictish masterpiece and its international connections (Dublin, 1998), pp 36–62.

Foster, Sally M., *Picts, Gaels and Scots: early historic Scotland* (London, 1996; rev. 2004).

Fouracre, Paul, 'The origins of the Carolingian attempt to regulate the cult of saints' in J. Howard-Johnston and P.A. Hayward (eds), *The cult of saints in late Antiquity and the Middle Ages* (Oxford, 1999), pp 143–66.

Fouracre, Paul, 'Conflict, power and legitimation in Francia in the late seventh and eighth centuries' in I. Alfonso, H. Kennedy and J. Escalona (eds), *Building legitimacy: political discourses and forms of legitimization in medieval societies* (Leiden and Boston, 2004), pp 3–26.

Fraser, James E., *The Battle of Dunichen, 685* (Stroud, 2002).

Fraser, James E., 'Ministry mission and myth in early Christian Fortriu', PhD, University of Edinburgh, 2003.

Fraser, James E., 'Adomnán, Cumméne Ailbe and the Picts', *Peritia*, 17–18 (2003–4), 183–98.

Fraser, James E., 'Strangers on the Clyde: Cenél Comgaill, Clyde Rock and the bishops of Kingarth', *IR*, 56:2 (2005), 102–20.

Fraser, James E., *From Caledonia to Pictland: Scotland to 795* (Edinburgh, 2009).

Fraser, James E., 'From ancient Scythia to the problem of the Picts: thoughts on the quest for Pictish origins' in S.T. Driscoll, J. Geddes and M.A. Hall (eds), *Pictish progress: new studies on northern Britain in the early Middle Ages* (Leiden and Boston, 2011), pp 15–43.

Gailey, C. Ward, and T.C. Patterson, 'State formation an uneven development' in J. Gledhill, B. Bender and M. Trolle Larsen (eds), *State and society: the emergence and development of social hierarchy and political centralization* (London, 1988), pp 76–90.

Gardner, John, *Law as a leap of faith: essays on law in general* (Oxford, 2012).

Geary, Patrick J., *Living with the dead in the Middle Ages* (Ithaca and London, 1994).

Geary, Patrick J., *Women at the beginning: origin myths from the Amazons to the Virgin Mary* (Princeton, NJ, 2006).

Gerriets, Marilyn, 'Economy and society: clientship according to the Irish laws', *CMCS*, 6 (winter 1983), 43–61.

Gerriets, Marilyn, 'The king as judge in early Ireland', *Celtica*, 20 (1988), 29–52.

Gildas: *De excidio Britonum, Gildas: The ruin of Britain and other works*, ed. and trans. Michael Winterbottom (London, 1978).

Gledhill, J., 'Introduction: the comparative analysis of social and political transitions' in J. Gledhill, B. Bender and M. Trolle Larsen (eds), *State and society: the emergence and development of social hierarchy and political centralization* (London, 1988), pp 1–29.

Goffart, Walter, *The narrators of Barbarian history (AD550–800)* (Princeton, NJ, 1988).

Gondek, Meggen, 'Investing in sculpture: power in early-historic Scotland', *MA*, 50 (2006), 105–42.

Gondek, Meggen, and Gordon Noble, 'Landscape with symbols', *British Archaeology*, 87 (Mar./Apr. 2006), 16–17.

Graham, A., 'Cultivation terraces in south-eastern Scotland', *PSAS*, 73 (1939), 289–315.
Graham-Campbell, James, *Pictish silver: status and symbol* (Cambridge, 2002).
Grant, Alexander, 'The province of Ross and the kingdom of Alba' in E.J. Cowan and R.A. McDonald (eds), *Alba: Celtic Scotland in the Middle Ages* (East Linton, 2000), pp 88–126.
Grigg, Julianna, 'The role and status of the metalworker in Scotland and Ireland: in the 1st millennium AD', MA, University of Edinburgh, 1997.
Grigg, Julianna, 'Expulsion of the family Iona over the spine of Britain by King Necthon' in P. O'Neill (ed.), *Exile and homecoming: papers from the 5th Australian Celtic conference* (Sydney, 2005), pp 31–42.
Grigg, Julianna, 'Conquest and conformity in penannular brooch manufacture', *Journal of the Australian Early Medieval Association*, 3 (2007), 159–68.
Grigg, Julianna, 'The just king and *De duodecim abusiuis saeculi*', *Parergon*, 27:1 (2010), 27–51
Grigg, Julianna, 'The Nemed, *Uraicecht Becc* and early Irish governance' in P. O'Neill (ed.), *The land beneath the sea: essays in honour of Ander's Ahlqvist's contribution to celtic studies in Australia* (Sydney, 2013), pp 87–100.
Haldane, A.R.B., *The drove roads of Scotland* (Edinburgh, 1968).
Halsall, Guy, *Settlement and social organization: the Merovingian region of Metz* (Cambridge, 1995).
Hamlin, Ann, 'The archaeology of the Irish church in the eighth century', *Peritia*, 4 (1985), 279–99.
Harrington, Christina, *Women in a Celtic church: Ireland, 450–1150* (Oxford, 2002).
Harrison, Kenneth, 'A letter from Rome to the Irish clergy, AD640', *Peritia*, 3 (1984), 222–9.
Harvey, David C., and Rhys Jones, 'Custom and habit(us): the meaning of traditions and legends in early medieval western Britain', *Geografiska Annaler. Series B, Human Geography*, 81:4 (1999), 223–33.
Helms, Mary W., *Craft and the kingly ideal: art, trade and power* (Austin, TX, 1993).
Hen, Yitzhak, 'The uses of the Bible and the perception of kingship in Merovingian Gaul', *EME*, 7:3 (1998), 277–90.
Henderson, Isabel, 'The origin centre of the Pictish symbol stones', *PSAS*, 91 (1957–8), 44–57.
Henderson, Isabel, *The Picts* (London, 1967).
Henderson, Isabel, 'The meaning of the Pictish symbol stones' in E. Meldrum (ed.), *The Dark Ages in the Highlands: ancient peoples, local history, archaeology* (Inverness, 1971), pp 53–67.
Henderson, Isabel, 'The monuments of the Picts' in P. McNeill and R. Nicholson (eds), *An historical atlas of Scotland, c.400–c.1600* (St Andrews, 1975), pp 9–11.
Henderson, Isabel, 'Early Christian monuments of Scotland displaying crosses but no other ornament' in A. Small (ed.), *The Picts, a new look at old problems* (Dundee, 1987), pp 45–58.
Henderson, Isabel, *The art and function of Rosemarkie's Pictish monuments* (Rosemarkie, 1990).

Henderson, George, and Isabel Henderson, *The art of the Picts: sculpture and metalwork in early medieval Scotland* (London, 2004).
Henning, Joachim, 'Slavery or Freedom? The causes of early medieval Europe's economic advancement', *EME*, 12:3 (2003), 269–77.
Herbert, Máire, *Iona, Kells and Derry: the history and hagiography of the monastic familia of Columba* (Oxford, 1988).
Herbert, Máire, 'The legacy of Columba' in T.M. Devine and J.F. McMillan (eds), *Celebrating Columba, Colm Cille Á Cheiliúradh: Irish–Scottish connections, 597–1997* (Edinburgh, 1999), pp 1–14.
Herren, Michael W., and Shirley Ann Brown, *Christ in Celtic Christianity: Britain and Ireland from the fifth to the tenth century* (Woodbridge, 2002).
Higgitt, John, 'The Pictish Latin inscription at Tarbat in Ross-Shire', *PSAS*, 112 (1982), 300–21.
Hill, Peter, *Whithorn and St Ninian: the excavation of a monastic town, 1984–91* (Stoud, 1997).
Hillgarth, Jocelyn N., 'Ireland and Spain in the seventh century', *Peritia*, 3 (1984), 1–16.
Hingley, Richard, 'Ancestors and identity in the later prehistory of Atlantic Scotland: the reuse and reinvention of Neolithic monuments and material culture', *World Archaeology*, 28:2 (1996), 231–43.
Hobsbawm, Eric, 'Introduction: inventing traditions' in E. Hobsbawm and T. Ranger (eds), *The invention of tradition* (Cambridge, 1983), pp 1–14.
Hodges, Richard, 'Peer polity interaction and socio-political change in Anglo-Saxon England' in C. Renfrew and J.F. Cherry (eds), *Peer polity interaction and socio-political change* (Cambridge, 1986), pp 69–78.
Hoskins, William G., *The making of the English landscape* (London, 1955; repr. 1985).
Hudson, Benjamin T., *Kings of Celtic Scotland* (Westport, 1994).
Hudson, Benjamin T., *The prophecy of Berchán: Irish and Scottish high-kings of the early Middle Ages* (Westport, 1996).
Hughes, Kathleen, *The Church in early Irish society* (London, 1966).
Hughes, Kathleen, *Early Christian Ireland: introduction to the sources* (London, 1972).
Hunter, J.R., *A persona for the northern Picts* (Rosemarkie, 1997).
Innes, Cosmo, *Sketches of early Scottish history and social progress* (Edinburgh, 1861).
Innes, Matthew, *State and society in the early Middle Ages: the Middle Rhine Valley, 400–1000* (Cambridge, 2000).
Innes, Matthew, *Introduction to early medieval Western Europe, 300–900: the sword, the plough and the book* (London and New York, 2007).
Innes, Thomas, *A critical essay on the ancient inhabitants of the northern Parts of Britain or Scotland*, 2 vols (London, 1729).
Isidori, Sancti: *Collectio Canonum*, ed. J.P. Migne (Paris, 1850).
Isidori, Sancti: *Sententiae*, ed. J.P Migne (Paris, 1862).
Jackson, Kenneth, 'Two early Scottish names', *SHR*, 33:115, pt 1(1954), 14–18.
James, Edward, 'Bede and the tonsure question', *Peritia*, 3 (1984), 85–98.
Janes, Dominic, 'The golden clasp of the late Roman state', *EME*, 5:2 (1996), 127–53.
Jaski, Bart, 'Early medieval Irish kingship and the Old Testament', *EME*, 7:3 (1998), 329–44.

John of Fordun: *Chronica Gentis Scotorum: John of Fordun's chronicle of the Scottish nation*, trans. Felix J.H. Skene and ed. William F. Skene, 2 vols (Edinburgh, 1872; repr. Lampeter, 1993).

Jones, C.W., 'The Victorian and Dionysiac Paschal tables in the West' in W.M. Stevens (ed.), *Bede, the schools and the computus* (Aldershot, 1994), pp 408–21.

Jones, Glanville R.J., 'Multiple estates and early settlement' in P.H. Sawyer (ed.), *Medieval settlement: continuity and change* (London, 1976), pp 15–40.

Jones, Glanville R.J., 'The Dark Ages' in D.H. Owen (ed.), *Settlement and society in Wales* (Cardiff, 1989), pp 177–97.

Jones, Rhys, 'Mann and men in a medieval state: the geographies of power in the Middle Ages', *Transactions of the Institute of British Geographers*, 24:1 (1999), 65–78.

Keeley, Lawrence H., *War before civilization: the myth of the peaceful savage* (Oxford and New York, 1996).

Kelly, Fergus, 'An Old Irish text on court procedure', *Peritia*, 5 (1986), 74–106.

Kelly, Fergus, *A guide to early Irish law* (Dublin, 1988; repr. 1991).

Kelly, Fergus, *Early Irish farming: a study based mainly on the law-texts of the 7th and 8th centuries AD* (Dublin, 2000).

Kemp, Eric Waldram, *Canonization and authority in the western Church* (London, 1948).

Kershaw, Paul, *Peaceful kings: peace, power and the early medieval political imagination* (Oxford, 2011).

Kidd, Colin, 'The ideological uses of the Picts, 1707–*c*.1990' in E.J. Cowan and R.J. Finlay (eds), *Scottish history: the power of the past* (Edinburgh, 2002), pp 169–90.

Kirby, David P., 'Bede and the Pictish church', *IR*, 24 (1973), 6–25.

Kirby, David P., '... Per universus Pictorum provincias' in G. Bonner (ed.), *Famulus Christi: essays in commemoration of the thirteenth centenary of the birth of the Venerable Bede* (London, 1976), pp 286–324.

Kosto, A.J., 'Hostages in the Carolingian world (714–840)', *EME*, 11:2 (2002), 123–47.

Lacey, Brian, *Cenél Conaill and the Donegal kingdoms, AD500–800* (Dublin, 2006).

Laing, Lloyd R., *Settlement types in post-Roman Scotland* (Oxford, 1975).

Lane, Alan, 'Trade, gifts and cultural exchange in Dark-Age western Scotland' in B.E. Crawford (ed.), *Scotland in Dark-Age Europe* (St Andrews, 1994), pp 103–15.

Lane, Alan, and Ewan Campbell, *Dunadd: an early Dalriadic capital* (Oxford, 2000).

Lapidge, Michael, 'Gildas's education and the Latin culture of sub-Roman Britain' in M. Lapidge and D. Dumville (eds), *Gildas: new approaches* (Woodbridge, 1984), pp 41–3.

Lapidge, Michael, 'The career of Archbishop Theodore' in M. Lapidge (ed.), *Archbishop Theodore: commemorative studies on his life and influence* (Cambridge, 1995), pp 1–29.

Lapidge, Michael, and Michael Herren, *Aldhelm: the prose works* (Cambridge, 1979).

Liber epistolarum Sancti Patricii episcopi, ed. and trans. D.R. Howlett (Dublin, 1994).

Lowe, Christopher, *Inchmarnock: an early historic island monastery and its archaeological landscape* (Edinburgh, 2008).

Lynch, Joseph, *Christianizing kinship: ritual sponsorship in Anglo-Saxon England* (Ithaca, NY, and London, 1998).

Mac Eoin, Gearóid, 'On the Irish legend of the origin of the Picts', *Studia Hibernica*, 4 (1964), 138–54.

MacDonald, Aidan, 'Caiseal, Cathair, Dùn, Lios and Ràth in Scotland: 3*', *Ainm*, 2 (1987), 37–54.

MacDonald, Aidan, *Curadán, Boniface and the early church of Rosemarkie* (Alness, 1992).

MacKinlay, James M., *Ancient church dedications in Scotland: scriptural dedications* (Edinburgh, 1910).

MacKinlay, James M., *Ancient church dedications in Scotland: non-scriptural dedications* (Edinburgh, 1914).

MacLean, Douglas, 'The status of the sculptor in Old Irish law and the evidence of the crosses', *Peritia*, 9 (1995), 125–55.

MacNéill, Eoin, 'Ancient Irish law: the law of status and franchise', *PRIA*, 36C (1923), 265–316.

Macquarrie, Alan, 'Early Christian religious houses in Scotland: foundation and function' in J. Blair and R. Sharpe (eds), *Pastoral care before the parish* (Leicester, 1992), pp 110–33.

Macquarrie, Alan, 'The kings of Strathclyde' in A. Grant and K.J. Stringer (eds), *Medieval Scotland: crown, lordship and community: essays presented to G.W.S. Barrow* (Edinburgh, 1993), pp 1–19.

Macquarrie, Alan, '*Vita Sancti Servani*: The Life of St Serf', *IR*, 44 (1993), 122–52.

Macquarrie, Alan, *The saints of Scotland: essays in Scottish Church history, AD450–1093* (Edinburgh, 1997).

Maddicott, J.R., 'Two frontier states: Northumbria and Wessex, *c*.650–750' in J.R. Maddicott and D.M. Palliser (eds), *The medieval state: essays presented to James Campbell* (London and Rio Grande, 2000), pp 25–45.

Maldonado, Aidán, 'Burial in early medieval Scotland: new questions', *MA*, 57 (2013), 1–34.

Mann, Michael, 'The autonomous power of the state: its origins, mechanisms and results', *European Journal of Sociology*, 25 (1984), 185–213.

Mann, Michael, *The sources of social power, 1: a history of power from the beginning to AD1700* (Cambridge, 1986).

Márkus, Gilbert, 'Iona: monks, pastors and missionaries' in D. Broun and T.O. Clancy (eds), *Spes Scotorum, Hope of Scots: Saint Columba, Iona and Scotland* (Edinburgh, 1999), pp 115–38.

Markus, R.A., 'The Latin fathers' in J.H. Burns (ed.), *The Cambridge history of medieval political thought,* c.*350*–c.*1450* (Cambridge, 1988), pp 94–6.

Markus, R.A., 'Gregory the Great on kings: rulers and preachers in the *Commentary on 1 Kings*' in D. Wood (ed.), *Studies in Church history, Subsidia* 9 (Oxford, 1991), pp 7–21.

Marsden, Richard, *The text of the Old Testament in Anglo-Saxon England* (Cambridge, 1995).

Martin, Richard P., 'Hesiod, Odysseus and the instruction of princes', *Transactions of the American Philological Association*, 114 (1984), 29–48.

Mc Carthy, Daniel, 'The lunar and paschal tables of *De ratione paschali* attributed to Anatolius of Laodicea', *Archive for History of Exact Sciences*, 49:4 (1996), 285–320.

McCone, Kim, *Pagan past and Christian present in early Irish literature* (Naas, Kildare, 1991).

McKerral, Andrew, 'What is a Davach?', *PSAS*, 82 (1947–8), 49–52.

McLeod, Neil, *Early Irish contract law* (Sydney, 1995).

McLeod, Neil, 'The metalworking tradition in medieval Irish law' in P. O'Neill (ed.), *Between intrusions: Britain and Ireland between the Romans and Normans* (Sydney, 2004), pp 103–13.

McNamara, Jo Ann, 'Women and power through the family revisited' in M.C. Erler and M. Kowaleski (eds), *Gendering the master narrative: women and power in the Middle Ages* (Ithaca, NY, and London, 2003), pp 18–21.

McNamara, Martin, *Glossa in Psalmos: the Hiberno-Latin gloss on the Psalms of Codex Palatinus Latinus 68 (Psalms 39:11–151:7)* (Vatican, 1986).

McNeill, John T., and Helena M. Gamer, *Medieval hand-books of penance: a translation of the Principal Libri Poenitentiales and selections from related documents* (New York, 1965).

Meeder, Sven, 'The early Irish Stowe Missal's destination and function', *EME*, 13 (2005), 179–94.

Metcalfe, W.M., *Pinkerton's Lives of the Scottish saints* (Paisley, 1889).

Middleton, Neil, 'Early medieval port customs, tolls and controls on foreign trade', *EME*, 13:4 (2005), 313–58.

Miller, Molly, 'Eanfrith's Pictish son', *Northern History*, 14 (1978), 47–66.

Miller, Molly, 'The disputed historical horizon of the Pictish king-lists', *SHR*, 58 (1979), 1–34.

Miller, Molly, 'The last century of Pictish succession', *Scottish Studies*, 23 (1979), 39–67.

Miller, Molly, 'Royal pedigrees of the insular Dark Ages: a progress report', *History in Africa*, 7 (1980), 201–24.

Miller, Molly, 'Matriliny by treaty' in D. Whitelock, R. McKitterick and D. Dumville (eds), *Ireland in early medieval Europe* (Cambridge, 1982), pp 133–61.

Moreland, John, 'Concepts of the early medieval economy' in I.L. Hansen and C. Wickham (eds), *The long eighth century* (Leiden, 2000), pp 1–34.

Moreland, John, 'Ethnicity, power and the English' in W.O. Frazer and A. Tyrrel (eds), *Social identity in early medieval Britain* (London, 2000), pp 23–51.

Moreton, Jennifer, 'Doubts about the calendar: Bede and the eclipse of 664', *Isis*, 89 (1998), 50–65.

Morris, Ian, 'Gift and commodity in archaic Greece', *Man*, 21.1 (1986), 1–17.

Morrison, A., 'Field survey and excavation at Dunbeath, Caithness', *PSAS*, 123 (1993), 458–60.

Mulville, J., M. Parker-Pearson, N. Sharples, H. Smith and A. Chamberlain, 'Quarters, arcs and squares: human and animal remains in the Hebridean later Iron Age' in J. Downes and A. Ritchie (eds), *Sea change: Orkney and northern Europe in the later Iron Age, AD300–800* (Balgavies, 2003), pp 21–33.

Näsman, Ulf, 'Exchange and politics: the eighth–early ninth century in Denmark' in I.L. Hansen and C. Wickham (eds), *The long eighth century* (Leiden, 2000), pp 35–68.

Nelson, Janet L., 'Aachen as a place of power' in M. de Jong, F. Theuws and C. van Rhijn (eds), *Topographies of power in the early Middle Ages* (Leiden, 2001), pp 217–39.

Nennius: *British history and the Welsh annals*, ed. and trans. John Morris (London, 1980).

Ní Dhonnchadha, Máirín, 'The guarantor list of the Cáin Adomnáin, 697', *Peritia*, 1 (1982), 178–215.

Nieke, Margaret R., 'Penannular and related brooches: secular ornament or symbol in action?' in R.M. Spearman and J. Higgitt (eds), *The age of migrating ideas: early medieval art in northern Britain and Ireland* (Edinburgh, 1993), pp 128–34.

Nieke, Margaret R., and H.B. Duncan, 'Dalriada: the establishment and maintenance of an early historic kingdom in northern Britain' in S.T. Driscoll and M.R. Nieke (eds), *Power and politics in early medieval Britain and Ireland* (Edinburgh, 1988), pp 6–21.

Noble, Gordon, and Meggen Gondek, 'Symbol stones in context: excavations at Rhynie, an undocumented Pictish power centre of the 6th–7th centuries AD?', *MA*, 55 (2011), 317–21.

Noble, Gordon, and Meggen Gondek, '"A very royal place" Rhynie and the Picts', *Current Archaeology*, 289 (2014), 22–8.

Ó Corráin, Donnchadh, Liam Breatnach and Aidan Breen, 'The laws of the Irish', *Peritia*, 3 (1984), 382–438.

Ó Cróinín, Dáibhí, 'Mo-Sinnu Moccu Min and the computus of Bangor', *Peritia*, 1 (1982), 281–95.

Ó Cróinín, Dáibhí, 'The Irish provenance of Bede's computus', *Peritia*, 2 (1983), 229–47.

Ó Cróinín, Dáibhí, '"New heresy for old": Pelagianism in Ireland and the papal letter of 640', *Speculum*, 60:3 (1985), 505–16.

Ó Cróinín, Dáibhí, *Early medieval Ireland, 400–1200* (New York, 1995).

Ó Néill, Pádraig, 'Irish transmission of late antique learning: the case of Theodore of Mopsuestia's commentary on the Psalms' in P. Ní Chatháin and M. Richter (eds), *Ireland and Europe in the early Middle Ages: texts and transmissions* (Dublin, 2002), pp 68–77.

O'Grady, Oliver J.T., 'The setting and practice of open-air judicial assemblies in medieval Scotland: a multidisciplinary study', PhD, University of Glasgow, 2008.

O'Brien, Elizabeth, 'Burial practices in Ireland: first to seventh centuries A.D' in J. Downes and A. Ritchie (eds), *Sea change: Orkney and northern Europe in the later Iron Age, AD300–800* (Balgavies, 2003), pp 63–72.

O'Brien, Elizabeth, and Charlotte Roberts, 'Archaeological study of church cemeteries: past, present and future' in J. Blair and C. Pyrah (eds), *Church archaeology: research directions for the future* (London, 1996), pp 159–81.

O'Keeffe, J.G., 'The Rule of Patrick [*Ríagail Pátraic*]', *Ériu*, 1:2 (1904), 216–24.

Oliver, Lisi, *The Body Legal in Barbarian law* (Toronto, 2011).

Oosthuizen, Susan, 'The roots of the common fields: linking prehistoric and medieval field systems in west Cambridgeshire', *Landscapes*, 4:1 (2000), 40–64.

O'Rahilly, Thomas F., *Early Irish history and mythology* (Dublin, 1946).

Ordnance Survey original name books for Scotland, ed. Ordnance Commission, Inverness-Shire no. 8, Parish of Ardersier in the Co. Inverness (Edinburgh, 1868–73).

O'Sullivan, P.E., 'Pollen analysis and radiocarbon dating of a core from Loch Pityoulish, Eastern Highlands of Scotland', *Journal of Biogeography*, 3:3 (1976), 293–302.

Pantos, Aliki, and Sarah Semple (eds), *Assembly places and practices in medieval Europe* (Dublin, 2004).

Parry, M.L., 'Secular climactic change and marginal agriculture', *Transactions of the Institute of British Geographers*, 64 (Mar. 1975), 1–13.

Patterson, Nerys Thomas, *Cattle-lords and clansmen: the social structure of early Ireland* (Notre Dame, 1994).

Patterson, Nerys Thomas, 'Self-worth and property: equipage and early medieval personhood' in W.O. Frazer and A. Tyrrell (eds), *Social identity in early medieval Britain* (London, 2000), pp 53–67.

Pelteret, David A.E., *Slavery in medieval England: from the reign of Alfred until the twelfth century* (Woodbridge, 1995).

Pinkerton, John, *An enquiry into the history of Scotland preceding the reign of Malcolm III or the year 1056* (London and Edinburgh, 1789).

Proudfoot, Edwina, 'Excavations at the long cist cemetery on the Hallow Hill, St Andrew's, Fife, 1975–7', *PSAS*, 126 (1996), 387–454.

Proudfoot, Edwina, 'The Hallow Hill and the origins of Christianity in eastern Scotland' in B.E. Crawford (ed.), *Conversion and Christianity in the North Sea world* (St Andrews, 1998), pp 57–73.

Pseudo-Cyprian: *De duodecim abusiuis saeculi*, ed. Siegmund Hellmann (Leipzig, 1909).

Ralston, Ian B., 'The Green Castle and the promotory forts of north-east Scotland', *Scottish Archaeological Forum*, 10 (1980), 27–40.

Ralston, Ian B., *The hill-forts of Pictland: since 'the Problem of the Picts'* (Rosemarkie, 2004).

RCAHMS, *North-east Perth: an archaeological landscape* (London, 1990).

RCAHMS, *In the shadow of Bennachie: a field archaeology of Donside, Aberdeenshire* (Edinburgh, 2007).

Reed, Teresa, *Shadows of Mary: reading the Virgin Mary in medieval texts* (Cardiff, 2003).

Reeves, William, 'Saint Maelrubha: his history and churches', *PSAS*, 3 (1857–60), 258–96.

Registrum Episcopatus Moraviensis, ed. Cosmo Innes (Edinburgh, 1837).

Rendell, Jocelyn, 'St Boniface and the mission to the Northern Isles: a view from Papa Westray' in B.E. Crawford (ed.), *The Papar in the north Atlantic: environment and history* (St Andrews, 2002), pp 31–7.

Repsher, Brian V., *The rite of church dedication in the early medieval era* (New York, 1998).

Reynolds, Roger E., 'Clerics in the early Middle Ages: hierarchies and functions' in R.E. Reynolds (ed.), *Clerics in the early Middle Ages: hierarchy and image* (Aldershot, 1999), pp 1–31.

Reynolds, Roger E., 'The de officiis VII graduum' in R.E. Reynolds (ed.), *Clerics in the early Middle Ages: hierarchy and image* (Aldershot, 1999), pp 113–51.

Reynolds, Roger E., 'The ordination of clerics in the Middle Ages XI' in R.E.

Reynolds (ed.), *Clerics in the early Middle Ages: hierarchy and image* (Aldershot, 1999), pp 1–9.

Reynolds, Susan, 'The historiography of the medieval state' in M. Bentley (ed.), *Companion to historiography* (Hoboken, 1997), pp 117–38.

Reynolds, Susan, 'The idea of the nation as a political community' in L. Scales and O. Zimmer (eds), *Power and the nation in European history* (Cambridge, 2005), pp 54–66.

Ritchie, G., and Anna Ritchie, *Scotland: archaeology and early history* (Edinburgh, 1991).

Robertson, Eben William, *Scotland under her early kings: a history of the kingdom to the close of the thirteenth century*, 2 vols (Edinburgh, 1862).

Robertson, Eben William, *Historical essays in connexion with the land, the Church &c.* (Edinburgh, 1872).

Robertson, Joseph, *Illustrations of the topography and antiquities in the shires of Aberdeen and Banff*, 5 vols, 2 (Aberdeen, 1847).

Rogers, John M., 'The formation of the parish unit and community in Perthshire', PhD, University of Edinburgh, 1992.

Rogers, John M., 'The formation of parishes in twelfth-century Perthshire', *Records of the Scottish Church History Society*, 27 (1997), 68–96.

Ross, Alasdair, 'The Dabhach in Moray: a new look at and Old Tub' in Alex Woolf (ed.), *Landscape and environment in Dark Age Scotland* (St Andrews, 2006), pp 57–74.

Ross, Alastair, 'Pictish matriliny?', *Northern Studies*, 34 (1999), 11–23.

Roymans, N., *Tribal societies in northern Gaul: an anthropological perspective* (Amsterdam, 1990).

Ryan, Michael, 'Early medieval Ireland: some archaeological issues' in K. McCone and K. Simms (eds), *Progress in medieval Irish studies* (Maynooth, 1996), pp 155–63.

Ryan, Michael, 'Furrows and browse: some archaeological thoughts on agriculture and population in early medieval Ireland' in A.P. Smyth (ed.), *Seanchas: studies in early and medieval Irish archaeology, history and literature in honour of Francis J. Byrne* (Dublin, 2000), pp 30–6.

S. Gregorii Magni: *Registrum epistularum: libri I–VII*, ed. Dag Norberg (Turnholt, 1982).

Sancti Columbani opera, ed. G.S.M. Walker (Dublin, 1957; repr. 1970).

Sanmark, Alexandra, 'Administrative organization and state formation: a case study of assembly sites in Södermanland, Sweden', *MA*, 53 (2009), 205–41.

Saunders, Tom, 'Class, space and "feudal" identities in early medieval England' in W.O. Frazer and A. Tyrrel (eds), *Social identity in early medieval Britain* (London, 2000), pp 209–32.

Scales, Len, and Oliver Zimmer, 'Introduction' in L. Scales and O. Zimmer (eds), *Power and the nation in European history* (Cambridge, 2005), pp 1–29.

Schulenburg, Jane Tibbetts, 'Female sanctity: public and private roles, *ca.*500–1000' in M. Erler and M. Kowaleski (eds), *Women and power in the Middle Ages* (Athens, GA, 1988), pp 102–25.

Scott, A.B., *The Pictish nation: its people and its church* (Edinburgh, 1918).

Seaver, M., 'Silent mills', *British Archaeology*, 87 (Mar./Apr. 2006), 40–5.

Seaver, M., 'Against the grain: early medieval settlement and burial on the Blackhill. Excavations at Raystown, Co. Meath' in C. Corlett and M. Potterton (eds), *Death and burial in early medieval Ireland: in light of recent archaeological excavations* (Dublin, 2010), pp 277–95.

Seebohm, Frederick, *Tribal custom in Anglo-Saxon law* (London, 1911).

Semple, Sarah, 'Locations of assembly in early Anglo-Saxon England' in A. Pantos and S. Semple (eds), *Assembly places and practices in medieval Europe* (Dublin, 2004), pp 135–54.

Serres, Michel, and Bruno Latour, *Conversations on science, culture and time*, trans. Roxanne Lapidus (Ann Arbor, MI, 1990).

Sharpe, Richard, 'Armagh and Rome in the seventh century' in P. Ní Catháin and M. Richter (eds), *Irland und Europa: die Kriche im Frümittelalter* (Stuttgart, 1984), pp 58–72.

Sharpe, Richard (trans.), *Adomnán of Iona: Life of St Columba* (London, 1995).

Sharples, Niall, 'From monuments to artefacts: changing social relationships in the later Iron Age' in J. Downes and A. Ritchie (eds), *Sea change: Orkney and northern Europe in the later Iron Age, AD300–800* (Balgavies, 2003), pp 151–65.

Shaw, Lachlan, *The history of the province of Moray: comprising the counties of Elgin and Nairn, the greater part of the county of Inverness and a portion of the county of Banff – all called the province of Moray before there was a division into counties*, 3 vols, 1 (London and Glasgow, 1882).

Shennan, Hay, *Boundaries of counties and parishes in Scotland: as settled by the boundary commissioners under the Local Government (Scotland) Act, 1889* (Edinburgh, 1892).

Sherry, John F., 'Gift giving in anthropological perspective', *Journal of Consumer Research*, 10:2 (1983), 157–168.

Simpson, W.D., 'Lesmoir Castle and the Church of Essie: with some further notes on Auchindoir', *PSAS*, 66 (1932), 86–101.

Skene, Felix J.H. (ed.), *The Book of Pluscarden*, 2 vols, 2 (Edinburgh, 1880).

Skene, William F., *Chronicles of the Picts, chronicles of the Scots and other early memorials of Scottish history* (Edinburgh, 1867).

Skene, William F., *Celtic Scotland: a history of ancient Alban: history and ethnology*, 3 vols, 1 (Edinburgh, 1876).

Skene, William F., *Celtic Scotland: a history of ancient Alban: church and culture*, 3 vols, 2 (Edinburgh, 1877).

Skene, William F., *Celtic Scotland: a history of ancient Alban: land and people*, 3 vols, 3 (Edinburgh, 1880).

Small, Alan, 'The site: its history and excavation' in A. Small, C. Thomas and D.M. Wilson (eds), *St Ninian's Isle and its treasure* (Oxford, 1973), pp 1–7.

Small, Alan, Charles Thomas and David M. Wilson (eds), *St Ninian's Isle and its treasure* (Oxford, 1973).

Smith, Anthony, 'War and ethnicity: the role of warfare in the formation, self-images and cohesion of ethnic communities', *Ethnic and Racial Studies*, 4:4 (1981), 375–97.

Smith, Ian, 'The archaeology of the early Christian Church in Scotland and Man, AD400–1200' in J. Blair and C. Pyrah (eds), *Church archaeology: research directions for the future* (London, 1996), pp 19–37.

Smith, J. Beverley, 'Judgement under the law of Wales', *Studia Celtica*, 39 (2005), 63–103.
Smyth, Alfred P., *Warlords and holy men: Scotland, AD80–1000* (Edinburgh, 1984).
Spall, Cecily, 'All that glitters: the case for goldworking at the early medieval monastery at Portmahomack', *Historical Metallurgy*, 40:1 (2006), 42–8.
Spearman, M.J., 'Early Scottish towns: their origins and economy' in S.T. Driscoll and M.R. Nieke (eds), *Power and politics in early medieval Britain and Ireland* (Edinburgh, 1988), pp 96–110.
St Augustine: City of God, trans. Henry Bettenson (London, 1972; rev. 2003).
St Bernard of Clairvaux's Life of St Malachy of Armagh, ed. H.J. Lawlor (New York, 1920).
Stacey, Robin Chapman, 'Law and order in the very old west: England and Ireland in the early Middle Ages' in B.T. Hudson and V. Ziegler (eds), *Crossed paths: methodological approaches to the Celtic aspect of the European Middle Ages* (Lanham, NY, 1991), pp 39–60.
Stacey, Robin Chapman, 'Speaking in riddles' in P. Ní Catháin and M. Richter (eds), *Ireland and Europe in the early Middle Ages: texts and transmission* (Dublin, 2002), pp 243–8.
Stacey, Robyn Chapman, *Dark speech: the performance of law in early Ireland* (Philadelphia, 2007).
Stafford, Pauline, *Queens, concubines and dowagers: the king's wife in the early Middle Ages* (Athens, GA, 1983).
Stancliffe, Clare E., 'Kings and conversion: some comparisons between the Roman mission to England and Patrick's to Ireland', *Frühmittelalterliche Studien*, 14 (1980), 59–94.
Stancliffe, Clare E., 'Kings who opted out' in P. Wormald, D. Bullough and R. Collins (eds), *Ideal and reality in Frankish and Anglo-Saxon society: studies presented to J.M. Wallace-Hadrill* (Oxford, 1983), pp 154–76.
Stevens, Wesley M., 'Bede's scientific achievement' in W.M. Stevens (ed.), *Cycles of time and scientific learning in medieval Europe* (Aldershot, 1995), pp 1–58.
Stevenson, R.B.K., 'Further notes on the Hunterston and "Tara" brooches, Monymusk Reliquary and Blackness Bracelet', *PSAS*, 113 (1983), 469–77.
Stevenson, R.B.K., 'The Celtic brooch from Westness, Orkney, and hinged-pins', *PSAS*, 119 (1989), 239–69.
Stocking, Rachel L., 'Martianus, Aventius and Isidore: provincial councils in seventh-century Spain', *EME*, 6:2 (1997), 169–88.
Sutherland, Elizabeth, *In search of the Picts* (London, 1994).
Tacitus: *The Agricola and the Germanica*, trans. Harold Mattingly (London, 1970).
Tacitus: *The Annals of Imperial Rome*, trans. Michael Grant (London, 1996)
Taylor, Simon, 'Place-names and the early church in eastern Scotland' in B.E. Crawford (ed.), *Scotland in Dark-Age Britain* (Aberdeen, 1996), pp 93–110.
Taylor, Simon, 'Seventh-century Iona abbots in Scottish place-names' in D. Broun and T.O. Clancy (eds), *Spes Scotorum: Hope of the Scots* (Edinburgh, 1999), pp 35–70.
Taylor, Simon, 'Place-names of Fife' in D. Omand (ed.), *The Fife Book* (Edinburgh, 2000), pp 205–20.

Taylor, Simon, *The place-names of Fife: west Fife between Leven and Forth*, 1 (Donington, Lincolnshire, 2006).
Taylor, Simon, 'The toponymic landscape in the Gaelic notes in the Book of Deer' in K. Forsyth (ed.), *Studies in the Book of Deer* (Dublin, 2008), pp 275–308.
Taylor, Simon, 'Place-names of Lesmahagow', *Journal of Scottish Name Studies*, 3 (2009), 65–106.
Taylor, Simon, and Gilbert Márkus, *The place-names of Fife: discussion, glossaries and edited texts, with addenda and corrigenda of volumes 1–4*, 5 (Donington, Lincolnshire, 2012).
Thacker, Alan, 'Monks, preaching and pastoral care in early Anglo-Saxon England' in J. Blair and R. Sharpe (eds), *Pastoral care before the parish* (Leicester, 1992), pp 137–70.
Thacker, Alan, '*Membra Disjecta*: the division of the body and diffusion of the cult' in C. Stancliffe and E. Cambridge (eds), *Oswald: Northumbrian king to European saint* (Stamford, 1995), pp 97–127.
Thacker, Alan, '*Peculiaris Patronus Noster*: the saint as patron of the state in the early Middle Ages' in J.R. Maddicott and D.M. Palliser (eds), *The medieval state: essays presented to James Campbell* (London and Rio Grande, 2000), pp 1–24.
The anonymous history of Abbot Ceolfrith, in D.H. Farmer and J.F. Webb (eds and trans.), *The age of Bede* (London, 1965; repr. 1998).
The Historia Brittonum; the Vatican recension, ed. David N. Dumville (Cambridge, 1985).
The Irish penitentials, ed. and trans. Ludwig Bieler (Dublin, 1975).
The Mabinogian, trans. Jeffrey Gantz (London, 1976).
The Patrician texts in the Book of Armagh, ed. and trans. Ludwig Bieler (Dublin, 1979).
The Rule of Benedict: a guide to Christian living, ed. and trans. monks of Glenstal Abbey (Dublin, 1994).
Thomas, Charles, 'Sculptured stones and crosses from St Ninian's Isle and Papil' in A. Small, C. Thomas and D.M. Wilson (eds), *St Ninian's Isle and its treasure* (Oxford, 1973), pp 8–44.
Thurston, Tina L., *Landscapes of power, landscapes of conflict: state formation in the south Scandinavian Iron Age* (New York, 2001).
Tilley, Christopher, *A phenomenology of landscape* (Oxford, 1994).
Tipping, Richard, Althea L. Davies and Robert McCulloch, 'Introduced woodlands in northern Scotland: pollen-analytical evidence for early historic plantations' in A. Woolf (ed.), *Landscape and environment in Dark-Age Scotland* (St Andrews, 2006), pp 29–47.
Trench-Jellicoe, Ross, 'The Skeith Stone, Upper Kilrenny, Fife, in its context', *PSAS*, 128 (1998), 495–513.
Tsurushima, Hirokazu, 'What do we mean by "Nations" in early medieval Britain' in H. Tsurushima (ed.), *Nations in medieval Britain* (Donington, 2010), pp 1–18.
Tyrrell, Andrew, 'Early medieval bodies and the corporeal identity' in W.O. Frazer and A. Tyrrell (eds), *Social identity in early medieval Britain* (London, 2000), pp 137–55.
Veitch, Kenneth, 'The Columban church in northern Britain, 664–717: a reassessment', *PSAS*, 127 (1997), 627–47.

Venerabilis Baedae: Historiam ecclesiasticam gentis Anglorum, historiam abbatum, epistolam ad Ecgberctum una cum historia abbatum auctore anonymo, ed. Charles Plummer, 2 vols (London, 1896; repr. 1956).

Wallace-Hadrill, John M., *Early Germanic kingship in England and on the Continent* (Oxford, 1971).

Wallis, Faith, *Bede: The reckoning of time* (Liverpool, 1999).

Walsh, M., and Dáibhí Ó Cróinín, *Cummian's Letter de controversia paschali: together with a related Irish computistical tract, De ratione conputandi* (Toronto, 1988).

Wareham, Andrew, *Lords and communities in early medieval East Anglia* (Woodbridge, 2005).

Wickham, Chris, *Framing the early Middle Ages: Europe and the Mediterranean, 400–800* (Oxford, 2005).

Wood, Susan, *The proprietary church in the medieval West* (Oxford, 2006).

Woolf, Alex, 'Pictish matriliny reconsidered', *IR*, 49:2 (1998), 147–67.

Woolf, Alex, 'Community, identity and kingship in early England' in W.O. Frazer and A. Tyrrell (eds), *Social identity in early medieval Britain* (London, 2000), pp 91–109.

Woolf, Alex, 'The Verturian hegemony: a mirror in the north' in Michelle P. Brown and Carol A. Farr (eds), *Mercia: an Anglo-Saxon kingdom in Europe* (London, 2001), pp 106–12.

Woolf, Alex, 'Dún Nechtain, Fortriu and the geography of the Picts', *SHR*, 85:2 (2006), 182–201.

Woolf, Alex, 'AU729.2 and the last years of Nechtan mac Der-Ilei', *SHR*, 85:1 (2006), 131–7.

Woolf, Alex, 'The cult of Moluag, the see of Mortlach and church organisation in northern Scotland in the eleventh and twelfth centuries' in S. Arbuthnot and K. Hollo (eds), *Fil súil nglais – A grey eye looks back: a Festschrift in honour of Colm Ó Baoill* (Ceann Drochaid, 2007), pp 299–334.

Woolf, Alex, *From Pictland to Alba, 789–1070* (Edinburgh, 2007).

Wormald, Patrick, 'Celtic and Anglo-Saxon kingship: some further thoughts' in P.E. Szarmach and V. Darrow Oggins (eds), *Sources of Anglo-Saxon culture* (Kalamazoo, MI, 1986), pp 151–83.

Yorke, Barbara, *Kings and kingdoms in early Anglo-Saxon England* (London and New York, 1990; repr. 2005).

Yorke, Barbara, 'Political and ethnic identity: a case study of Anglo-Saxon practice' in W.O. Frazer and A. Tyrrell (eds), *Social identity in early medieval Britain* (London, 2000), pp 69–89.

Yorke, Barbara, *The conversion of Britain: religion, politics and society in Britain, c.600–800* (Harlow, 2006).

Index